An insider's guide to eco-renovation & newbuilding

Understanding
design

Choosing
materials

Maximising
insulation

Generating
energy

Managing
water

the
sustainable
building
bible

TIM PULLEN

D1340542

Includes 'How to heat and power your home for free!'

C015288208

Title, illustrations and this edition © Ovolo Books 2011
Text © Tim Pullen 2008-2011

Originally published as *Simply Sustainable Homes* 2008
New edition revised and expanded as *The Sustainable Building Bible* November 2011

Print edition: ISBN: 978 1 9059 5914 3
eBook ISBN: 978 1 9059 5928 0

Printed in the UK

The paper used in this book is FSC certified and totally chlorine-free.
FSC (the Forest Stewardship Council) is an international network to promote
responsible management of the world's forests.

www.ovolobooks.co.uk

ABOUT THE AUTHOR

Tim Pullen is an expert in sustainable building and
energy efficiency. He works at green homes consultancy
Weather Works (www.weatherworks.co.uk) advising
clients on renewable energy and efficiency in the home.

Contact: tim@weatherworks.co.uk

The author wishes to acknowledge the contributions and help given to him in writing this book and would
like to extend his gratitude to all of the following for their help.

Nicole Jones, Architect of Carmarthen – for her ideas, encouragement and enthusiasm.
Meiron Jones, Architect with Carmarthenshire County Council – for how sustainability is viewed.
Colin King, Head of Building Research Establishment, Wales – for technical assistance and an insight to the
workings of The Code and Ecohomes.
Andrew Teitge MSc, renewable energy consultant and environmentalist – for his technical corrections.
Amanda Pullen, my daughter, for her extensive and invaluable research work.
Monica Margarite Midgley, without who's spelling, grammar and punctuation this book would be
incomprehensible.

CONTENTS

INTRODUCTION

This book is an expanded and updated edition of 'Simply Sustainable Homes' which was originally published more than three years ago and needed updating due to a number of factors. These include the recession of 2008-2009 - which has had a significant impact on the housebuilding industry generally, as well as self-builders and renovators – and the fact that government is getting more firmly behind sustainable building and renewable energy. All of which changes the way we need to think about what we do.

If you are building, renovating or converting a property and want to do it sustainably you will need to make decisions, lots of them, and this book provides the information necessary to help make them good decisions.

HOW THE BOOK WORKS

The book looks at every aspect of a self-build or renovation project from design to lighting to renewable energy. It sets out the key issues, what can work, what might not work, what to avoid and, in some areas, what sustainability will cost. The book takes a pragmatic approach, dealing with what is realistically achievable for the majority of self-builders. It starts from the point that we live in Western Europe in the twenty-first century and have grown used to little luxuries like flushing toilets and electric lights. Reverting to a former lifestyle – 'living like Granny' – recognises the failings of the way we live but denies any of the beneficial advances of the twentieth century, and there have been many. My Granny lived in an East End slum and as far as I remember it was neither pleasant nor sustainable.

Working through the book from beginning to end will give an insight to each element of the project and enable the reader to make an informed decision as to whether that is a feature they wish to include in their project.

NEW BUILD, RENOVATION, EXTENSION OR REFURBISHMENT

The intention is that this book provides information and guidance that is relevant and useful, whatever your project is. In some cases the distinction is clear, in others less so. The '100 per cent Sustainable' chapter will have little relevance to the refurbisher, for instance, but the Insulation chapter will apply to any project. Where there is a possibility of confusion the subject of the chapter is dealt with in general terms and its application to new build, renovation, refurbishment, etc. dealt with separately at the end of the chapter. The anticipation is that this will give all the background information and allow the reader to pick out the bits that apply to his or her project.

PROJECT FINANCING OR 'THE SUSTAINABLE BUILDER'S DILEMMA'

Most well run projects, new build and renovation, will have a carefully calculated budget, abstracted from the design drawings and specification. That budget will routinely be exceeded and it is as the budget begins to run out that hard decisions have to be made. It usually goes something along the lines of 'Shall we have the recycled bamboo flooring and the solar panels or the Aga and the fifth bedroom – because we can't have it all?'

Having a good, honest grip on what motivates the idea of sustainability will be of immense help. If the heart is crying out for a big house above all other things then that will come to the fore and sustainability will be sacrificed on the altar of expediency. The time, effort and money spent on designing in those sustainability features will have been wasted. Conversely, considering what sustainability means to you, and what it is likely to cost, may just cement the idea and make it the issue around which the whole design revolves.

Size matters and for the sustainable builder it is foolish to think otherwise. A sustainable home will cost more to build but as we get richer we want bigger houses. A 1930s three-bedroom semi will be around 100 sq m floor area and in its time would then have been considered roomy. Today a self-build of less than 150 sq m is a rarity.

Consider: A typical 200 sq m floor area, four-bedroom house, built to a reasonable standard of finish might cost £1,250 per sq m or £250,000 to build. Making it a sustainable house might add £35,000 to the build cost, raising the rate to £1,425 per sq m. Building a 175 sq m four-bedroom sustainable house to a reasonable standard of finish at £1,425 per sq m would also cost £250,000. This really is the question that most self builders aspiring to some level of sustainability have to face. Which is most important, a sustainable home or the extra 25 sq m? What this book will do is help you with that fundamental decision.

ASPIRATIONS

Making good decisions is generally a matter of knowing exactly where you are headed – knowing what your targets are. This is equally true of sustainable house building. You, dear reader, will do well to sit down and think about what it is that motivates you. It may be:-

- The desire for a more comfortable home
- Lower running costs
- Lower CO_2 footprint
- A desire to 'do your bit' in saving the world
- The belief that this is a good way to increase the value of your home
- A desire to go your own way – get off the housing estate
- The sense of accomplishment

It may be none of these or all of these, or something else entirely. The reality is that it does not really matter. Saving cost is just as valid a motive as saving the planet. Whichever road we take, we all end up at the same place. The key is to know what truly motivates you and what you are prepared to pay to get it.

The last few years has seen significant rises in energy prices which in turn has led to a key motivator being to reduce running costs. Returning to 'the sustainable builder's dilemma' it is often the aspiration to lower running costs that get dropped in favour of a lower build cost. The thinking is that today's problem is getting the house built within budget. Dealing with escalating running costs is tomorrow's problem.

Or is it? From 2016 (2013 in Wales) all new houses will be built to zero carbon dioxide emission standards, i.e. highly efficient with very low running costs. We can argue whether, in the light of the 2009 recession, that legislation will come forward but dramatically improved efficiency in the thermal performance of a house is inevitable.

On average we move house every seven years. You probably won't because the house you are building is your dream home and you intend staying in it, but it will eventually be sold. Let's say it is 10 years before the house you are building now is on the market. By then the big builders will have been building and selling energy efficient homes for at least three years. They will have ironed the wrinkles out of the process and be building those energy efficient houses at good prices. That is the market your house will have to compete in. The house you are building today, that doesn't get those energy efficiency features because the budget was not there, will have to compete with houses that have those features and the lower running costs that go with them. What impact will that have on the value of your house, and its saleability in that market in 10 years time?

So maybe dealing with escalating running costs is today's problem, just as much as getting the house built in budget.

WHAT IS A SUSTAINABLE HOUSE?

I live in a house built in 1817 which, except for the addition of central heating, double glazing and indoor plumbing, functions in largely the same way as Mr Jonathon Morgan, its builder, intended. As I travel around the country I see many examples of 100 year old, 200 year old and even 400 year old homes that still provide good accommodation. In most cases these were and are ordinary houses for ordinary people. They had minimal embodied energy and CO_2 when they were built and they meet the definition of a sustainable building, although in those days it was probably just called a building.

The biggest problem lies in houses built in the last 60 years. The need for cheap, quick houses post-Second World War followed in the 1960s by an abundance of cheap fuel in the form or North Sea oil has led us down the wrong path. Houses were built to a standard formula for the nuclear family. The cheap, bright three-bed estate semi of the Sixties and Seventies, and then, as we got richer, the cheap, bright four-bed detached of the Eighties and Nineties. All built to a minimum price and maximum profit, with little or no consideration of CO_2, running costs or whole-life cost. In the last few years we have finally realised that oil is not an infinite resource and that a 60-year design life is just not good enough.

PEAK OIL – OR WHY BUILD A SUSTAINABLE HOME?

We live in an oil driven economy. Pretty much everything we do, every move we make, is affected by the price of oil. In early 2007 the headlines were Oil Prices Set To Fall 30 per cent! They promptly rose from about $60 a barrel to $140 a barrel. It fell again in early 2009 to $40 due to a world recession, but before the year was six months old it was back to $75

As a result of the 2009 recession the oil importing countries – us, the Americans, the Germans, all the rich bits of the world – were flying less, buying fewer cars and spending less on products that need to be transported across the world. The slowdown in the global economy, as credit to consumers and businesses dried up, hit demand for oil hard. But still the price rose by almost 100 per cent within the year.

Oil is a finite resource. It will run out (effectively if not actually) and the only question is when. The rate at which we are finding new sources of oils is now being outstripped by the increase in demand from developing countries. Demand is still increasing faster than supply and while market forces still operate the price will continue to rise. So while the academics argue about which definition of peak oil is the right one and when we will reach it, we have effectively passed it.

In the UK consumption of oil has risen by a fairly steady two per cent per year since the 1940s. Until 2005 when it appears to plateau. And a similar story can be seen across most of western Europe, which may be why pundits are suggesting a fall in price.

The past three years has seen the price of domestic heating oil rise by some 84 per cent across the country. Distributors of heating oil are predicting a rise of 30 per cent plus in the next 12 months. It has to be said that history, geology and market laws are all pointing against a significant and lasting fall in oil prices.

That fossil fuels generally and oil specifically are contributors to global warming is increasingly becoming accepted as fact. As is the idea that global warming is a reality. In the past five years or so there has been a shift in the position of the global warning deniers. They first denied that global warning was a reality, it did not exist and was all the figment of over-excited imaginations. They then moved to a position of saying that it does exist but is nothing to do with CO_2 or human intervention; it is a natural phenomenon that will go away in time. They now maintain that it does exist, it is related to CO_2 and human intervention, but there is no point in doing anything while China, India, or anyone far away, is building a new coal-fired power station every two minutes.

It is the sort of argument that might more usually be found in a junior school playground. If we, the people who created the problem, are not prepared to do anything, why should anyone else?

KEY DESIGN ISSUES

There are three key issues surrounding the sustainable home. These are

Size: The bigger the house the more resources it uses. Obvious but usually ignored. The sustainable builder will be designing a house that is big enough to meet current needs but with the ability to extend (or shrink!) to meet future needs. He will tend to avoid size as a status symbol, preferring other ways of demonstrating his prowess and sensitivity.

Energy: Putting energy at the centre of the design. Making energy a key design parameter is standard across most of Europe. In Germany one of the first decisions will be for a 15kW, or 20kW or 25kW house. We in the UK do not even have the language. We don't know what a 15kW house is (but you will before you finish the book).

RUNNING COST ANALYSIS

for 200 sq m house for space heating only

Year	Part L1A 55kWh/m²/year	Best Practice 35kWh/m²/year	Passivhaus 15kWh/m²/year	Zero Carbon 10kWh/m²/year
2009	£540 pa Oil-fired boiler	£340 pa Oil-fired boiler	£90 pa Heat pump	£80 pa Wood pellets
2010 20% price rise	£648 pa Oil-fired boiler	£408 pa Oil-fired boiler	£108 pa Heat pump	£96 pa Wood pellets
2011 20% price rise	£778 pa Oil-fired boiler	£490 pa Oil-fired boiler	£130 pa Heat pump	£115 pa Wood pellets
2012 25% price rise	£972 pa Oil-fired boiler	£612 pa Oil-fired boiler	£162 pa Heat pump	£144 pa Wood pellets

Lifespan: Until the mid 1980s the accepted design life of a house – effectively what Building Regs compliance would achieve – was 60 years. After a couple of year's consultation the Building Research Establishment decided to extend that to 80 years. Not a massive change maybe but a step in the right direction. Bear in mind that my own home, 200 years old and with its life's end still not in sight, is far from unique.

RUNNING COST ANALYSIS

At the turn of the millennium the idea of petrol costing more than £1 per litre was unthinkable. In 2003, when petrol and diesel first went over £1 per litre, there were demonstrations, rolling convoys and refineries blockaded across the country. Today, in 2011, petrol over £1.30 per litre is the norm. We used to get distressed when it went over £1.20, but we've learnt to live with it.

The price rises discussed in the table above may seem unreasonable but consider that today the price of electricity is up to 15p per kWh. In 1999 the average price was just 4.7p per kWh. What might it be in 2020?

SET TARGETS AND ACHIEVE THEM

Any movement towards sustainability is a movement in the right direction, so don't beat yourself up over how far to go. We each of us have different motives, different constraints, different fears and desires. Setting a low target and hitting it is likely to lead to learning and success. Setting a high target and missing could lead to the abandonment of the whole idea. We start from the premise that 100 per cent sustainability is not possible. We have to accept that copper pipe, cables, light fittings, plug sockets etc. are more or less unsustainable (although potentially recyclable) and move on from that.

SUSTAINABLE, ZERO CARBON, ECO AND LOW ENERGY HOMES:

What is the difference in all these names? The answer is that it is largely a matter of degree. No building can be eco-friendly, by definition. What ever you build, even an earth shelter, will not have a positive impact on the ecology. The best we can hope for is to reduce the level of unfriendliness. All of these terms set-out to describe something other than the conventional brick-and-block, energy guzzling house.

Things described as eco-homes or green homes tend to have features like a green roof and rainwater harvesting while the low-energy house will tend to focus on energy consumption, sometimes to the exclusion of all else.

A sustainable home will tend to focus on materials and provide accommodation and facilities in a way that has the lowest possible impact on the ecology and on natural resources. That will apply to the build process, the operation of the building and its eventual demolition and/or re-use.

A zero carbon home is a Government idea for moving us towards energy efficiency. In July 2009 a white paper re-affirmed the Government's intention that all new housing from 2016 must have net zero CO_2 emissions. At this stage the requirement is for all new houses in Wales to have net zero carbon emissions from 2013. The move to zero carbon homes is reinforced by a few local authorities requiring new planning applications to meet Code for Sustainable Homes Level 3 as a minimum. Which is likely to be Level 4 by 2012 and is broadly in line with Building Regulation requirements. Until 2009 Code Level 3 was the 'advanced' standard, imposed by just a small number of local authorities. The 2010 revision to Part LIA of the building regulations (the bit dealing with energy efficiency) requires a 25 per cent reduction in CO_2 emissions compared to 2006 Part LIA standard, meaning that all local authorities will require broadly Level 3 standard as a minimum and the 'advanced' standard, imposed by the few local authorities moves to Level 4.

In practical terms this means increasing insulation levels by possibly 25 per cent (depending on the project and the method of construction – some methods, like SIPS for example, will achieve the standard as normal) and possibly adding solar thermal panels. In terms of energy efficiency Level 4 is not a particularly difficult target, although even three years ago it would have been considered near impossible.

RENEWABLE ENERGY

Any home claiming sustainability credentials will incorporate renewable energy in some form.

There is a lot of talk about wind turbines and heat pumps, most of which is at best misleading. Wind turbines in urban locations do not work well, if at all. The managing director of a major wind turbine manufacturer (products available at your local DIY shed) stated in February 2007 that only one in five customers have a suitable site. Even that figure seems a bit optimistic.

Similarly, heat pumps are becoming big news on the back of advertising that claims reductions in heating bills of 'up to 70 per cent'. There are heat pump customers out there whose electricity bills have trebled or even quadrupled as a result of poor designs based on poor information. These disaster situations are not the fault of the technologies but rather of the people selling them. Heat pumps are, generally, great technology. They work extremely well in properly insulated houses when they are used to power underfloor heating.

In almost all circumstances renewable energy is site specific. What will work well in one location will not necessarily work in the next. To look at any renewable energy technology as you would a gas-fired boiler is always a mistake. They are just not that well understood. If you want a condensing gas boiler your local plumber need only stick his nose in the door to be able to say, with some certainty 'What you need here is a Galaxy Superstar PDQ123.' and he would be right. Ask him if your ground conditions are suitable for a 12kW heat pump and he will suck his teeth, shuffle his feet and tell you to install a gas boiler instead.

In fairness that is becoming less true as heat pumps (and other technologies) move nearer the mainstream and more plumbers become more acquainted with them. But, a little knowledge being a dangerous thing, it is easy to believe the manufacturer's hype and the salesman's puffs. Heat pumps are routinely advertised with a COP (efficiency) of in excess of 400 per cent. That is the basis on which they are sold and on which we buy them. The Building Research Establishment (BRE) published a paper in late 2010 with data gathered over a 12 month period for air and ground source heat pumps. It showed that when used for space heating and hot water efficiency for air source heat pumps could be as low as 230 per cent. That may still seem pretty good but the reality is that at that level, as it runs on mains electricity, it will be more expensive to run than a gas boiler and emit more CO_2. More and more plumbers are getting switched on to new technology and recognising that heat pumps need to be used with solar panels.

Designing in the right renewable energy technology requires a careful consideration of your site, the property you are building or renovating, and the way you live in that property. It is second in importance only to designing in the right insulation. There is no magic about it. The right system will work well. The wrong system poorly installed will not work and will cost a lot of money.

FINANCIAL IMPLICATIONS

It is inarguable that building a sustainable home is more expensive than building a conventional gas-guzzling house. It is equally inarguable that the sustainable house will be cheaper to run (see the table on page 12).

It can be argued that building an energy efficient house is in effect capitalising running costs. The extra cost of building in a sustainable, energy efficient way is only a tiny proportion of the cost of the energy needed to run a similar, conventionally built house across its life.

Sustainable homes are also beginning to command a premium price, which has been shown in developments from Tyne & Wear to Cornwall. In effect recovering the extra build cost. People are becoming ever more aware of rising energy costs and are now actively wanting to buy sustainable, energy efficient homes.

IN SUMMARY

There are possibly four main reasons why you and I should build sustainable, energy efficient homes:

Money – if achieving sustainability, energy efficiency and zero CO_2 emissions cost no more than staying as we are, there would be no argument we would all do it. But we are all affected by financial considerations and achieving those goals can be expensive. If we look at the whole life cost of the house, sustainability, and energy efficiency, will always save money. Maybe we need to take a longer term view and make the investment for our children's sake.

Save the planet – it is difficult to deny that what is good for the planet is good for the individual. Each of us, as we walk across the world, leave a footprint, however small and the effects of global warming will not be limited to those that cause it. Houses use 27 per cent of the UK's energy each year and as a consequence account for 22 per cent of the CO_2 emissions. Which actually represents a fall of 2.9 per cent since 1999. So what we are doing with sustainable building is beginning to work.

THE **SUSTAINABLE** BUILDING BIBLE

Insurance – specifically using renewable energy as protection against the oil industry. The price of oil, gas and electricity will only rise, and the less we need of it the less we are affected by what those huge companies decide to do.

Smugness – or perhaps self-satisfaction would be a better expression. Creating a more sustainable home with lower carbon emissions (and lower running costs) is difficult and an achievement in itself. Building your own home is a great adventure – it is a project that will fill your life for a number of years. Doing it at all will make you feel good. Doing it sustainably will, quite rightly, make you feel great.

If we act and are wrong and global warming turns out to be a just a scare storey, the result is that we end up living in better homes. If we do nothing and global warming is a reality, the result is water lapping around our nostrils.

THE STANDARD FOUR-BED, FOUR-PERSON HOUSE

Throughout this book we will be referring to the 'standard house' and drawing comparisons based on that typical size. By the 'standard house' we are taking a 200 sq m floor area property, slightly larger than the average house which is about 130 sq m to 140 sq m. It will be on two floors, with four bedrooms, 2.5 bathrooms, and four people in occupancy, with a typical work /school occupancy pattern.

Construction details (for comparison purposes – not because it is a good idea) are: a one tenth of an acre plot with the rear of the house having a south-facing aspect. Patio doors to the rear give access to the lounge and construction will be block inner skin, brick outer skin, under concrete roof tiles. Part L standard levels of insulation through-out. Solid concrete slab ground floor, with suspended timber first floor with chipboard flooring. Glazing will be uPVC double glazed with 12mm air gap. The house will have a conventional gas condensing boiler with standard pressed steel radiators. Mid-range kitchen and bathroom fittings with tiled floors and tiling to walls. Other floor coverings to be carpet. Gardens to the property will be laid to lawns with flower borders. A driveway of some 15m length to be hard paved, leading to a double garage.

Your house will obviously be different but hopefully you can 'scale off' from this standard.

INTRODUCTION

1 GETTING STARTED

The idea for building your own home can come from many places – a long held desire, an opportunity, a sudden windfall, a change of life circumstances. Often that initial idea – more often a pipe-dream – will lead to a bit of research – visiting exhibitions, reading magazines, reading books like this one. The idea becomes an evolutionary process. There will be many decisions to be made - whether to buy a plot of land or not is often the first - but then the design process begins and the first, and arguably most important, of many decisions has to be made – to build to a budget or to a design. To put it another way, build to a price or to a standard. The reality is usually a compromise.

Both budget and design will be influential and sometimes budget will win and sometimes standard. The sustainable builder has another element — a target outside the ordinary that will impact on budget and design. The targets for a traditional project will be to get the house finished broadly on budget, on time and looking like the plans. The sustainable builder or renovator will also have targets around sustainable materials, energy consumption, energy generation – essentially the level of sustainability.

A sustainable project is not like a traditional project – a fixed standard, black or white, succeed or fail, completed on not completed. A sustainable project proceeds through shades of grey (or green?) from the wholly un-sustainable to the wholly sustainable. Where any project sits on that scale will be influenced by many things – the site, the budget, the support or otherwise of the architect and the local authority, the skills available local to the site, the materials available – but most of all by what the individual self-builder or renovator believes to be realistically achievable. It has been said before and will be said again that it is better to successfully build a 10 per cent sustainable house than to fail to build a 100 per cent sustainable house.

The key to any successful project is balancing the budget with obtaining the desired outcome. Unsurprisingly, going over budget is far easier and far more common than getting the project finished on or under budget. For the sustainable builder or renovator the problem can be even more acute.

A traditional build will, of its nature, be well understood. Most elements of the build will be familiar to the relevant contractor and easy to price and schedule accurately. The sustainable build is dealing with methods, materials and products that may be either unknown or less well known to the contractor and therefore less easy to price accurately. The contractor may feel he is taking on a risk and price accordingly. It is here that the 80/20 rule starts to apply. Planning is the key and 20 per cent of the time will be taken up with planning 80 per cent of the project; 80 per cent of the time will be spent on the remaining 20 per cent – those small but vital tricky bits. The essential issue is to expect and accept this disparity. Allow the time for planning the project – getting comparison prices, sourcing the right materials and methods, finding the best contractors, then revisiting the design in the light of incoming information and doing it all again. Ensuring that so far as possible every detail of the entire project, right up to a key in the door and a smoking chimney, has been considered, priced and added to the schedule.

It is a wise self-builder or renovator that adds at least 20 per cent to the final, most accurate price available and makes sure that that sum can be funded. And it is certainly foolish to start a sustainable project without that contingency budget.

We are all prone to moments of whimsy and what seemed like exactly the right look at the outset of the project will change as the project progresses. New ideas occur, new products pop up, the original product is no longer available, fashions change and white is this year's black. Quite often the changes just represent a way of staying involved in the project. For any number of reasons the spec will almost certainly change, and changes in themselves add time and cost, beyond the simple cost difference in the product. Factoring these into the schedule can be tricky, but anticipating delays is essential if the budgeted build cost is to be near accurate.

Sustainable projects will have the double whammy of client-driven desire to achieve a standard and delays forced by a lack of familiarity with the material, method or product. It is these delays that are likely to be the biggest factor in budget overrun. Delays cost money principally because the wages of the people being delayed still need paying.

Any successful build project requires commitment and attention to detail. A sustainable project has more detail and requires more commitment. All this time spent planning provides the opportunity to give proper attention to those details and to maximise the probability of success. It allows the potential problems to be revealed and for targets to be adjusted accordingly.

It needs to be recognised that the planning and project management process is different for a new-build from a renovation project. The big issues will remain broadly the same but they start from different places, have different considerations and probably different outcomes.

As costs rise it proves a real test of the green credentials of those driving the project. When cash gets tight are you going to build a smaller house or build a less sustainable one? It is a crucial decision and if you can honestly face your priorities it will make decision-making easier.

SELF-BUILD

Sustainable builders fall into three main categories. Those who:
- want to use as high a percentage of sustainable material as possible
- want to minimise energy use, CO_2 and running costs
- want both of the above.

Whichever category you fall into the rules for achieving what you want will remain broadly the same. Even a 100 per cent sustainable house will follow these same rules:

1. Set achievable targets

Be prepared to change your targets in the light of incoming information. The right target for any given project might be the 100 per cent sustainable home with zero carbon emissions or it might be simply a 10 per cent improvement on building regulations (the minimum legal requirement you have to build to in the UK and Northern Ireland). At this stage it does not really matter. What matters is having a clear idea of what you consider satisfactory, together with the knowledge that it is achievable and affordable.

2. Take an holistic approach

A house is a machine like any other, and everything connects to everything else. Bigger windows will look good, bring in more light and give an airy feel, but what effect do they have on the heating and ventilation systems? Will solar gain mean some shading is needed for the summer, or will the extra heat loss mean more insulation? If you think about it long enough you can figure out how the size and orientation of the windows relate to the size of the heat pump. This is, perhaps, a fairly obvious example but the principal extends throughout the house. Within the context of design if we change one thing there will be consequences. What we seek to avoid are unanticipated consequences. We want a machine that works in the way the design intended.

3. Put energy at the centre of the design

Make energy consumption a design criterion, along with the number of bedrooms, size of lounge, etc. It allows an understanding of how much the house will cost to run, and consequently if you can afford to live in it. It influences virtually every detail of the house, from the construction system, to the glazing, to the orientation.

The traditional house building process usually follows the following steps:

■ Create a design – based largely on the client's requirements the architect will come up with a look and layout that should please the client and satisfy the local planning authority.

■ Get planning consent – fill out the forms, pay a fee and, if required negotiate with the planners on detail, consent should follow.

■ Complete the SAP calculation – your architect or house designer prints off a standard specification, known to meet Building Regulations and sends this with the drawings to an approved assessor. The Client pays another fee and if the architect has been done his or her job properly the plans get a Pass – and some indication of the notional annual energy consumption of the house.

■ Get Building Regulations approval. This confirms that the house meets the officially required minimum standards of construction, and it involves another fee.

■ Build the house – six, 12 or 18 months of toil, sweat, heartache, anxiety, joy, delight, anger, frustration and, finally a warm glow of satisfaction. And lots and lots more bills to pay.

■ Find out what it actually costs to run. 12 months after the build is finished, as the fuel bills start to roll in, you find out how much energy the house uses, what the current running costs are. If you are feeling brave, calculate what the running costs are likely to be in 10 years time.

Putting energy at the centre of the design needs a different approach:

■ Set out primary design criteria – what is really important in terms of size, number of rooms, layout, orientation. Communicate this to the designer, in a way he or she can understand. Remember it is your project, not theirs.

■ Decide on acceptable heating energy demand – 15, 20, 25kWh/m2/yr, whatever suits (we'll go into what that means in Chapter 4). Ensure that the designer understands that this is a design criterion with the same level of significance as the number of bedrooms. Before engaging the architect, architectural technician or draughtsman it is important to ensure that they understand your environmental requirements and know how to deliver the standard you require. By reading this book you should be in a position to ask pertinent questions and be able to judge from their reply if they are capable of delivering. It is much easier to ascertain this before the design process begins rather than at the point where they have spent several thousand pounds

1

of your money on a pretty (or not so pretty) design that is incapable of meeting your sustainability goals.

■ Design house – As with the traditional approach but here the construction method, levels of insulation, amount and orientation of glazing, heating system will have to be taken into account. These would have been done anyway, for Building Regs approval, but now they need to be done earlier. Part of this process will be to establish how the house will be built; the complexity of construction detail and whether this is practically achievable. Having the building contractor on board at this stage will be useful, as will having other experts or consultants.

■ Calculate what it will actually cost to run. Having set a target heating energy demand it is important to check that the architect has achieved it. Establish the design heat load, and other energy demands for hot water, lighting, power and calculate actual running costs (How you do this will be explained in Chapter 2).

■ Calculate what the house will cost to build. It is essential to have a clear idea of costs and having at least the main contractor on board will ease the process. There will be a strong possibility that the design and specification will mean that it exceeds the budget, so…

■ Return to Step 1. and repeat until satisfied. The temptation is always to rush through this process and self-builders quite naturally want to get to the building bit. There is an understandable sense of urgency. If possible, resist. Time and money spent on the planning stage will be returned many-fold.

■ Get planning consent, SAP Calculations and Building Regs approval. A largely rubber-stamp process as the work that has gone before should ensure approval.

■ Build house – with all the anxiety and joy as in the traditional approach, but with a much clearer idea of the outcome.

It is likely that this approach will be more difficult than the traditional approach, largely because the sustainable builder is asking the designer and contractors to work outside their comfort zones. The architect cannot reach to the shelf and pull down a standard design or a standard specification (or, more likely, reach into the bowels of their PC) but actually has to think, be creative, calculate, be an architect. The same applies to the contractor. They know to two decimal places how many bricks can be laid in an hour, but ask the cost per square metre for lime render and the confidence disappears.

The responsibility lies with the client to ensure that all parties know and understand what the objectives are and why the client is setting them. Which perhaps highlights the main difference between a sustainable and a traditional build. The self-builder wanting a traditional house, built to Building Regs and no more, can, and often does, walk away from the construction process. Personal involvement may extend no further than a concern over finishings – kitchen fittings, paint, tiles etc. The self-builder wanting a sustainable house is likely to be far more involved in the construction technology. They may be lucky and find an architect completely up to speed on sustainability and energy consumption. Then the self builder can relax. There are an increasing number of such people and the chances of getting lucky are improving, but the sustainable self-builder still needs to be prepared to get involved.

Resource use

The sustainable builder will be aware of the need to be careful with the use of resources. That is, not using more resources in terms of materials and energy than is necessary, and ensuring that all the resources that the site has to offer are used to the full. The sustainable builder will be thinking about using timber from sustainable sources, natural insulation, using recycled materials. He or she may also make use of the sun on a sunny site or plant trees as a windbreak on a windy site. But it will also mean thinking outside the box. For example, we might question the purpose of an external brick skin to a timber-frame construction. It has no structural benefit, adds a bit to the weather-proofing but its main purpose is aesthetic. To get that look adds a great deal in terms or resources and embodied CO_2. Or the sustainable builder might be planning a vegetable garden with a little greenhouse perhaps and maybe a few chickens. All well and fine, a great idea, fun and productive. The veg garden will produce waste material as well as veg (or instead of in my case) as will the chickens. Combine the two in an insulated box and you have a hot-composting system that will provide sufficient usable heat to warm the greenhouse and nutrients for the veg garden. A beautifully elegant cycle that is maximising resource use.

Design-in the renewable energy.

Knowing how much energy the house will need and what resources are available will allow informed decisions on what renewable energy can be incorporated, what can be afforded, it will minimise the capital cost and maximise its effectiveness.

If energy use has been set as a design criterion and that approach to design taken, the renewable energy aspects will have been considered, but it may mean revisiting the house design a number of times to allow better use of the energy resources available.

Do your own research

Architects and designers don't know everything. In my day-job as a sustainable building

THE SUSTAINABLE BUILDING BIBLE

1

consultant I get the opportunity to meet many people trying to build houses in a more sustainable way. I am told regularly that the house has been designed to be really efficient . Now maybe the fact that they have come to me means that these are only the ones who are feeling that the brief is not being met – but I doubt it. It's not because architects and designers are bad people – or even bad at their job . But in many cases they are designing houses that they know can be built – generally to a budget and in a way they are familiar with. Increasing numbers of architects have a growing, even expert, knowledge of sustainability and how it applies to house design. The Association of Environment Conscious Building (www.aecb.net) keeps a list of them.

Building in a sustainable way is not a black art, the knowledge is available to anyone. It will be down to you to make decisions around fundamentals like which construction system to use, what constitutes a good level of insulation, how the use of sustainable materials impacts on budget and quality, and which renewable energy systems are the best idea. Those decisions are best based on first-hand knowledge and a bit of research (well, quite a bit probably) will help find the information needed for confident decisions. But talking to those who have already done it and as much research as possible also helps.

There was a time when most of those involved in supplying sustainable materials and technology were like-minded souls who were making a living delivering something they believed in passionately. But sustainability is now big business and they have been joined by many who see it as good business. Nothing at all wrong with that – but with it have come those who make claims for their products which at best are wildly optimistic and at worst are simply 'unsustainable'! Nowadays, even with lots of convincing-looking calculations you should check the facts. In later chapters we'll take a look at the technologies in more detail and suggest which are likely to offer the best solutions in various circumstances. For instance wind generation may look vey good on the top if a hill on a large site but not so good in a densely-built low-lying urban environment.

There are two basic elements to a self-build project; the plot and the house. Deciding on the targets that you want to achieve will help determine which of those comes first. The self-builder wanting to build a free-energy house must have the right plot, one with the resources necessary to generate that energy. If free energy is not so important then neither is the plot and then the house design, the materials and maybe energy-efficiency can take centre stage.

Setting targets is about more than a desire for six bedrooms, a swimming pool and tennis court. For the sustainable builder it is about how well the machine will work, how it will fulfil its function. It will not be easy, but by giving yourself realistic objectives you stand a greater chance of success.

RENOVATION

The approach to a renovation project varies slightly in that the building and the plot are what they are. The scope to adjust orientation or glazing, for instance, will be, at best, limited. As a consequence any targets will be, to some extent, dictated by the building and the plot. The renovator does not have the same freedom of choice. Otherwise the process is largely the same – but there are subtle differences.

1. Property audit

Understand what you have and how it works. What is more or less significant will depend on the age and functionality of the building. A big old stone barn with 600mm thick walls will work in a different way to a Victorian terrace. The barn will be fairly fixed in the way it works and any modifications need to enhance rather than interrupt that functionality. A Victorian terrace is much more adaptable as the idea of building functionality into the fabric had largely been lost in the drive for speedy, profitable construction when it was built.

An audit allows informed decisions as to what to keep, what to change and what to remove. The renovator will also set targets around the preferred level of sustainability and that will influence those decisions.

2. Insulate to the max

The renovator does not have the same freedom to install the optimum levels of insulation to all elements as the self-builder does. All that can be asked is that the renovator puts in as much insulation as is practically possible, maybe going a step further in those areas that lend themselves to insulation to compensate for those areas that don't.

3. Calculate energy consumption

Depending on the scale of the renovation a SAP calculation may or may not be needed but will be even less reliable than for a new build, in terms of actual energy consumption. It will be necessary for the renovator (or the renovator's consultant of choice) to calculate these figures and probably to calculate the U-values of each element.

Putting energy at the centre of the design is still a good idea - but in practice more difficult to achieve because it is usually a case of compromising between what is desired and what the

1

building is capable of. Carrying a target heating energy consumption figure in mind helps to keep focused. They say that the point of a railway timetable is to let you know how much the train is late by. The same principle applies to energy consumption.

4. Consider renewable energy

What is possible will be entirely dependent on the site and the energy resources it has available. Considering all the options, from wind turbines to biomass boilers, will help to ensure that the best decisions are made. It also impacts on other decisions around heating and ventilation, and going into the project with a pre-conceived idea of the system to be installed can be problematic. Renewable energy systems work best in one of two ways:

■ Design the system to meet the house. The conventional route is to design the house to meet the need and then design-in the renewable energy systems. But letting this be a circular process, so that the renewable energy systems feed into the house design is typically a more successful approach.

■ Design the house to meet the system. If, for instance, a heat pump seems like a good idea, and the site has the right conditions, then design the house to suit. Accept that this may or may not be possible in a renovation where design options can be constrained.

5. Decide on heating and hot water systems

There will be many factors affecting this decision; location, size of property, levels of insulation and peak heat load, as well the resources available on or near the site. Taking this decision early in the design process may equally influence other factors; a heat pump needs underfloor heating, which means lifting the ground floor, which gives the opportunity to install more insulation, which reduces the size of the heat pump..

6. Water & the outside

For some reason renovators tend to express more concern about the garden and what to do with it than the self-builder does. Maybe because it is the one area over which they have full control or because it's already a garden – not a building site or field?

Reducing water consumption presents exactly the same opportunities to the renovator as it does the self-builder. Both will be thinking about aerated taps, flow regulators and the like. Dealing with grey water recycling (where you reuse some of the water used in the house) or rainwater harvesting can present the renovator with more of a problem, and more cost. Pipe-work may already be in place, as will drains and soakaways. Changing pipe routes or adding more pipes can be difficult and can involve un-burying them from walls, floors or the garden making it more expensive – possibly unrealistically so.

If one or other of these systems is to be installed then the services of a reputable plumber need to be engaged early in the planning stage. Unless it is clear that there is no issue, (a barn conversion would be an example – where there is no existing pipe-work and therefore no problem) then the implications of installing a system need to be investigated, costed and included in the plan.

While it is true that in terms of sustainability the renovator starts a step or two ahead of the self-builder, the greater flexibility of a new build project allows them to catch up quickly. The Government, BRE, The Energy Saving Trust, The Carbon Trusts, as well as many private companies are all spending huge sums trying to come up with ways of moving the existing housing stock to a greater level of sustainability. Maybe indicative that a really sustainable renovation is no easy task.

It could all be a matter of degree. If these Government sponsored projects are trying to achieve Passivhaus standard or Code for Sustainable Homes level 6 then the problems they face are big, and warrant the huge sums being spent. But if the individual renovator merely wants to make the house better than before it is reasonably easy to achieve the desired level of improvement. Giving up a bit of internal space and properly insulating a Victorian terraced house will have a significant impact on the efficiency, the running costs, the comfort and the sustainability. Pop a solar panel on the roof and install a condensing gas boiler and the house is likely to move from Code level 1 to level 3.

But setting realistic targets is the key. Targets need to be based on the property audit, geared towards personal desire and balanced with the budget

EXAMPLES

The examples to follow are what has been achieved. The projects are not particularly extraordinary but serve to illustrate the process that lead to success.

Barn Conversion.

A large nineteenth century timber-frame barn, most recently used as a grain store. The building had a single floor of some 250m^2 floor area, with height to comfortably accommodate a second floor. The intention was to build a five-bedroom house for a growing family. Overall the planned accommodation to be around 420m^2. The building is on a north-south axis so that the

1

roof elevations are east and west. An adjacent shed was to be upgraded, and helpfully provide a south-facing roof elevation. The garden extends to around a third of an acre, more than enough to accommodate a ground source heat pump.

The original construction was a 4in x 2in timber frame on a 2ft brick plinth. This was not capable of supporting a second floor and the first set of plans proposed a blockwork inner skin to allow some insulation to the walls and to support the second floor.

The clients took the view that they wanted to build as sustainably as possible and to utilise as much renewable energy as possible. Budget was not inexhaustible but was not, at the outset, a primary consideration. Planning consent was obtained based on the original drawings but the clients quickly realised that those plans did not lend themselves to sustainability.

A new architect was brought in, together with a sustainability consultant. The new architect was fully behind the ideas and immediately understood that radical changes would be needed.

The first, and most significant of these, was to change the proposed blockwork inner skin to a green oak frame. This had two affects: firstly, it added a huge aesthetic appeal, and secondly, it allowed for far more insulation to the walls than had previously been the case. It also allowed for that insulation to be sustainable.

The original calculations indicated a peak heat load of 23kW and an energy consumption of around 60kWh/m^2/yr. The clients considered this unacceptable and after some discussion with the consultant, in which Passivhaus was briefly mentioned, a figure of 30kWh/m^2/yr was settled on. While Passivhaus was perhaps a desirable objective it was, in all practical terms, unachievable within the constraints of a nineteenth century barn.

As plans were being finalised the main contractor came on board. He was happy to confess that he knew little about sustainability but was keen to learn. It became clear that he genuinely saw building houses sustainably as the way of the future. He needed to learn and was happy to go the extra mile to do so. Oddly, for a builder, he was very budget-conscious and pointed out the likely extra costs involved in the high level of sustainable materials being used.

The clients' decision was to use as much sustainable material as possible, but to ensure that enough budget remained to fund a renewable heat source. As a consequence the decision was to use FSC timber through out and a mix of sustainable and non-sustainable insulation materials. Confidence in the builder grew and it was considered that far more attention to detail would be given and that a higher level of air-tightness could reasonably be achieved. New calculations based on the new insulation and air-tightness levels gave a peak heat load of 12kW and a predicted energy consumption of 28kWh/m^2/yr.

A lot of thought was given to the principal heat source. Installing solar thermal panels was almost a given, but the decision around a ground source heat pump or a biomass boiler was not easy. A biomass boiler was finally opted for, principally for the greater flexibility it offered. The oak frame put some constraints on heating to the first floor and these were most easily overcome by using radiators.

The building has a huge roof area and from the outset it was planned to install a big rainwater harvesting system. The clients took the view that this would meet around 50 per cent of the water demands of the house, including the vegetable garden. Therefore they could afford to be a little profligate with water use in the house and treated themselves to power showers.

The completed property looks really impressive, is welcoming and retains all of its original character. The heat load at completion was actually lower than predicted as the contractor had become a bit obsessive about air tightness and instead of the required 5m3/hr the blower test came in at 2.9m^3/hr – to everyone's great joy. The project came in near budget, although the project started before the budget was finally set. The clients have, deservedly, a huge sense of satisfaction, from a successfully completed project and from the level of sustainability they were able to incorporate.

2. New build family home

A family taking advantage of the relaxation in planning regulations to build a new home in the rear garden of their existing home. The budget was firmly fixed and not over generous, and the design criteria well defined. A four-bedroom home with two bathrooms, a kitchen, a lounge and a large music room. To have a light, airy feel and to be as energy efficient as possible. The original target was for a Passivhaus with solar thermal and PV arrays on a south-facing roof, but the available budget meant that this was not a practical option and AECB Silver standard was taken as a more achievable target. Discussions between the client and the architect around budget and probable build cost continued for some weeks (drifting into months). For these clients, energy consumption was more important than size. They wanted to build the most efficient house possible rather than the largest possible.

The solution was a house big enough to meet the design criteria, using SIPS panel construction with a truss roof. This allowed for high levels of insulation and excellent air-tightness, bringing the energy consumption down to less than 25kWh/m^2/yr. The final design was a house of 180m^2 floor area, down from 270m^2 in the first set of plans, but still providing all the accommodation needed. A glass atrium was added to the front, south-facing elevation,

1

which increased the natural lighting and the passive solar gain. This not only reduced the heating requirement but also improved the performance of a passive ventilation system. Existing tress to the east and west were considered sufficiently large to provide summer shading and prevent overheating, but internal blinds were also incorporated. Solar thermal panels were installed in the roof and the principal heat source was a 5kW air source heat pump. Wood burning stoves were installed in the lounge and music room for highlight heating. The option to install solar PV was incorporated in the design but not taken up initially due to budget. It is an option that the clients can revisit as technology changes, prices drop and maybe more funds become available.

The key issues in this project were budget and energy efficiency. Addressing those issues determined the size of the house and the construction system. They in turn informed the decisions around the heating system. Initially the drive to minimise CO_2 emissions led to a desire for a wood pellet boiler, but budget and convenience tended to mitigate against that. In the final analysis an air source heat pump was significantly cheaper, the house had a low energy demand and underfloor heating meant that the heat pump could achieve good efficiency. If, when, the option to install solar PV is taken then the heating system will be largely CO_2 free.

The clients made an early decision that they were prepared to sacrifice size to achieve the level of energy efficiency they wanted. The architect's attitude was based on potential resale value, in that a larger house would be worth more (in that location) than a smaller, more energy efficient house. It has to be recognised that the architect had the clients' best interest at heart but was missing the point that the clients intended to live in the house for the long term, when rising energy cost are likely to have more influence on house prices. Also that it was the clients' lifestyle choice. They wanted to feel that they had taken this one opportunity to do all they could.

3. Extension to suburban semi

The clients have occupied the house for some years and want to extend in two directions. They want to extend the lounge into the rear garden and add utility space to the side, as well as adding a ground-floor bathroom. In addition they want to do this work as sustainably as possible and to minimise the energy consumption of the house. Installing a rainwater harvesting system is a key issue and they wanted to re-landscape the garden from largely floral and decorative to incorporate some vegetable production.

The budget is fixed, cannot be exceeded and is reasonably modest for the scale of the project. Initial considerations were for a straw-bale construction to the extension, for the sustainability and the perceived thermal performance. This proved unworkable for a compact suburban location and the construction method was changed to a single skin timber frame, externally rendered and incorporating 200mm of hemp insulation. The roof was of reclaimed tiles on FSC timber rafters. Similarly the new floors were FSC timber with 200mm of hemp insulation. The opportunity was taken to lift the existing suspended timber floor to install more hemp insulation and to deal with draughts. Loft insulation to the existing house was increased by laying 200mm sheep wool on top of the existing 100mm mineral wool.

Changes had to be made to the plans to ensure the project came in on budget. Some of these were fairly small, like reducing the width on the rear extension by 500mm and the length of the side extension by 1m. Others were larger and more significant. The plan was to change the existing timber, single-glazed windows for new double-glazed units. When prices were obtained it was realised that this one feature would absorb a large proportion of the budget. The existing timber frames were in good repair and calculations showed that installing secondary double-glazing would more than halve the heat loss through the windows and cut the cost by 80 per cent. The affect of this was to give more financial elbow room for dealing with the heating.

The property had a small gas boiler, dealing exclusively with domestic hot water, space heating being provided by two old and very inefficient gas fires. The decision was to install solar thermal panels to the south-facing roof, install high-efficiency radiators and a small air source heat pump.

Laying out the garden was a fairly simple matter, and the budget even allowed for a greenhouse and a pond. The natural slope to the garden allowed a rainwater harvesting tank to be installed with minimal excavation.

When the plans were finalised the clients felt that they had achieved all their goals. The extensions provided the extra accommodation they needed and would be constructed sustainably; they had incorporated all the energy and resource saving features that were possible; they had reduced the overall running costs of the house, and its CO_2 emissions, and would have a larger, lighter, warmer, more functional and more valuable home.

COMMERCIALITY

Many books have been written on how to make money from self build and renovations. That is not the point of this book but it has to be recognised that commerciality will always be a factor in the equation. Some self-builders and renovators are happy to spend more than the finished property is worth – but they are the exception. They may take the view that they are

1

building the house they want to live in. They can afford it, their children and perhaps their grandchildren will also enjoy it so perceived monetary value is not a key issue.

The fact remains that, on average, the great British public move house every seven years. That will generally involve selling the house you live in and realising its monetary value. It is at this point that the commerciality of the project comes in and the effect is likely to be greater on the renovation project than a new-build. The renovator's property could be surrounded by other properties that will set a ceiling on the value of the house being renovated. You won't get a million when every other house in the street is worth £250,000 – whatever you have spent on sustainability.

Building sustainably is not (yet) all about money – but taking a view on the probable value of the house on completion at least allows an informed decision on how much to invest. The sustainable builder may take the view that seven, 10 or 20 years-on having built anything other than a sustainable, energy efficient house would have been folly. With higher energy bills highly likely to come will potential buyers choose an energy-guzzling or energy-efficient house to buy?

What we seek to achieve are successful, sustainable projects. Houses that are appealing and comfortable, use less energy, fewer resources, have less impact on the local ecology and able to realise their true value. That is a successful project and a happy self builder.

GETTING STARTED

1

2 DESIGN RIGHT

A good product starts with a good design. A conventional house design can almost be taken off the shelf as, beyond shape, style and size there is little to consider and all the technical bits, like how to build it and what to build if from, are a well trod path. But a sustainable home needs a bit more thought. To be sustainable means able to be kept in existence, to be maintainable, to endure. A sustainable home goes further even than that. To reiterate, Sustainability means meeting our needs today without compromising the ability of future generations to meet their own needs.

If we accept that statement as a guide to what designing a sustainable house means then it leads us to two conclusions :

We need to minimise our use of natural resources – that is, materials used in the construction of the house and fuel used in its operation.

We need to design houses that can be adapted to meet future needs and/or can be recycled when they are demolished.

The 'average' UK house uses around 200 tonnes of materials in its construction. Of that 164 tonnes is virgin material (never before used), 12 tonnes is material from industrial waste and 24 tonnes is recycled material (figures from Building Research Establishment (BRE)).

In addition, on average 13 per cent of that virgin material will not be used in the property but is defined as "accidental waste" - broken, lost, off-cuts, over-order, etc. – that goes straight to landfill. That is 21.3 tonnes of new materials lost, at a cost to the builder estimated at between £3,600 and £4,500.

The conventionally built average family home will use around 1,040,000kWh of energy in its life (assuming a life of 80 years and built to 2006 Building Regulations standard). That equates to around 450 tonnes of CO_2 emissions per house and there are some 23 million houses in the UK. The Government suggest an immediate reduction of 40 per cent in CO_2 emissions from 2002 levels, and an overall reduction to zero by 2016. With those figures you can see why.

DESIGN RIGHT

A sustainable house is a house that minimises consumption of materials and fuel. It makes good environmental sense but good commercial sense as well. Use less, spend less.

HOW TO PICK THE DESIGNER

There is a presumption that a house must be designed by an architect. It is not an unreasonable presumption but it is not accurate. There is no legal requirement that plans be drawn or designs created by any particular person. You are at liberty to design your own home (if you feel qualified) or to retain anyone else you want. The choice extends to Architectural Technicians, Architectural Designers, Structural Engineers, Design Consultants, Builders, yourself, the bloke next door. Anyone is legally able to, but the question is should you allow anyone to do it?

An architect will bring seven years of training in what makes a building work and, perhaps more importantly, how to make sure it stands up, which should not be ignored. But they may or may not bring the creative spark, and the enthusiasm for sustainable construction that you need.

As a self-builder you will need three things from your designer:

■ You need to know he or she has done something similar before. Ask for reference projects and go and see them. Speak to the owners and get a view as to how they got on with the designer.

■ Empathy. Does the designer hear what you say and understand? Does he or she tend to tell you what you need rather than listening to what you want?

■ Insurance. Architects are required to carry the appropriate insurance so that if it all goes wrong you can sue them with some confidence of getting some recompense.

The sustainable builder will want a designer / architect that is sympathetic to the ideal and has some experience in the materials and methods. It is accepted that an architect will be versed in traditional building methods and materials. He or she will know how different things will perform in different circumstances. That knowledge will guide the design process from a technical as well as aesthetic view point.

Some sustainable materials will perform the same as their non-sustainable alternatives and some will perform quite differently. Your designer needs to know which is which for the design to work properly. When you are picking your designer you will go through the same process - checking references, viewing other projects the designer has done – but with an emphasise on sustainable building. But most of all you will be checking for empathy. Does the architect/designer understand what you want and why you want it?

2

You will be working with the architect/designer for 12 months or more and it is important that you get on with them. That you feel able to deal with them on a, possibly, daily basis. If they are not empathetic towards your ideals, if they do not share your objectives but try to impose their own, then they may be difficult to get along with.

ASSEMBLING THE RIGHT TEAM

A good architect/designer will also know their own limitations and the experts needed to fill the gaps. That is likely to include a structural engineer and quite possibly a heating and ventilation engineer. The project will also need a builder, and maybe a lighting engineer, a project manager and an interior designer, maybe a sustainability consultant too. In which case they too must have proper knowledge of, or the enthusiasm to learn about, sustainability and renewable energy.

Decide early on what the team needs to consist of and what their total fees are likely to be. The client, the architect/designer and the builder are the basic minimum and of these only the architect wants fees. The architect can call in structural and heating engineers as necessary, and they also will want fees. A sustainability consultant will want fees but can significantly reduce the time the architect/designer spends working things out.

A critical factor in deciding on your team will be the construction method you choose. If you choose timber frame construction using all sub-contractors you will need more people in your team than if you opt for off-site manufacture. Off-site manufacturers do pretty much everything for you – from the drawings and planning consent to fitting the light bulbs. So you won't need anyone else in the team.

Most clients consider themselves adequately qualified project managers, interior designers and lighting engineers, but is that really the case? As an instance, the interior designer needs to be more than a make-over artist. They need to be able to help with use of light, flows around living spaces, juxtaposition of one room to another as well as the more usual things like colour, texture and mood. All these things may be within the architect/designer's capability but are they really within the capability of the untrained client? The client wants, above all things, a successful project and to achieve that they have a responsibility to recognise their own limitations, just as the professionals they engage do.

There is an old Native American saying – If you want to go quickly, go alone. If you want to go far, go together. Building a sustainable home is not a sprint and you will go further, achieve more with the right team around you.

DESIGN ISSUES

As the owner / builder you will be making decisions around open plan living or private space; is the kitchen the hub of the house; do you need a boot-room or mud room by the back door, or maybe a shower room; do you need to consider cats and dogs sharing your space; what are the circulation issues – is the dining room used daily or for special occasions; do you want the potential for extending the property as a whole, extending the living areas into the garden or potential for a granny annex?

All these issues will be discussed with the architect and all will influence and be influenced by the materials to be used, the heating and lighting requirements and the construction method to be used. Designing a home is usually an evolutionary process, and designing a sustainable home will add a couple of key issues into the mix. For the conventional self-builder the issues will be shape, size and style (not necessarily in that order), for the sustainable builder the key issues will be energy, size and resources (in that order).

I. Energy

What generally happens is that the house is designed and built. We move in and maybe, if we are a bit anal, we retain the heating and electricity bills and at the end of a year work out what the house is costing to run. We then either blow our cheeks out in horror and decide to do something about it or put the bills away again and try to earn a bit more money.

The alternative for the self builder is to make energy consumption a primary design parameter.

At the first meeting with the architect or designer all the issues listed above will be discussed, maybe the budget as well, so that the designer gets a good idea of the sort of house you want. Add energy consumption to the list. If your designer knows immediately what you are talking about, you have probably picked the right designer.

* The 'Insulation For Varying Standards' table on page 55 shows that building to Part L standard will mean that the house will consume 55kWh of energy per m^2 floor area per year, EST Best Practice standard will reduce this to 35kWh, Passivhaus to less than 15kWh. From that you can work out what your house will cost to heat thus:

Total floor area x energy/m^2 x cost of energy

Say, 200m^2 x 55kW/m^2/yr x 5p/kWh = £550 p.a.

Do the maths properly, extrapolating running costs over, say, 10 years and you will arrive at a number of kWh per m^2 that you think will be affordable in 10 years time. When you have arrived at a number of kWh/m^2 that is acceptable, give that figure to the designer as a key

2

parameter. If you have picked your designer well he or she will know what to do with the figure and how to achieve it.

Bear in mind that from 2016 (2013 in Wales) the Government will be doing this for you. From then all new houses will have to be zero carbon, which effectively sets heating energy consumption at less than 10kWh per m² per year.

2. Size

Above all things, size matters. The average UK family home is now 130m² floor area which compares to just 85m² in 1950. A 53 per cent increase in size (and consequently materials and energy) in 60 years. This is a reflection of the increasing wealth of the nation and we have always used our house more than anything else to make a statement about our wealth and status. Size has become the principal method of measurement. Put simply the bigger it is the more material it consumes, the more energy it uses and the more CO_2 it embodies and emits.

A method of gauging a build budget is by the cost per square metre. It will vary with the quality of finish, the location and the construction method and will currently be something between £500 per m² to £2,500 per m² – of course it can go on up significantly from that, but that is for a different book. The temptation is to start with the overall budget, say £250K and swiftly arrive at the conclusion that a 4-bedroom, upper-mid range level of finish will allow a house of 200m² at £1,250 per m².

Making it a sustainable house might add £35,000 to the build cost, raising the rate to £1,425 per m² and pushing the total budget to £285,000. Or, reduce the size to 175m², retain the planned sustainability and the standard of finish and the budget returns to £250,000. This really is the question that most self builders aspiring to some level of sustainability have to face. Which is most important, a sustainable home or the extra 25m²? The question is, does a warm, welcoming, functional, strikingly designed house that makes clever use of space and is efficient in its use of fuel but only 175m² say less about the owners than a conventional home of 200m²? Opinions will be divided and it has to be recognised that we now live in a 'I want it all' world. But maybe that is an illusion and actually we can't have it all and maybe, like the kid having a paddy on the supermarket floor, we are better off not having it.

3. Resource Use

Sustainability is about finding materials appropriate to the design

2

as locally as possible but there is an issue to do with marrying aspiration to budget. There is no question that sustainable, 'green', materials are more expensive than their conventional alternatives. As the design evolves there will be decisions to be made about what materials to use, and where is best to use them. As an example; is it better to have a timber-frame house using timber from a non-sustainable source than a brick-and-block house? Or; sustainable insulation is a great idea but too expensive. What to do?

The answer is usually compromise. There is not much personal advantage in using sustainable insulation under the floor slab where you don't come into contact with it, but plenty in having it in the loft where you may come into regular contact. A timber frame house will have lower embodied energy and use less energy to run it than a brick-and-block house, irrespective of where the timber comes from.

It has to be recognised that the level of success will be a product of the amount of effort put in. Some people love the opportunity to do the research and find the materials they want, others don't. Sustainable building is still an idea in its infancy, but it is maturing. Architects, engineers, builders, tradesmen, builder's merchants all tend towards the conventional, because it is safe. It leaves them in their comfort zone. Building sustainably means getting outside that zone. It means finding new design ideas, new materials, new sources of material, new ways of working with that material. It requires thought and effort and it can be a bit scary.

4. Land Use

The sustainable builder will be looking to include renewable energy in some form, and that will be dictated to some extent by what the plot is capable of offering – is it sunny, is it windy, does it have a stream. But the amount of renewable energy needed will be dictated by the design and that has to take account of the potential of the site.

Let's assume that the site has the potential for a south facing elevation. So building a sun room to get some passive solar heat will be a good idea. It will make the house brighter and warmer, and reduce the overall heating load. In turn reducing the investment in the heating system.

But too much solar heat is a bad thing as it may mean investment in a cooling system. The designer of a sustainable house will calculate the solar gain and design-in any counter-measures necessary. Planting deciduous trees close to the sun-room will provide summer shading and will remove the need for cooling.

If yours is an excessively windy site keeping the wind off will improve thermal performance

2

and reduce wear-and-tear. Evergreen trees will work better as a wind-break.

But get the trees in the wrong place – too close or too far away – and they can do more damage than good.

The point is to consider the plot and what it can offer. Think of it as part of your home, use the features is has to offer and design in the things it needs.

5. Location

The location of the property will be driven by a range of personal factors, from where you want to live (region of the country, rural, urban, sub-urban) to proximity to schools, shops, road and rail networks. In sustainability terms, all these issues have a role to play.

A brown-field site has obvious ecological advantages over a green field site but may not be in the preferred area. Proximity to essential services and communications links have the potential to reduce car use, but may deny the attraction of a rural location.

Location will also be driven by availability, finding the right plot is not easy and there is often a compromise to be made. It is such a personal issue that it is probably sufficient to know that there are sustainability issues around it. The choice of location will be a factor in the level of sustainability being aimed at.

Shelter belt max 3X height of house from the house

6. Orientation

There are two main orientation factors to consider; external, i.e. the compass orientation of the building, and internal i.e. the location of the rooms within the building.

In renovation projects it is a matter of working with the existing

2

external orientation but there may be some potential to alter the internal orientation.

Providing a south facing elevation and a south facing roof plane enables access to solar power in all its forms; solar panels, passive solar heat gain and more natural light. It is equally important to arrange the room layout to suit – circulation rooms (living room, kitchen etc.) on the south and operational rooms (utility room, garage, bathrooms) on the north.

This allows the circulation rooms to have large, tall windows that allow in plenty of natural light (tall windows get more light to the back of the room) and operational rooms to have small windows (less heat loss).

Rooms with windows on the east are useful as bedrooms, benefiting from morning sun, but living rooms with west facing windows will be affected by glare from the low setting sun – but will get a good view of the sunset.

Proximity of trees to windows can provide shading which can be beneficial if they are deciduous trees in front of south facing windows by providing summer shading and winter sun, but detrimental if they are evergreen or in front of east-facing windows.

Orientation also needs to fit in with the topography of the site to take advantage of views and, so far as possible, keep road, rail or other noise as far away as possible and to provide access to the outside space.

Orientation and room layout can make or break the comfort and the sense of well-being in the home. Ultimately they will determine how you live in the house.

7. Quality of Life

Dealing effectively with noise, daylight, views of the sky, easy access to outside space and good ventilation will improve the comfort of the house and the quality of the lives of the people in it.

Noise is the biggest potential nuisance to any home owner, with the greatest potential to cause discomfort and annoyance. Limiting adverse noise, both incoming and outgoing, has an obvious benefit. It has also been shown that allowing daylight into the house without glare and providing views of the sky improves the sense of well-being for the occupants, as well as displacing the need for electric lights. Similarly good ventilation, natural or mechanical, improves oxygen levels and prevents a damp, musty atmosphere, again improving the sense of well-being. Poor ventilation has been recognised as a factor in sick building syndrome.

None of these issues are difficult to deal with at the design stage, but can prove impossible to deal with later. There is a balance between light and glare, light and solar heat gain, ventilation and draughts. Get the balance wrong and at best there is a cost of rectification, at worst the house is unpleasant and possibly unhealthy to live in.

THE **SUSTAINABLE** BUILDING BIBLE

2

THE HOLISTIC APPROACH

Everything connects to everything and a house, any building, is like a machine with many connecting parts. Changing one part will tend to affect the whole. In design terms it means that each decision needs to be considered in the light of its possible impact on every other part of the building.

The usual example is that a house designed to be air-tight will have a high level of thermal efficiency, if the occupiers live their life in a way that doesn't need windows to be opened. The holistic designer will start with the lifestyle of the occupiers, and their aspirations, and design a house and heating system to suit. (NOTE: This idea that air tight houses cannot have open windows is a bit of a myth. The rationale is that if it is air tight when a window is opened the heating system will go into overdrive. That is true, but if a window is being opened then it will either be for a short time or it is warm enough outside to not need the heating system to be switched on. Heat recovery ventilation systems are clearly affected by open windows, but can equally clearly be switched off when the window is open.)

But obviously it goes much further than that. A house is a large, complex machine with many issues relating to its performance, maintenance and efficiency. The Code for Sustainable Homes require that a manual be produced to set out all those issues on paper, recognising the importance of understanding the house and how it was designed to be run. Future occupiers, as well as the current ones, will need a good understanding of how the house was designed to operate for it to be operated efficiently.

CONSTRUCTION METHODS

There are two basic construction methods: Light & tight, which is usually timber-frame with maximum insulation and minimum air permeability; or Mass and glass, which is masonry walls and floors with lots of glass to enable high levels of solar heat to be absorbed. The 'mass' is often termed 'thermal mass', as it is used to absorb heat. Mass and glass does not preclude high levels of insulation or automatically mean more air leakage. However it is difficult to argue that mass-and-glass has higher embodied energy and therefore starts from a worse position in terms of eco-credentials.

The main recognised construction methods are:-

Brick-and-block: By which we mean standard masonry, cavity wall construction. This is the archetypal heavyweight construction method but fails to really achieve the thermal mass required for thermally efficient construction. The standard construction is a 100mm inner skin of high density or aerated concrete blocks with 70mm of insulation and 50mm clear cavity, with brick or rendered block outer skin. The issue is that each kilogram of concrete, stone, whatever can absorb a given quantity of heat energy and 100mm concrete block skin cannot absorb enough energy to constitute effective thermal mass.

The advantages are that this is a universally recognised construction method. You can buy bricks and blocks today and start work tomorrow. It is relatively cheap, robust and needs minimal maintenance. And is a highly flexible construction medium.

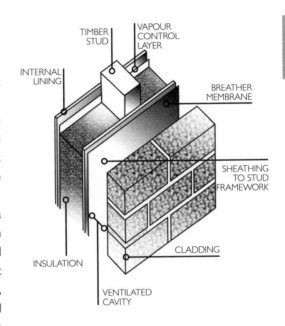

On the downside it has huge embodied energy and CO_2, construction is slow and subject to the vagaries of the weather. It is difficult, and expensive, to move beyond Part L1A and a U-value of 0.35 and difficult to adapt to meet future needs.

Brick-and-block walls are structurally robust so the roof can be almost anything you want. Trusses or cut timber roof with slate or tile covering would be normal, but it could also support a green roof or things like zinc or copper.

Timber Frame: In terms of sustainability, timber-frame carries good credentials, especially if the timber is from a sustainable source and the construction uses sustainable insulation. Typical construction will be a 140mm inner skin, filled with usually mineral wool insulation, a vapour barrier and an external skin, usually brick or rendered block. The inner skin alone will typically give a U-value of 0.24 (30 per cent better than brick-and-block). Change the insulation to high density foam and the U-value will drop to 0.17. The masonry outer skin has next to no effect on the U-value.

The illustration on page 27 shows a typical timber-frame construction method, which epitomises the challenge facing the sustainable builder. In a nutshell, is it the right way round?

Ask yourself why the brick is on the outer skin and consider the effect of having the masonry

2

cladding on the inside. It may sound weird but think about it. The structural stability would not be changed, nor would the thermal performance or the air tightness. Being on the outside it provides weather-proofing but there are lots of ways to do that. The affect of having the masonry on the inside would at least provide some thermal mass able to absorb and release heat and thereby reduce the amount of energy put into the house. Putting the insulation outside the brick means that you get a tea-cosy effect.

Sustainability is often about challenging the accepted norm. The brick outer skin is actually there to convince the rest of the world that you have built in bricks and mortar. It has nothing to do with the performance of the wall.

The principal advantages of timber frame are speed of construction and thermal performance. Taken together these can lead to lower build cost than brick-and-block. In addition, of course, timber is a renewable resource with significantly lower embodied energy and CO_2 than brick-and-block.

On the downside it is not as flexible as brick-and-block and needs planning. The design needs to be sent to a timber frame manufacturer, who will work it into their manufacturing diary and expect to deliver and erect the timber frame on a given date. Any delay to the delivery and erection dates can lead to disaster.

Stick Build: Essentially the same as timber frame, but built on-site rather than pre-assembled in the factory. U-values tend to be slightly poorer than timber frame but this is to do with construction quality rather than an inherent function of stick build.

Stick build is used in areas with difficult access (where lorries cannot get close enough to offload) or where the design makes pre-fabrication of timber frames too tricky. Tends to be more expensive than timber frame, uses more timber and takes longer to build.

Stick build and timber frame both present the opportunity to use timber from sustainable sources as, in both cases, the cost of the timber is a fairly small factor and the cost of upgrading to sustainable timber will make only a small difference. What that does, more than anything, is send the message that this is a sustainable build and that you are serious about using responsibly sourced materials. In itself a big statement of intent.

POST AND BEAM:

Post and beam construction is making something of a resurgence with the traditional post and beam house, as illustrated right, being replaced with the more modern green oak frame.

This traditional post-and-beam construction method has been

used for thousands of years. Until the mid to late 18th century it was still the most popular form of construction used in Britain. Changes in fashion, cheaper alternatives and (ironically perhaps) a shortage of oak led to the method falling out of favour. There are many examples of houses built up to 500 years ago to be seen in this country and in sustainability terms this construction method still has a lot going for it.

In this case the "green" in green oak frame is not used to describe colour, or its eco-credentials but to indicate that it is young, not dried or seasoned, oak. From a green viewpoint, green oak can be considered very green. It has low embodied energy, low embodied CO_2, uses no chemicals or preservatives, has a long life and can come from a sustainable source (although it doesn't always). But sustainable building is not just about green products.

For the self-builder looking for sustainability green oak frames have three key features:

The material is, or can be, truly renewable. In many parts of Northern Europe, and increasingly in the UK, oak is a managed crop.

The material has very low embodied energy. Oak is used green for two reasons – it is cheaper than seasoned oak because you don't have to pay for the time and energy needed to season it. Secondly because green oak is softer than seasoned oak and therefore easier to work with. Both these features lead happily to a lower energy and CO_2 content.

COURTESY MARK WELSH

COURTESY OAKWRIGHTS.CO.UK

Left: typical timber-frame construction method. Right: Post and beam construction also gives more flexibility with the room layout, as none of the internal walls will be load bearing.

2

German companies such as Hanse Haus specialise in off-site manufacture

Post-and-beam is a very flexible construction method. Internal walls can be moved at will as they are not load-bearing and it is relatively simple to extend (or shrink) a building. All of this leads to a longer useful life for the building.

On the down side, the fact of it being green oak means that it will dry over time and cracks will appear. The drying period could be upwards of 12 years and will see the moisture content fall from around 60 per cent to around 16 per cent. That is obviously a huge change so it is not surprising that the oak shrinks and that cracks appear. The transverse shrinkage – across the width – can be as much as 10 per cent. In structural terms this shrinkage will have no affect at all. It is a normal process and allowed for in the design. In terms of thermal efficiency it is rather a different matter.

Green oak frames have come back into fashion principally for aesthetic reasons. They are attractive, they have a real appeal and they differentiate the property. But to get those qualities the posts and beams need to be exposed and that means they are difficult to make thermally efficient.

2

Traditionally the panel between the posts and beams would be filled with something to keep the rain out – wattle and daub, timber, clay and brick were all used. Nowadays we need to do a bit better than merely keep the rain out and insulated panels are often used. Typically these panels will have a U-value of at least 0.3 as that is the maximum allowed under Building Regs. But the posts and beams will have a U-value of probably 0.5 (it will vary with the size of the timber) which means that it needs cladding on either the inside or the outside merely to conform to Building Regs. A design purporting to have green credentials will be looking for a U-value across the wall possibly as low as 0.2 (a Passivhaus wall will be down to 0.12). To achieve that will need at least 120mm of Kingspan or Celotex insulation cladding to the frame. Essentially that is a SIPS panel and these are often used with green oak frame construction.

Green oak frames highlight a major decision for the sustainable builder; which is most important sustainable materials or energy conservation?

Structural Insulated Panels

Essentially SIPS are a refinement of the timber frame idea. Two sheets of Oriented Strand

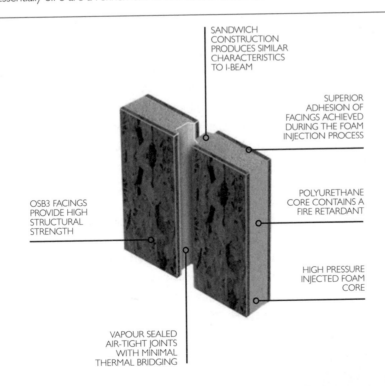

SANDWICH
CONSTRUCTION
PRODUCES SIMILAR
CHARACTERISTICS
TO I-BEAM

SUPERIOR
ADHESION OF
FACINGS ACHIEVED
DURING THE FOAM
INJECTION PROCESS

OSB3 FACINGS
PROVIDE HIGH
STRUCTURAL
STRENGTH

POLYURETHANE
CORE CONTAINS A
FIRE RETARDANT

HIGH PRESSURE
INJECTED FOAM
CORE

VAPOUR SEALED
AIR-TIGHT JOINTS
WITH MINIMAL
THERMAL BRIDGING

2

Board (OSB) sandwiching foam or polystyrene insulation. As with timber frame, the panels are manufactured in a factory, delivered and erected on site. Unlike timber frame, the SIPS panels rely on the sheets of OSB for their structural stability rather than the timber frame – which is often omitted from SIPS.

As shown in the illustration on page 30, SIPS panels usually have a tongue-and-groove connection which improves air-tightness. This together with the insulation in a 150mm SIPS panel will commonly achieve a U-value of 0.15 or better.

SIPS construction is usually more expensive than timber frame and brick-and-block, but has much faster erection time. This means that the potential for delaying follow-on trades in minimised and the overall build time is reduced.

In terms of eco-credentials, SIPS have a couple of question marks. The option for sustainable insulation is not easy to find, and tends to be even more expensive, and the source of the timber making up the OSB is questionable. However these are relatively small matters in the overall scheme of things. The energy efficiency is very good so energy consumption and CO_2 emissions are very low.

Off-Site Manufacture

Off-site manufacture is where the whole house – walls, floors, roof, windows, doors, electrics, plumbing, the lot – is manufactured in a factory and effectively assembled on site. The raison d'être of OSM's is to build more energy efficient houses. Notable manufacturing companies are Baufritz, Hanse House, Huf House, Scandia House mostly German companies but there are a couple of UK firms, Potton, famous for their Lighthouse but now marketing the Zenit, and RuralZed, a company set up specifically to provide energy efficient, sustainable housing.

The illustration on page31 shows the erection of a house nearing completion. In this case a team of nine men erected the whole house in just seven hours. As can be seen windows and doors are all installed and, once the last piece is lowered into place the house is wind and water-tight.

According to the Energy Saving Trust a traditional brick and block house built to Building Regulations standards will consume up to 85kWh of energy per year, per square metre of floor area for space heating and hot water. The off-site manufactured (OSM) house can get that figure down to below 30kWh p.a.

Triple glazed windows, heat pumps, heat recovery systems, solar panels and pellet boilers are either included as standard or available options. In all cases the levels of air tightness are excellent all achieving 5m³/hr or better – twice as good as Building Regs call for.

From an energy efficiency point of view there is no contest, OSM's beat brick & block and timber frame every time. The illustration shows a typical OSM wall section, in this case using a combination of wood fibre and mineral wool insulation, with timber external cladding.

If what you want is the hands-on involvement of building your own home then OSM is probably not for you. If you want an energy efficient house, delivered on time and on budget then OSM may be the way to go. The reality is that by 2016 when zero carbon houses are mandatory, we will all be doing something similar.

A combination of the above

It may well be that budget, aspiration, design all conspire to prevent any one system being just right. They all have some eco-merit and all have their own advantages, and their constraints. There is no reason not to be creative and use particular systems where they are most appropriate, mixing and matching to suit the design and the terrain.

Designing a sustainable home is about challenging the conventions. It is about asking if the methods and materials used are actually the best option available, or are they just being used because 'it is the way we have always done it?' It is often a matter of determining which of construction method and design is the cart and which the horse.

QUALITY CONTROL

Actually achieving what is set out in the drawings and specification is becoming increasingly important as we continually improve the design. The most important issue is achieving the level of air tightness specified. Air tightness has the single biggest impact on heat loss and missing the design specification not only means that the heat loss target is missed and the efficacy of the heating system put in danger, but it also means potentially expensive remedial work.

Increasingly, and specifically in the 2010 Building Regulations, there is a requirement to demonstrate that what was specified is actually achieved. In the case of air tightness the design figure will be included in the SAP calculation and tested with a blower test, carried out when the house is nearing completion. The figure specified MUST be achieved, so if the house fails there will be costly and time consuming remedials to find where air is leaking and to fix the leaks.

On site quality control is not something we have been used to in the UK. In broad terms, yes

2

the build is checked, but not in detail. Failures – cracks in plaster, stairs moving away from the wall, gaps around wall penetrations, floor tiles that ring hollow – are attributed to settlement or drying where in fact they are the result of poor quality construction.

A high performance house cannot tolerate poor quality construction and need good quality control. The design and specification have been carefully worked out and need to be implemented as stated – not as near as the tradesmen feels able to do on that day.

The point is that the self builder needs to understand this at the outset and organise with the architect, designer or builder who will be responsible, and then ensure it happens.

SOLAR ENERGY

Solar energy has been harnessed by humans since pre-history, using a range of ever-evolving technologies. Some 1.4kW of solar energy falls on each square metre of the Earth's surface, but only a minuscule fraction of that energy is used.

Solar technologies are either passive or active, depending on the way they capture, convert and distribute sunlight. Active solar techniques include photovoltaic and solar thermal panels and convert sunlight into electricity or useful heat respectively. Passive solar techniques include orienting a building to the sun, selecting materials with good thermal mass and designing spaces that naturally circulate air.

To calculate the amount of heat produced by a south facing window multiple the area of the window in square metres by 868 and divide the answer by 3.4 for a result in Watts.

For example:

A room with a 4m² patio door and a 1.6m² window both on the south elevation of a room with a floor area of 20m²

Heat gain in Watts = 5.6m² x 868 / 3.4 = 1429 Watts

An acceptable level of solar heat gain is 25W per m² of floor area. In this case a 20m² floor area room will be receiving 71.5W per m². It will therefore need some cooling in summer and there are a number of ways of dealing with it:

■ Mechanical cooling, i.e. air conditioning

■ Retractable blinds to provide shading

      ■ Planting – trees or other plants to provide shading

        ■ Open the patio doors

          ■ Distribute the heat

            Obviously designing a room that will require air conditioning

2

does not fall within the sustainable remit, although it might well be the conventional builder's first choice.

Retractable blinds fitted over the window and patio door provide an acceptable and effective solution, but they add cost and increase the embodied CO_2 of the house.

Planting deciduous trees in front of the south elevation (poplar, plane or similar) will provide dappled shade in summer and allow sunlight though in winter. Although poplars have a high growth rate, there may still be a short term issue with shading until the trees are up to height. An alternative may be to plant clematis or similar on a pergola-type structure outside the patio doors. This will not only provide adequate shading but will also encourage greater use of the outside space.

Simply opening the patio doors will have a marked cooling affect, as will using passive ventilation to distribute the heat through the house – which may be why the sun-room was built in the first place.

It is likely, essential even, that a house claiming sustainability credentials will utilise solar energy in a positive and considered way, be that passive solar energy used to heat and light the house or active solar energy collection to heat and power the house. It is difficult, not to say impossible, to conceive of a sustainable house that has not designed in solar energy. The only question is how much.

THERMAL MASS

Building in thermal mass is often the reason given for using traditional brick-and-block construction, but the truth is that it doesn't provide much useful thermal mass. Or, at least, it has to be very carefully designed and constructed to be of value.

The thermal mass in the house has to absorb heat that can later be released. If that heat comes from the gas boiler it is providing no advantage in that it is the same heat that could have been used in the house. To be useful the thermal mass needs to be able to absorb solar (free) heat and is therefore best designed in around windows and patio doors.

Each kilogram of concrete, brick, stone that is being used to provide the thermal mass has a finite capacity to absorb heat. Therefore the amount of material needed needs to be calculated to ensure it is able to absorb enough heat to have a real impact when that heat is released.

It is, however, true that thermal mass will tend to flatten the peaks and troughs of heating the house. That in itself can tend to save energy, and used properly in a well insulated building can be of value.

2

WINDOWS & DOORS

The current choice of material for windows and doors, in probable order of popularity, is : u-PVC, Aluminium, Wood – solid, Wood – engineered, Steel.

It has to be said that steel has little to recommend it. Thermal performance is poor, cost relatively high and it is inherently high maintenance. Except where there is a structural need, there is always a better alternative.

Similarly with aluminium. Although it is a recyclable material, in its powder coated form (usual for windows and doors) it is practically unrecyclable due to the cost and energy used in getting the coating off. And thermally it is outperformed by both u-PVC and wood.

For the past 30 years u-PVC has been the standard as it offers a functional, relatively cheap product that is perceived to have a long life and be maintenance free. But the environmental impact of PVC, based on published research, can only be considered controversial. The two camps, being environmentalists and the PVC manufacturing industry, unsurprisingly take widely different views. To try and put the argument in a nutshell :

■ 1. PVC uses large amounts of fossil fuel (worldwide production of PVC is currently around 18 million tonnes per year, about 57 per cent of which is oil, as a raw material). It also uses large amounts of chemical additives. The argument seems to revolve around the amount and potential toxicity of the by-products and waste. There seems to be no argument that they are produced, it is a question of how much and how poisonous?

■ 2. The Building Research Establishment has recently accepted that PVC is a recyclable material. However, there are currently two post-consumer PVC recycling facilities in the UK and regulation restrict the amount of recycled material that can be used in a new u-PVC window or door. For most people the only practical way to dispose of a defunct u-PVC window is to landfill.

■ 3. PVC is said to be long-life and maintenance free. Dulux, amongst others, now offer paints for PVC designed to block ultra violet light, preventing discolouration and extending the life of the product. Again, a cynic might ask why this is necessary if the product is inherently long-life and maintenance free? And we are all aware of double glazed units that have "popped" – that are no longer sealed and have condensation on the inside. Generally this will be in windows 10 to 12 years old. It can be fixed but the reality is that fixing it costs virtually as much as a new window.

It perhaps comes as no surprise that the only really eco-option is wood. In the past wood has had something of a bad press: said to be expensive, to warp, rot, and need lots of maintenance. But

2

modern manufacturing methods mean that none of this is necessarily true.

Eco-windows and doors are generally made from durable timber; Douglas fir, Redwood or oak. The ones with true eco-credentials are Forestry Stewardship Council certified, meaning that the timber comes from responsibly managed forests. Whether they are solid timber or engineered timber, they tend to not twist or warp (engineered timber being especially good in this respect) and modern design and manufacturing methods mean that rain water is conducted away, preventing rot.

Eco windows are treated with non toxic, usually water based, compounds to prevent fungal or insect attack. The Green Building Store supply the EcoPlus System windows and doors which use boron. This is an organic compound, first used by the Romans as a timber treatment, which also improves the fire resistance. In addition, paint or stain finishes are also organic or water based. This means that, worst case, at the end of the window or door's life it can be composted as there are no chemicals in the wood that might be considered. harmful.

Thermal performance of timber windows and doors is at least as good as u-PVC. As an example EcoPlus System standard windows have a U-value of $1.2W/m^2$ compared to a u-PVC standard of $1.8W/m^2$. They also offer a Passivhaus standard window with a U-value of just $0.5W/m^2$. The attention to detail is also quite something, with "warm-edge" spacers in windows, double sealed letter-boxes and even specially designed cat-flaps that ensure low air permeability and good thermal performance (although even that does not get up to Passivhaus standard).

The maintenance required is not what it used to be either. Modern micro-porous paints and stains are absorbed by the wood rather than layered on it, so that they don't blister or flake. They do require maintenance but this generally amounts to wiping clean and applying a single coat of paint or stain, once every 5 or 6 years.

And as to cost, good quality wooden windows from a major manufacturer like EcoPlus or Allan Brothers will vary from £250 per m^2 for standard windows to £600 per m^2 for windows of Passivhaus standard. Solid timber windows from your local joiner might cost £200 to £500 per m^2 and u-PVC £200 to £350 per m^2. It is quite likely that wood, engineered or solid, will cost more, but perhaps not as much as you might think.

To quote Dr Gillian Menzies of Heriot Watt University, 'To build sustainably, we are not required to sacrifice comfort and well being, but to act responsibly in the way we select materials and design components for construction.' In this case acting responsibly probably means no more than questioning what the marketing men have been telling us for the past 30 years.

2

PASSIVE VENTILATION

Before Building Regs called for increasingly air-tight houses and mechanical ventilation became the norm, people kept cool fresh air in the house using natural methods: walls that 'breathe', breezes flowing through windows, as well as large amounts of stone and brick absorbing daytime heat. These ideas were developed over thousands of years and became a standard, integral parts of building design. Today they are called passive ventilation and, ironically perhaps, are considered alternative technology to the 'normal' mechanical ventilation systems.

There are two basic types of passive ventilation, which can be described as pressure and buoyancy systems. Pressure systems rely on the positive pressure on the windward side of the building causing a lower pressure on the leeward side, causing air movement through the building from the windward to the leeward side. There are obvious design implications in that vents, window openings and room layouts have to be positioned appropriately to ensure air movement is possible and in the right direction.

Whole House Passive Stack Ventilation Systems – or PSV – work on the buoyancy principal. They are recognised by BRE, included in Building Regs Part FI and the Scottish Technical Standard 3.

Hot air is buoyant in cooler air and tends to rise. This is often called the "stack effect", which also describes the equipment. A simple example is an open fire with a chimney stack, which is a passive ventilation system. The chimney air is heated by the fire and the smoke carried away on the warm, rising air. In the same way a PSV system will draw warm, moist air through ducts from a bathroom or kitchen and out through the roof. Fresh air can be introduced through vents in walls or windows in habitable rooms (living room, bedroom etc.) or ducted in from the roof.

In some cases, as with the Monodraught Windcatcher, both extract air and fresh air use a single roof vent, the stale air coming out of the leeward side of the stack and fresh air introduced on the windward side. Arup have developed a PSV system where a specially designed cowl and ducting system allows the fresh air being introduced to be warmed by the air being extracted – effectively passive heat recovery.

Refinements have been added to the standard PSV system to provide greater control. Systems are available that use humidity controlled extract and inlet valves which open and close according to internal conditions. So that air is only extracted from the bathroom, for instance, when the bath or shower have been used.

Monodraught also offer a system with a solar PV powered fan. This provides the added benefit of more precisely controlling the

2

volume of air being extracted and introduced, but still without the need for extra energy.

An alternative way to warm the incoming air and thereby minimise the heat loss inherent in ventilation systems is to use "supply-air windows". Essentially these are double glazed windows with a third pane of glass on the outside with an inlet at the bottom of the third pane and an outlet at the top of the double-glazed unit. So that incoming air passes behind the third pane, gaining a little solar heat and a little of the heat leaving the house through the double glazing and enters the house a little warmer. Dwell-Vent Ltd offer supply-air window PSV systems with non-return valves on the air vents to prevent warm air leaving the house.

Passive ventilation is little more than a new twist on an old idea. With the drive to achieve zero carbon homes, building every more air-tight houses is becoming critical, and with it the need for controlled ventilation. Passive ventilation systems can meet the bill, usually have no moving parts and are relatively inexpensive. A basic system being little more than ducting and valves. Adding sophistications like supply-air windows or PV powered fans is a matter of personal choice but as with all these things design is critical. A well designed system will extract air from the right places and introduce the right amount of fresh air. Get the design wrong and we have either a damp, stuffy house or a cold, draughty house.

NATURAL VENTILATION

Natural ventilation used to be a matter of opening the window or trickle vents and air brick but has moved on a bit from there. Thermostatic window actuators (electric opening when the room gets too hot) are becoming more trendy as are passive roof cowls – either the old middle-eastern wind towers that push air down into the building or cowls that use the wind to draw air from the building. All these systems provide a fair degree of control over the amount of air moving through the building and the direction of its movement, either mechanically through dampers or electronically. They also use little or no energy to do it.

Simply opening the windows can achieve the same thing but with a good deal less control. If windows are to be used then it is necessary to design the right openings in the right places to achieve proper ventilation.

Horizontal pivot openings offer the best ventilation capability as they tend to be effective in any wind direction. Vertical pivot openings work well as air scoops when the wind direction is parallel to the wall but need articulation to the building elevation (e.g. bay windows) to create a local pressure difference.

With any of the natural ventilation options a good understanding of the systems, heating and ventilating, and the design issues around them is essential. As we move towards ever more air-

2

tight buildings the issue of ventilation becomes increasingly important. The old rule of 5 per cent of floor area as opening windows no longer applies and it is no longer something that can be left to guesswork or luck. Airtightness beyond $7m^3/hr$ needs the expert advice of a heating and ventilation engineer to ensure safety and health. See Assembling the Right Team, this section.

ENERGY USE

We are required by building regulations to provide a SAP rating (Standard Assessment Procedure) at the design stage of the project. The SAP calculation will come up with a figure of up to 100 (the higher the number the lower the running cost, with figures over 100 being

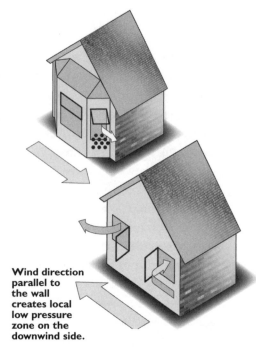

Wind direction parallel to the wall creates local low pressure zone on the downwind side.

net energy exporter). It may be 64, 82, 47 or whatever but unfortunately very few of us know what that figure means. We know that a high figure is good and a low figure bad but it takes a detailed examination of the SAP calculation to find out how much energy the building will actually use.

The SAP calculation will give a figure in kWh per year which needs to be divided by the total floor area. We are looking for a figure of less than 55kWh/m² to comply with 2010 Building Regulations insulation standards. A property looking for sustainability credentials will want to go some way past this.

The SAP calculation is a retrospective look at the probable energy consumption, in that it is a result of design rather than an influence on design. What the sustainable builder will want to do is put energy consumption at the front of the design process.

INSULATION FOR VARYING STANDARD

The point of this is two-fold: The figure relates directly to the amount of fuel the property will consume and what it will cost to run; if some or all of that fuel is fossil fuel the figure also translates into CO_2 emissions.

Our standard house, conventionally insulated will emit a total of

2

4.23 tonnes of CO2 every year. So our standard house of 200m² will use 11,000kWh of natural gas heating and 5,000kWh of electricity each year. That is:
- Gas – 11,000 × 0.19 = 2090kg or 2.09 tonnes
- Electricity – 5,000 × 0.43 = 2150kg or 2.14 tonnes

CONVERT KWH TO CO₂ :

For natural gas multiply by 0.19
For oil multiply by 0.25
For grid electricity multiply by 0.43

A point that is shown in the table (above right) and is probably blindingly obvious is that a zero carbon house is not zero energy. If all the energy for the zero carbon house came from grid utilities it would emit 2.64 tonnes of CO_2. Reducing the heating load significantly reduces the potential CO_2 emissions but still leaves some heat load and all the electrical power to be dealt with.

Designing the energy efficiency rating of the home is still something of a new idea, we are usually more interested in the sale value. It is only in the last year or two that energy use and running cost have come in to the equation at all. A sustainable home will put energy use at the heart of the design process. Not only the amount of energy used but also the source of that energy.

INSULATION FOR VARYING STANDARDS

	Part LIA	UK Best Practice	Passivhaus	Zero Carbon
Walls Polyurethane	50mm	100mm	175mm	200mm
Floor Polystyrene	100mm	100mm	200mm	200mm
Roof Mineral wool	270mm	350mm	400mm	400mm
Windows U-value	1.8	1.3	<0.8	<0.8
Air Tightness	10m³/hr	<3m³/hr	<1m³/hr	<1m³/hr
Energy For heating per m²	<55kWh p.a.	<35kWh p.a.	<15kWh p.a.	<50kWh p.a.
Annual Consumption for 200m² house	11,000kWh	7,000kWh	3,000kWh	2,000kWh

THE **SUSTAINABLE** BUILDING BIBLE

2

AIR TIGHTNESS

It is mandatory for all houses gaining planning consent after April 2006 to meet the Building Regulations Part L1A standard on air tightness. That standard is a 'leakage' of not more than 10m³/h/m²@50pa. That is, 10 cubic metres of air per hour escaping for every square metre of the envelope surface area with the air at a pressure of 50 Pascals. What that actually means is a bit of a mystery and whether it is a good idea is another thing altogether. We are being forced to adopt air-tightness which means, increasingly, that mechanical ventilation is needed for dehumidification and the introduction of fresh air.

The 2003 Building Regulations stated that we had to have a maximum of 1.5 air changes per hour (ach). It was in the late 1980s that the standard changed from a minimum to a maximum. Until then 1.5ach was considered to be the minimum amount of air need to maintain oxygen levels, clear out exhalation CO_2, pollutants and smells. The 2006 regulations are based, at least in part, on the Canadian R2000 standard which calls for 0.8ach at 50pa.

Achieving permeability of less than 10m³/hr is still a matter of choice – for the time being at least. By 2016 the permitted permeability will be less than 3m³/hr, possibly less than 1m³/hr. The problem for the self-builder lies in the attention to detail needed to achieve those levels of air tightness. It is a quality control standard that the UK house building industry is just not used to.

HEATING CONTROLS

In a house built to 2006 Building Regulations standards 77 per cent of the energy used in the building will go to space and water heating and 23 per cent to power – lighting, TV, computer, etc.

The big energy user is space heating, accounting for up to 60 per cent of the total. A good control system could reduce the energy bill by 15 per cent, will cost perhaps £300 (if installed with a new heating system) and will allow different temperatures and different heating times for each room or each zone of the house. Why heat a bedroom from 5pm. when there is no intention to use it until 11pm? Why heat a guest bedroom to the same temperature as other bedrooms when it is not going to be used at all?

Designing the right systems for heating, lighting and ventilation is critical but having control over those systems is the only way to make sure they work efficiently.

The latest Building Regulations Part L1 specifies that in new houses with a total heated living space floor area of over 150m² the heating circuit must be split into at least two, fully controlled, separate

2

zones along with a separately controlled hot water zone.

Each zone should have its own independent time and temperature control and each zone can fire the boiler independently. The first zone to require heat switches the boiler on and the last zone to reach the required temperature switches it off.

Ideally each room or separate area of the house will be considered as a separate zone, and separately controlled.

ENERGY EFFICIENT LIGHTING

With legislation that came into force in January 2009, 100W lamps are no longer available, 60W went in 2011 and all high energy incandescent lamps off the shelves by 2013. Why? Put simply because 85 per cent of the electricity consumed by incandescent lamps produces heat rather than light. If we swapped all the incandescent lamps in the UK for low-energy lamps, we would save 5 million tonnes of CO_2 emissions every year.

Compact Fluorescent Lamps

The technology in compact fluorescent lamps (CFL's) has improved massively in recent years. Because we are increasingly buying them, there is value to the manufacturers in developing better technology. In the past the colour of CFL's was limited to 'cold blue' light but they are now available in the full range from 'cold blue' to 'warm white'. Look for the Energy Saving Trust logo on the packaging as these lamps have to emit the same quality of light as an incandescent lamp.

CFL's can be used anywhere that an incandescent would have been used, and they don't have to be ugly. Go to www.ecostreet.com/blog/green-art/ and click on "Low energy bulbs like you have never seen them before" for an idea of what is possible. Or take a look at www.greenpeace.org.uk/climate/light-bulb-gallery/ to get an idea of the full range. There are now CFL's for every application.

Light Emitting Diode

To some extent this is the new kid on the block. LED lights have been around since 1979 but getting a good quality white light was always a problem. LED's naturally emit blue, red or green light and that needs to be altered in some highly technical way to produce white light. In commercially viable terms LED's giving a good white light have only been available since the late 1990's.

LED's have generally been used for highlighting – downlighters particularly – as they emit a

2

fairly tight beam of light. But again technology is moving on and there will soon be LED lamps available that look like a traditional light bulb and give a similar, diffuse light.

A 5W LED lamp will give the same amount and quality of light as a 35W halogen – and would be used in the same application. At around £8 each they are two to three times the price of halogen lamps but with a life in excess of 40,000 hours they will last five to six times as long.

Take a look at www.ecocentric.com click on eco lighting and take a look at their Lightening Rod for the sort of thing that is possible with LED's. Because they are small, dimmable and have a range of colours, LED's offer a design flexibility that is unsurpassed.

Halogen Lamps

With the advances in LED technology and the range of LED lamps now available, it is difficult to see the point of halogen. They are a bit cheaper but you will need to buy five during the life of one LED lamp. And the LED will cost about £9 less per year to run.

Low Voltage Lighting

The advantage of low voltage lighting is that it gives the lighting designer more flexibility, more scope. It is not about saving energy. The light emitted by a lamp is a factor of the number of Watts of electricity delivered to that lamp. O-level physics tells us that Watts = Volts x Amps. Reducing the voltage makes the lighting circuits less dangerous to handle and therefore more adaptable to interesting designs but does not reduce the amount of energy needed. If a lamp is rated at 5W or 50W, that is the amount of energy it will consume, irrespective of whether that energy comes from a 12v or 240v supply.

IS IT WORTH CHANGING?

A new four bedroom house has maybe 20 to 25 lamps, usually being a mix of incandescent, CFL's and halogens. They will consume about 1800kWh of electricity per year at a cost of £220. Switching to all CFL's and LED's will reduce the consumption to about 450kWh and the cost to £60 per year. To say nothing of saving 0.6 tonnes of CO_2 emissions. Taken across the UK that would equate to not needing eight power stations.

LIGHTING DESIGN

Lighting is, perhaps, the single most important design issue in the home. It has obvious health and safety issues but also sets a mood.

2

It will highlight the features, low-light the faults, make the room relaxing or vibrant. It is the lighting that makes a room function – be it natural or artificial lighting. As a consequence we use a lot of it.

With the choice of lighting types and the effects that can be created, giving due attention to lighting design is even more important. Combining CFL's with LED's overcomes the problems with both and can provide a lighting system that is effective and able to meet varying demands. But it probably needs input from a professional.

SELECTING SUSTAINABLE MATERIALS

A pre-determination for a particular material will go a long way towards determining the overall design. For example, the client who wants a turf roof will strongly influence everything that goes under it. A pre-disposition for ship-lap cladding will make the decision for straight walls as ship-lap does not do curves well.

In terms of sustainability the only essential prerequisite is that as many materials as practically possible should be from sustainable sources.

Unless the architect and/or builder are particularly enthusiastic the use of recycled or reclaimed materials will be limited to those that the client finds. Local research of architectural salvage yards and demolition yards can be extremely revealing. From mundane roof slates to the more esoteric - interesting wall or floor tiles – it is truly amazing what can be found with a little effort. Just knowing what is potentially available will help in the decision making process and may open up whole new lines of thought.

There are sustainable alternatives to just about every item that goes to the construction of a house: timber – FSC timber; slates – recycled slates; ceramic tiles – recycled glass tiles; concrete – recycled aggregate concrete; PVC windows – wooden windows. The scope of the sustainable materials available will be a product of the research and effort that the client puts in. And a cost comparison to non-sustainable alternatives is inevitable and advisable. But the cost comparison needs to be properly conducted to be meaningful. There is no material difference, in terms of quality or durability, between standard concrete and concrete made from recycled aggregate – so price and desire are the only issues. There is a material difference between PVC gutters and copper gutters. PVC will be significantly cheaper but will have a significantly shorter life so the whole-life cost of copper gutter will actually be less than that of PVC. That is in addition to the environmental and maintenance issues. As a self-builder aspiring to a sustainable home, you must decide what is practically achievable in your project. There is no pre-requisite to use only sustainable materials and as will be seen in

2

further chapters there is a sound argument for using the right material in the right place, irrespective of whether it is sustainable or not. The targets for a sustainable build must be practical and achievable. It is better to succeed in a small way than fail in a large way.

Listed below are just some of the many web sites selling sustainable materials.

■ www.rounded-developments.org.uk

■ www.greenconsumerguide.com

■ www.greenshop.co.uk

■ www.aecb.net

■ www.fsc.org

WATER

Did you know that the average household with four people uses 175,000 litres of water each year? And that each litre needs 0.005kWh of energy to get it to the tap. That is 875 kWh of energy to deliver drinking quality water to each house.

Did you also know that up to 35 per cent of that high quality water, and energy, goes straight down the toilet?

Each toilet will use, on average 61,000 litres of water per year. A low flush cistern will reduce that to 40,000, an ultra low flush to under 30,000 litres. Showers use, on average, 35,000 litres per year. Again, an aerated shower head reduces the quantity of water used to around 17,000 litres.

The same story is true of taps, dishwashers and washing machines. How far anyone goes in terms if saving water is still a matter of personal choice and it has to be considered that grey water or rainwater harvesting systems will take a long time to recover their cost in terms of reduced water bills. A rainwater harvesting system will cost around £4,000 installed but against that needs to be stacked the convenience of having a water supply that is free of any energy input, available to water the garden or wash the car and not subject to hose-pipe bans.

EXTERNAL SURFACE TREATMENTS

Asphalt drives, slab patios, concrete footpaths are not the only options. As with most elements of the house there are alternatives. Water permeable options are available for all external surface treatments and they have a number of benefits:

■ They reduce the rainwater run-off to drains reducing the risk of overloading the drainage system and of flash flooding.

■ They allow more water back into the water-table, making it available for extraction as drinking water.

■ They challenge the way we look at external surfaces to provide potentially more aesthetically pleasing treatments.

■ They improve the local ecology.

Unlike most other sustainable alternatives the benefit of permeable surface treatments does not come directly or immediately to the home owner. To be blunt, it is something we do for the greater good. For the time being at least. The Code for Sustainable Homes requires that no more water runs off the site after the house is built that before the house was built, and that has been embodied in 2010 Building Regs.

WASTE & RECYCLING

In terms of the operation of the house it is simply a matter of providing adequate space for the separation of waste into recyclable stores. Certainly internally, but perhaps externally as well with the provision of space for more than one waste-bin and perhaps some composting bins is worthwhile.

In terms of construction, remember that some 21 tonnes of waste (to say nothing of excavation spoil) will be produced during the build project. A trial conducted by two major house builders in 2002 found that sorting and separating this waste reduced the build cost by an average eight per cent. Costs were saved in two ways: materials were recovered and reused, haulage and landfill charges were reduced. It makes obvious commercial sense as well as environmental sense to consider what actually is rubbish.

It is fair to say that some local authorities appear to be becoming obsessed with waste; its sorting, storage, collection and disposal. Eventually all local authorities will come to the conclusion that all waste is either reusable, recyclable or a source of energy, and that we have no need for landfill sites. In the meantime find out what your local authority's position is, and, as a minimum, comply.

EXTENSION, CONVERSION & RENOVATION

Renovating, converting or extending an old building is perhaps the most sustainable means of construction. If the outer shell is kept, and the project needs no major building effort, then the potential environmental damage of sourcing and bringing in new materials and machinery is at least reduced.

The renovation or extension project can give the owner a chance to examine the property in terms of its ecological impact:

2

■ What features of this property are geared towards sustainability?

■ Which features aren't, and should be changed?

■ Can renewable energy be incorporated?

■ Which elements of the project lend themselves to sustainable materials?

■ Would the property benefit from redesign?

Consider the shell of the building; what is the state of repair, what is its U-value, what is the potential to improve the thermal performance and what are the options for doing it?

What we are saying, in effect, is that whatever the scale of the project, from a simple extension to an otherwise comfortable house, to a major renovation, take the opportunity to consider or re-consider the property as a whole.

All the same issues discussed above apply it is merely a matter of scale.

THE DESIGN ISSUES IN SUMMARY

Put energy at the centre of the design process. Make energy consumption, and the running costs, as significant a design criterion as the number of bedrooms or the size of the kitchen.

Decide which is most important, size or sustainability – dealing honestly with the 'The Sustainable Builder's Dilemma' at the design stage will save a lot of heartache, and unnecessary expense. It will also put you on track to designing a house you can actually build.

Pick the right designer and let her/him be the guide as to the remainder of the team. Whoever the designer is, and whatever their qualification, you need to be on the same wavelength or yours will be a difficult and expensive project.

Quality of life. Recognise how you live and let that guide the design. Your perfect house may actually be difficult to live in.

Include the plot in the design. It is not just there to hold up the building, it makes a contribution to the house and the way it works.

Set yourself achievable targets. Better to succeed in a small way than fail in a big way.

The Holistic Approach – everything connects to everything. Your house is a machine and understanding how it works is the only way to make sure it does work.

DESIGN RIGHT

2

3 SUSTAINABLE MATERIALS

One of the principal decisions any builder makes is what materials to use. More accurately, perhaps, it is a set of decisions, or a decision process, as there are thousands of components to a house and many options for each one – some, if not all, using different materials.

SUSTAINABLE MATERIALS – V – SUSTAINABLE DESIGN

If materials selection forms an integral part of the design process there is no conflict. For the sustainable self-builder or renovator, there has to be an expectation that more time, effort and money will be expended in the design phase of the project than would be the case for a conventional build.

A conventional build will require decisions on the size of the property, the construction method (timber-frame or masonry) and style. That will be about it. The architect will specify the materials and the builder will find the cheapest options.

The first area of research for the sustainable builder is to find an architect who understands, and enjoys, sustainability. That in itself may not be easy but an architect who has no knowledge of sustainability and takes no pleasure from the challenge will make the task impossible.

Once an architect has been found the next stage of the process will be to start researching materials – at the same time keeping an idea as to the type of house preferred. But a pre-determination for a particular material may not be helpful as it will go a long way towards determining the overall design. For example, the client who insists on straw-bale construction will strongly influence everything else about the house – the construction method, the options for roofing, virtually all other materials, the thermal performance, to say nothing of the look .

In terms of sustainability the only essential prerequisite is that as many materials as practically possible should be recycled or from sustainable sources. The design process then becomes a cycle of finding materials to suit the design and changing the design to suit the materials. Do

MATERIALS

3

Resource	Quantity per house	Kg CO$_2$ per house	Comments
Spoil	12m^3	750	
Blocks	1,586	6,823	High density concrete
Bricks	6,940	4,164	3kg brick
Reinforced beams	26m	800	
Plasterboard	148m^2	180	Weight taken from COSHH sheets
Mortar	3m^3	690	
Glass	27m^2	2,109	Based on UPVC double glazing.
Timber	6m3	1,096	At 400kg/m^3
Paint	75ltr	457	Acrylic paint
Roadway	52m^2	16,783	Concrete with tarmac over
Concrete roof tile	93m^2	2,700	Data from the BRE elemental tables
Concrete floor	72m^2	1,173	
General insulation	500kg (estimated)	1,303	Assumes polyurethane foam
Membrane	80m^2 8kg	66	Assumes plastic sheet, 120 microns
Ancillaries		5,000	Wiring, pipes, drainage etc.
Total CO^2		**43,914**	

not be fooled. This will be neither quick nor cheap. What it will produce is a building that gives the owner a strong sense of self-satisfaction; a building that can be boasted about and displayed; and a building that will more than repay its extra design cost in many ways other than financial.

The sustainable builder will be looking to incorporate at least some sustainable materials, complicating that decision-making process still further. The first question is what sort of sustainable builder you aspire to be; energy focussed or materials focussed? Of course these are not mutually exclusive but the energy focus will look at building the most energy efficient property possible which might mitigate against some sustainable materials. A case in point would be insulation. The energy focus wants excellent thermal performance and so lots of insulation. Sustainable insulation tends to perform less well than non-sustainable options and so more insulation is needed to achieve the same level of performance. Which is all well and fine but in practice it may be difficult to install the amount needed. There may just not be enough room. So the compromise is guided by the focus. The energy focus will tend towards non-sustainable insulation and the materials-focus will stick with the sheep wool.

THE **SUSTAINABLE** BUILDING BIBLE

3

SUSTAINABLE OPTIONS

Element	Preference	Options	Avoid
Foundations	Reclaimed aggregate concrete	Concrete and block	
Ground floor	Suspended timber with reclaimed aggregate blinding	Foamed concrete on reclaimed aggregate sub base	Block and beam
Intermediate floors	FSC timber joists with reclaimed timber boards	FSC timber	Concrete
Walls	FSC timber frame, reclaimed brick	Masonry	Steel frame
Wall cladding	FSC timber, lime render	Masonry	PVC
Windows & doors	Durable timber frames with Low-E double glazing	Aluminium frames	uPVC or PVCu
Roof structure	FSC timber trusses	non-sustainable timber	Steel
Roof covering	Reclaimed slates or tiles, new timber shingles	Concrete roof tiles, clay roof tiles	Copper or Zinc
Finishes	Natural paint on lime plaster	Natural paint on flue-gypsum plaster	Alkyd paint on phospho-gypsum plaster
Floor covering	Linoleum, natural carpets	Ceramic tiles	Vinyl
Gutters, pipes	Galvanised steel	Coated aluminium	PVC, zinc, copper

That is a fairly easy and perhaps obvious example. When we get to things like pipes, cables, floor coverings the decisions can get more complex.

The case for using sustainable materials is a good one. 50 per cent of material resources taken from nature are for buildings. 50 per cent of waste production in the UK comes from the building industry. The biggest single source, 28 per cent, of the CO_2 embodied in buildings is in the stone, sand and aggregates used. 82 per cent of the material used in the conventional house is virgin material – never before used – and currently a huge proportion of that is from non-sustainable sources. And around 13 per cent of that virgin material will not ever be used – off-cuts, broken slates, etc. – but will go straight to landfill.

3

For the table above we are using a UK average house which is about 130m² to 140m² in floor area, is on two floors, with three to four bedrooms, one-and-a-half bathrooms, and four people in occupancy. This is slightly smaller than the 'standard' house we are using elsewhere in the book but useful for the comparison of national data. This average house will use some 200 tonnes of materials and up to 44 tonnes of CO_2 will be embodied in those materials. The carbon footprint calculation below is for this average UK house and has been calculated using data from BRE Wales. As this information is very general in its nature, it has been supplemented by referring to the Bath University Inventory of Carbon and Energy (ICE) data sheets. The 'average house' is assumed to be of brick and block cavity walls on traditional foundations and concrete ground floor topped off with a concrete tile pitched roof.

This models the main structure of an 'average' house and so the figures are an extrapolation from quantities used across the UK. It takes the property to a weatherproof condition with painted walls but does not account for decorative finishes, fixtures or fittings or landscaping. If we add a proportion of CO_2 for waste materials and CO_2 emitted during the construction process, the figure climbs to 54 tonnes.

A conventionally built zero carbon house – that is a house emitting zero carbon dioxide, as proposed by the Government for 2016 – will take some nine years to recover the carbon dioxide embodied in it.

A study of the figures in the table show that merely switching from brick and block construction to timber frame and using reclaimed roof tiles would reduce the embodied carbon of our average house by almost 12 tonnes.

CHOOSING THE RIGHT MATERIALS

The construction method chosen will directly affect the choice of materials to be used, and that will be a result of the decision on the level of thermal efficiency (see Chapter 2, Design Right, page 41). Post & beam could be concrete, steel or wood but timber frame can, by definition, only be timber. A green roof is a green roof but it will affect the materials used to support it and potentially affect the design of the building and the materials used in the main structure.

Increasingly the press, the Government and the major house builders are talking about Modern Methods of Construction (MMC) as being the way forward. MMC's are essentially pre-fabrication, but without the negative associations of post-war pre-fabs. MMC's can be steel, concrete, timber, brick or block – any of the standard construction materials – but pre-fabricated in a factory for on-site assembly. All of the super-efficient German house manufacturers, like Hanse Haus, Huf House, Baufritz et al, are MMC manufacturers and there

3

is nothing wrong with their products. If fact they are some of the best houses available.

MMC's are being developed for :

■ Better energy efficiency

■ Reduced build cost

■ Better materials usage – less waste

■ Reduced time on site – better productivity

Beyond energy efficiency, and they can be incredibly energy efficient, any sustainability improvements are purely incidental. So far as the UK is concerned MMC's are aimed at hitting the 2016 zero carbon target while at the same time reducing the build cost (or at least not letting it rise as a result of zero carbon).

There are hundreds of components to a house and thousands of options for the materials. There are simple choices – like whether to use sustainable insulation or plastics – and less simple choices – like whether to use reclaimed timber flooring from a local source or new flooring from a sustainable but distant source.

Sustainability starts from the point of reducing the drain on natural resources and clearly materials are fundamental to that, but over the past few years what is the right choice has become more complex. Ten years ago a sustainable building was a bit of a strange beast. It tended to focus on more esoteric building methods like straw-bale, rammed earth and the like, with a significant nod in the direction of energy efficiency. People that built them were dedicated souls fighting almost insurmountable problems. The sustainable materials were scarce, sustainable products almost unheard off and they were forced to be creative and inventive to achieve anything at all.

Thanks to them, the availability of sustainable materials has improved hugely. Architects are far more aware, some are even enthusiastic, builder's merchants stock growing ranges of sustainable products and the internet is full of sites with natural and sustainable products, materials and methods.

But the question as to what constitutes a sustainable material can be difficult. One definition is a material that has a lower impact on the environment than the non-sustainable alternative.

At one end of the scale there is material from a renewable source, e.g. sheep wool insulation or timber from a sustainable forest, that has a very small impact. The impact is not zero as there are issues around harvesting and transport, but in real terms it is the best we can do. Their use has caused no depletion of natural resources, minimal energy has been used in their processing and they have few or zero chemical additives.

SUSTAINABLE MATERIALS

At the other end of the scale is material that is just one step up the ladder from the non-sustainable alternative, e.g. polypropylene (PP) or polyethylene (PE), which are plastics that are used for pipes or cable insulation as an alternative to PVC. All three use oil as a base material but PP and PE use less energy in the manufacture, have fewer harmful additives and are more easily recycled. The manufacture of PVC can cause the emission of dioxins, PCB's and heavy metals, it is difficult to incinerate as it will emit chlorine and heavy metals and is virtually indestructible in landfill. None of them would achieve a 'good' rating in sustainability terms, one is just a bit better than the other.

In between are a host of materials with more or less sustainable credentials and again it can be difficult to choose between them. The difference between, say, plywood, chipboard and Oriented Strand Board (OSB) will lie in the glues or bonding agents used and the environmental credentials of the manufacturer. Chipboard and OSB use, primarily, waste wood from other manufacturing processes and plywood uses veneer that is taken from a log. In this case the answer might be that plywood using rainforest veneers is a no-no but there is a trivial ecological difference between chipboard and OSB – although a significant difference in terms of use. OSB is relatively durable and stronger than chipboard.

Lime is held up as something of a panacea by the eco-builder but the reality is that it is only marginally better than cement in terms of its embodied energy and CO_2. Each kg of cement will embody 0.83Kg CO_2 compared to 0.74Kg CO_2 in lime. The reality is that the CO_2 embodied in the cement is far outweighed by the CO_2 embodied in the sand and aggregate that it binds. Making lime concrete, or limecrete, is a particular skill that is scarce in the UK. It will be faster, easier and more environmentally effective to use recycled aggregate with cement to make concrete than to learn how to use lime to make limecrete.

There are a few alternatives to conventional concrete but not all work in every situation. Recycled aggregate is increasingly easy to find and it is possible to hire crushing machines to turn rubble into re-usable aggregate – if rubble is available in the first place. But even so, recycled aggregate and using lime may be impractical. Foamed concrete may be an answer for the floor slab. There are plenty of specialist suppliers around (Google "foamed concrete" to find some) and the product uses less aggregate, less cement and has better thermal properties than conventional concrete or limecrete. Concrete is generally a structural component of the building and its strength is usually critical to stability. In sustainability terms it is best not to use concrete at all, but if it is to be used, it has to be the right concrete for the job.

What will suit in any given project will vary with the circumstances of that project. The

3

material to use for the floor slab is an example of the decision that will face the builder. A choice between least bad options, or a potentially significant budget overrun.

But it is not always like that. Some of the choices are far clearer. Take flooring. Any rainforest timber is obviously a no-no. Even rainforest timber from a sustainable source is a bit iffy in that doubts exist over the sustainability of the forest and the extraction process usually has a high impact on the local ecology. Reclaimed timber, on the other hand, has excellent credentials and is available from virtually every salvage yard in the country. As it is reclaimed no profit is going to the rainforest timber producers and thereby encouraging the industry, and it has virtually zero embodied energy and CO_2 (that was all taken up in its first use).

Reclaimed timber also has the virtue of being available in a huge variety of sizes, colours and grades. It lends itself well to floor boards, as a decorative finish or to be covered with carpet or lino. The colours and grains that aged timber take on also allow more interior design options. Reclaimed timber is probably not suitable for structural elements, but for internal joinery, flooring and even external fascias and soffits it offers a good alternative.

The table on page 52 is a list of the main elements of the build with sustainable and less sustainable options and the materials to avoid, if possible. It will come as no surprise that many of the materials in the Avoid list are what would be considered "traditional"

The list is not exhaustive and is intended to provide an insight into the types of materials available for each element. And that sustainable options exist for all elements.

SET YOUR OWN TARGETS

It is better to have a building with some sustainable credentials than a building with none. It may be that some elements of the build have to be sacrificed on the altar of practicality or, more usually, finance to achieve a successful project. Personal research will determine which elements can be dealt with sustainably in any given location or project, and making that determination early in the design process will save time, cost and heart-ache.

For the self-builder or renovator, education is key. Researching sustainable and recycled materials available in the locality of the project will inform and influence the design of the building. Unless the architect and/or builder are particularly enthusiastic the use of recycled or salvaged materials will be limited to those that the client finds. Local research of architectural salvage and demolition yards can be extremely revealing. From the mundane, recycled roofing slates, to the more esoteric, interesting timber, wrought iron balustrades, landscaping features, antique tiles. It is truly amazing what can be found in good salvage yards. And talk to the guys in

3

the yard and find out what is coming in. You may be able to pre-book a batch of bricks or roof tiles. Knowing what is potentially available will help in the decision making process and may open up whole new lines of thought.

Recycling material has to be the first objective for a sustainable build, but doubts have been expressed over the transport costs, in terms of CO_2, of using reclaimed material. The following guide, produced by BRE, shows the distance a reclaimed material can be transported by road before it has a greater environmental impact than a new product manufactured locally (within 50 miles).

RECLAIMED MILES

Material	Distance (in miles)
Reclaimed tiles	100
Reclaimed slates	300
Reclaimed bricks	250
Reclaimed aggregate	150
Reclaimed timber	1000
Reclaimed steel products	2500
Reclaimed aluminium products	7500

Reverting to the opening statement that sustainability is about meeting our needs without impacting on the ability of future generations to meet their needs, then renovating an existing building is the ultimate in sustainability. It minimises the use of new resources, effectively recycles all the material contained in the building and adds zero transport CO_2. Is it not a shame that there are 1,000's of houses in cities across the country that are being pulled down because they are perceived to have no potential to be adapted and changed to meet modern needs? Which raises the question, how many modern estates will suffer the same fate?

One of the tenets of sustainability is to design in the potential to be adapted and changed. It is not always easy but as an example, post & beam construction builds a structure that covers a space with none of the internal walls carrying structural load so that they can be moved at will. The post & beam structure itself can be added to or even reduced and it provides a degree of flexibility not easily found in other construction methods.

The house you are building will last 100 or even 200 years and it is impossible to know what those future generations will need. Designing in adaptability and using materials that can be recycled will at least give them the chance of meeting those needs.

TIMBER

Timber-frame construction has become the de facto standard for a sustainable build. It uses principally a renewable material, minimises production and transport energy and CO_2, has good structural stability and good thermal performance. Doubts are still being expressed

3

over the longevity of timber-frame, which seems to fly in the face of the evidence that surrounds us. Throughout the UK there are houses 200, 300 or even 400 years old, still standing in good repair and still used on a daily basis. (The author has personal experience of a 600 year old house, still used as a domestic residence, occupied by descendents of the original builders, and still with all the original roof timbers.) In Japan there are temples over 2,000 years old, constructed entirely of timber.

The life of a building is determined by the quality of the materials, the quality of the construction and the care in its maintenance. The same factors apply irrespective of the construction method.

10 things to know about wood

■ 1. As trees grow they naturally absorb CO_2 from the atmosphere. A typical tree absorbs 0.9 tonnes of carbon for every cubic metre of growth.

■ 2. When a tree is felled, it continues to store carbon for the remainder of its life as a wood product or in part of a building. We grow more trees in Europe than we fell, thus creating an increase in forest across Europe by the equivalent of 100 football pitches per hour.

■ 3. Most of the wood we use for construction in the UK is softwood. Over half of the wood we import is certified to show it is sourced from a managed forest. The other half is not.

■ 4. The materials used in a typical three-bedroomed semi-detached house in England emit about 14 tonnes of CO_2 in their extraction and manufacture alone. By using timber frame, you can save up to nine tonnes per house

■ 5. Structural timber composites such as glulam and LVL (laminated veneered lumber), enable wood to compete successfully with steel or concrete in large structures.

■ 6. Achieving low-energy housing is cheaper and quicker using timber-frame construction than conventional brick and block. Well constructed timber frame houses can comfortably deliver significantly better levels of air permeability than required under building regulation

■ 7. Wood windows help to reduce energy demands at least as well as u-PVC and enhance the value of the property. Wood windows which are double glazed and painted in the factory have 30 year durability warranties, paint guarantees of up to 10 years.

■ 8. Wood floors not only look good, often cost less than other floor materials but have health benefits too in that it doesn't harbour mites and dust which can lead to allergies.

■ 9. Wood can be easily repaired and re-used. Many wood products are re-used or re-machined into other products, such as railway

TIMBER APPLICATIONS

3

Application	Species	Durability	Availability	Cost
Structural	Sitka Spruce	Not durable	Regular	Low
	Norway Spruce	Slightly	Regular	Low
Cladding	Oak	Durable	Variable	Medium
	Cedar (British)	Moderate	Limited	Medium
	Cedar (American)	Durable	Variable	Medium
	Larch	Slightly	Regular	Low
	Douglas Fir	Moderate	Regular	Medium
Ext Joinery	Oak	Durable	Variable	Medium
	Douglas Fir	Moderate	Regular	Medium
	Scots Pine	Slightly	Regular	Low
	Sweet Chestnut	Durable	Limited	Medium
	Siberian Larch	Moderate	Regular	Medium
Int Joinery	Ash	Not durable	Regular	Medium
	Beech	Not durable	Regular	Low to med
	Sweet Chestnut	Durable	Limited	Medium
	Pine (various)	Slightly	Regular	Low
	Hemlock	Slightly	Regular	Low
	Oak (European)	Durable	Variable	High
	Yew	Durable	Limited	High
Mouldings	Hemlock	Slightly	Regular	Low
Flooring	Ash	Not durable	Regular	Medium
	Beech	Not durable	Regular	Low to med
	Birch	Not durable	Regular	Low
	Oak	Durable	Variable	High
	Pitch pine*	Moderate	Variable	Medium
Decking etc.	Siberian Larch	Moderate	Regular	Medium

* Pitch Pine – source must be checked as in some areas it is at risk of extinction.

3

sleepers as a garden design material or re-machined from large sections into floor boards and wood profiles.

■ 10. Wood is renewable. Forest certification schemes and chain of custody help the wood industry to prove it.

Timber will always be a big part of a sustainable build and sustainable timber is fast becoming the accepted norm. Certified sustainable timber is timber that is produced from a forest that is managed to minimise the impact on the ecology and that is grown, harvested and replanted in an environmentally sensitive way. It is far more easily available than was once the case and there are many schemes certifying the sustainability of the timber, including Forestry Stewardship Council (FSC), the Finnish National Certification Scheme, and the UK Woodland Assurance Scheme. The FSC scheme is probably the most widely recognised in the UK but if in doubt contact Forests Forever for advice.

Another organisation, TRADA, have a very useful website at www.trada.co.uk It is free, and easy, to register and it has a wealth of information on all types and species of timber, including suppliers.

Timber for every application

All the species listed as available from UK grown sources will usually be managed sources but this is always worth checking. Other species are available for all applications but these will not necessarily be UK grown and may or may not be from sustainable sources.

This excellent website, www.trada.co.uk/techinfo/tsg/view/122 , lists many more species for each application.

Durable timber

The durability of timber (its ability to withstand weather) is a factor of three issues; its species, its growth and its processing.

Hardwood species – oak, iroko, sapele, chestnut – are naturally more durable than most softwoods. Some softwood species, e.g. Douglas fir, are also durable but to a lesser extent. Redwood is a softwood timber with good durability often used in external joinery. Straight grown softwoods, with no knots or shakes that has been slow dried will be far more durable than kiln dried knotty pine.

Durable timber is useful because it needs little or no treatment to be maintained in good condition, and it lasts. In window and door-frames it will outlast PVC with none of the ecological impact. In this country

3

we are lucky to have many examples of old timber buildings using what we would now call durable timber but in those days was just called timber. In the last 60 years the demand for ever increasing volumes of construction timber has led to ever falling quality. We are now accepting timber for structural and joinery purposes that would previously have been rejected as unfit for purpose. That poorer quality has a shorter life which means that it needs replacing more often, increasing the demand for timber still further.

It needs to be remembered that FSC, or any other certification, says nothing about the timber's quality, only that it comes from a sustainable source. BS5268 provides five classes of durability, plus non-durable and perishable. Classes 1 to 3 require no treatment, classes 4 and 5 may need treatment if used externally and non-durable should only be used internally.

Selecting the appropriate species, specifying the class of durability and designing around those issues will minimise the amount of wood needed, eliminate the need for unnecessary toxic treatments and extend the life of the building.

Timber treatments

Forest Forever (www.forestsforever.org.uk) or the Forestry Stewardship Council will also give advice on timber preservation. Again there are alternatives to the traditional approach of treating every piece of timber with chemical preservatives.

The last 40 years has seen the timber industry routinely using some highly toxic insecticides and fungicides. Much of the application has been to prevent or remedy the premature decay of timber that has come as the result of poor design, using inappropriate species, poor quality timber and inadequate maintenance.

The timber treatment industry has expanded massively and is now a significant sector of the building industry, and of course has its own vested interest. We are exhorted daily with TV ads to spray our fences and decking with chemicals to make them last. Remedial treatment of timber is undertaken routinely, at the slightest sign of any timber bio-deterioration, with treatment often a condition of a mortgage offer. Pre-treated timber is routinely specified in buildings where it is difficult to see any justification for it

Establishing the 'need to treat' underpins British Standards (BS5589 & BS5268 part 5), something that is routinely overlooked. BS5268 Part 5 emphasises good design and the use of appropriate timber: "where design is unlikely to provide adequate protection, a naturally durable timber or the use of an appropriate preservative treatment should be considered".

The careful selection of timber species, coupled with good design and good building practice, can eliminate the need for chemical treatment. New wood from Durability Classes 4 & 5, non-

3

Above: the turf roof houses the solar panels, while, in aesthetic terms, it allows the building to fit in with its environment.

This planted sedum roof has two high-performance membranes beneath it that cover 120mm of insulation placed above a vapour barrier.

Maintaining a grass roof can be a problem. He may have been better planting sedum, or similar, that needs no maintenance.

durable and perishable wood will require treatment when used in exposed situations such as windows, doors, roof tile battens, fascia boards etc. Even then, inorganic boron compounds will be as effective as the chemical alternatives. They are safer and far more environmentally sensitive.

There are a few joinery manufacturers offering naturally treated durable windows and doors. The Ecoplus System range is one that is pre-treated with a glycol borate. Inorganic borate pre-treated roof tile battens, fascias etc are available in certain parts of the country and The Association of Environment Conscious Building (AECB) have information on current availability.

For most applications, timber of any durability class does not require treatment for internal carpentry or joinery, although quality remains an issue to ensure it does not warp or bend as it dries in the house.

GREEN ROOFS

Green roofs are, without doubt, one of the more visible signals that what we have here is a sustainable build. And they do have some significant benefits; they absorb heat (from the sun), they absorb CO_2, they absorb a large proportion of the water that falls on them (up to 70 per cent) and, most importantly, they replace the ecology that the building stands on. London has brought in regulations to ensure certain types and sizes of building have a green roof, principally for the ecological and heat absorption reasons.

There are two basic types which can be described as thick (Intensive) and thin (Extensive). There is also a semi-extensive which is somewhere between the two.

Intensive: Consists of a thick layer of soil (200mm+) in which a variety of plants, vegetables, shrubs and trees can be grown. Such roof gardens are often accessible and can even be used for recreational facilities and useful spaces. They provide a valuable habitat for wildlife but place significant weight on the building and need substantial roof support. They offer good insulation and better water absorption than the thin types. Having a variety of plant species means that maintenance will be necessary (comparable to a ground-level garden), perhaps even mowing. People have been known to keep goats on the roof for this purpose, but you have to wonder.

Extensive

Generally a shallow layer (25-100mm) of substrate planted with low growing, stress-tolerant grasses, mosses and alpine species (e.g. Sedum). These light-weight systems require little or no

3

maintenance, and do not impose any significant weight on the building, but the roof structure will still generally need to be reinforced.

There are generally considered to be three different approaches to Extensive roofs:

■ Sedum roofs

Sedum is a low growing succulent plant that requires no maintenance in terms of mowing and will put up with short periods of drought. These are usually pre-grown sedum mats based on 20mm of substrate or systems of greater substrate depth (standard depth = 70mm) in which sedums can be seeded or planted.

■ Meadow roofs

These roofs are based on 70-100mm substrate depth. They involve the use of seeded or planted low, drought tolerant grasses, perennials and alpines, which can be native or ornamental species. Maintenance will be an issue and needs to be considered when deciding what to plant,

■ 'Brown' or 'Biodiversity' roofs

Such roofs are designed to recreate natural and often local habitats rich in birds, plants and insects. This is often done by using the by-products of the development process such as rubble and subsoil which are left to colonise naturally overtime or may be seeded with wildflowers. May have the same maintenance issues as an Intensive roof, unless you like the wild-and-free look.

Semi-extensive

Of slightly greater depth than extensive systems (100-200mm), allowing for a greater diversity of plants to be grown and local habitats created. Based on the same principles as extensive roofs they are generally low maintenance.

Any growing medium will attract other species – that is sort of the point - and maintenance is likely to remain an issue. The extensive green roof has little thermal benefits and good insulation will be needed under it, as will a water barrier. They will retain a proportion of the water that falls on them, but gutters and downpipes will still be needed. Although heavy compared to conventional roof coverings they are not so heavy that they cannot be laid on a timber roof structure. They can be used on pitched roofs, but there is not much point as it increases water run-off and they are generally laid to a single, fairly gentle, fall.

As with all things, the function of the roof needs to be considered. If it is to be walked on then sedum will not do; if getting to it for maintenance (potentially with a lawn mower) is a problem then an intensive roof is not the answer; if the wild-and-free look does not suit the building then a meadow roof is a non-starter.

3

The question as to whether a green roof should be an intrinsic part of a sustainable build is open to debate. The clear, incontrovertible, benefit of replacing the ecology that the building stands on can be countered by the over-bearing influence that it has on the overall design.

In situations where a green roof suits the design of the building and the topography of the site, especially where the roof can form part of the landscape, it is a great idea. Starting with the premise of a green roof exerts such a strong influence on the structure that it can end up looking out of place and pointless.

Cost of a Green Roof

The cost will of course vary with the type of green roof and the particular situation. As a guide prices can vary from £50 per m² for a sedum roof to £200 per m² for a fully planted Intensive roof plus, of course, the cost of any reinforcement needed to the roof and/or wall structures.

WASTE MANAGEMENT

It is an intrinsic part of both the Ecohomes standard and the Code For Sustainable Homes that a waste management plan be prepared and implemented. They are called Site Waste Management Plans (SWMP) and are likely to become compulsory for all building sites in the near future. The reason is that the building industry produces around 72 million tonnes of waste (figure from Chartered Institute of Building) each year and a good proportion of it goes to landfill. 13 million tonnes of that is waste material which is defined by the DTI as waste that was delivered to site, unused and sent to landfill. Just to emphasise that point – that is 13 per cent of the materials cost of the project that is sent straight to landfill.

A few statistics. The average skip leaving a building site costs about £150 and on average has materials to the value of £1,200 in it. The UK produces around 400 million tonnes of waste annually, of which about 72 million tonnes comes from construction sites (if we add demolition sites the figure rises to 109 million tonnes).

Avoiding, or even just reducing, waste has a direct affect on the build cost, as well as the environmental impact. But it is a particularly tricky problem to come to grips with. One method that has been used successfully, but that needs a lot of close management, is to order too little.

The standard process is to measure the amount needed and ADD a percentage for breakages, spillage, of-cutting, etc. The percentage will vary with the material so we might add 10 per cent to readymix concrete, 20 per cent to concrete blocks, 20 per cent to timber, and so one. This ensures that there is enough material to complete the job and keep the tradesman employed. But it leads to a waste culture as the tradesman knows that there is always enough

3

and he does not need to take much care with cutting or handling. After all a concrete block costs less than 50p so why worry?

Almost invariably this means that there will be some material left over but what can you do with 10 or 20 concrete blocks? They will lay about on site, being used as impromptu seating or something similar, until they are broken and thrown in the skip.

Order too little on the other hand and the tradesman will run out before the job is finished, will be able to count exactly how many more are needed, which are then bought and used. The left-over waste is virtually eliminated and the tradesman eventually become used to the system and start taking more care with their cutting and handling.

Studies have shown that under-ordering can halve the amount of waste going to landfill – that is a reduction of over six per cent in the materials cost of the project.

The Government web site www.netregs.gov.uk gives a lot of information on how to handle and manage waste, but in short it amounts to:

■ Only order enough material and have it delivered "just in time" to avoid losses during storage.

■ Sort the waste before it hits the skip and reuse everything possible.

■ Sort waste for recycling in separate skips or areas. Sorting metal waste separately may generate income.

■ Avoid "miscellaneous waste" disposal. Know what is in each skip and where it should be going.

A DTI project carried out by two major housing developers found that careful waste management could reduce the project cost by up to eight per cent.

Another good web site is www.wrap.org.uk (Waste & Resources Action Program) who provide advice and guidance on the efficient use and disposal of materials. They also maintain a directory of recycled aggregate suppliers across the UK.

FOR THE RENOVATOR & REFURBISHER

SUSTAINABLE FINISHING MATERIALS

Plaster

The only real alternatives are lime or to use a substrate that does not need plastering, like Fermacell.

Lime renders were traditionally applied to walls built of poor quality rubble, stone or porous brick or to walls in exposed locations facing driving winds. They help by acting like a sponge, absorbing rainfall then allowing it to evaporate rather than soak into the wall. Most cottages and houses built of rubble stone would have been rendered originally and they tend to suffer from penetrating damp if the lime render is removed or replaced with a cement rich render. For interiors a fairly smooth surface could be obtained using a coarse render mix, but for top quality internal plastering the final coat would be richer in lime and polished up to a smooth, close finish.

Fermacell board is easy to use and is ready for decoration without the need for plaster. For a 'glass' finish use FST (Fine Surface Treatment available from the manufacturer) to apply a skim coat finish. It's great for touching up, joints and the like to give a smooth finish.

Paint

All paints contain three main components: pigment (colour), a binder (holds the paint together) and a carrier (disperses the binder). With many modern paints these ingredients are made using toxic chemicals that are harmful to both the environment and human health. Cadmium, lead and chromium are frequently used in pigments; petrochemicals, solvents, benzene, formaldehyde and other volatile organic compounds (VOCs) are used in binders and carriers. Toxic, environmentally harmful, chemicals are also used in modern paints as preservatives, stabilisers, thickeners and driers.

Non-toxic paints are often called Low-VOC, No-VOC, VOC-Free, odourless, odour-free and green, natural or organic paints. There are no set standards for defining these labels, and they are widely misused for marketing purposes. To help consumers make informed decisions on their paint purchases, various ecological labels have been developed by different countries to indicate that the paint has fulfilled certain environmental requirements, in accordance with respective government regulations. These eco-labels can be found as logos on paint cans. In the UK, VOC labels are used, and indicate the content of VOCs using one of five classifications: Minimal (0-0.29 per cent), Low, Medium, High and Very High (VOC content greater than 50 per cent).

Natural paints are the only true non-toxic paint since they contain no VOCs, and are made from natural ingredients such as water, vegetable oils, plant dyes, and natural minerals. The main binders used in natural paints are: linseed oil (from flax seeds), clay, lime, and milk protein. Lime and milk paints give an authentic period look, and are often used in antique restoration projects. Chalk is used as an extender to thicken paint; turpentine (distilled from pine trees) is used as a

3

solvent; essential oils from citrus fruits (d-limonene) are used as a solvent and fragrance; and natural mineral and earth pigments are used as colorants.

Eco Paints (www.ecotopia.co.uk), Little Green Paint Shop (www.designercolours.com) and Earthborn Eco Paints (www.mylittleeco.co.uk) are all good suppliers, but Google Eco Paints and you will find a few dozen more.

Wallpaper

It may come as a surprise that PVC is often used in wallpaper; principally to give extra strength when it is wet with paste. But there are now a few ranges of PVC-free wallpapers. Check out Harland Organic Furnishings at www.organic-furnishings.co.uk/wallpaper/24/ for chemical-free wallpaper made entirely from chemical and PVC-free paper from sustainable sources.

Tiles

As a mark that virtually every component of the house can come from a sustainable source, floor and wall tiles are now available from recycled glass, recycled CD's, recycled tiles, recycled tyres, and even recycled carpet tiles and recycled leather.

Recycling is second only to re-use in terms of sustainability and sourcing these energy and resource rich products with recycled raw material is a great step forward. What particular look and material will suit is the province of the designer and once again amounts to a Google search for eco tiles.

Mouldings

By this we mean architrave, skirting boards and the like. The majority of the cost of these products go in the moulding process itself rather than in the raw material, so there is little excuse for using anything other the FSC certified timber.

But beware, there are ranges of veneered mouldings where the veneer is anything but sustainable – often rainforest timber.

Flooring

Floor covering is a bigger issue than we might think. Legislation is coming forward (albeit slowly) that will control the use of PVC and other chemicals in carpets and similarly to control the disposal of these materials, particularly to landfill.

But once again, there is a huge range of sustainable options – from natural linoleum to bamboo. Even recycled bamboo and recycled carpets. Cork features quite highly in the eco-flooring manufacturer's list but there has to be a question mark over cork as a sustainable material given its slow growth, long harvesting cycle and small global distribution. Wool carpets have always been considered the better quality alternative to acrylics but now they are the sustainable option as well. Check out www.sustainablefloors.co.uk/green-carpets.html for details.

The most often ignored, but perhaps most interesting source of timber flooring is, once again, the local architectural salvage yard. Exploration will often reveal old, interesting and beautiful wood, ideal for flooring or even doors and mouldings.

French oak is increasingly a managed crop, there is even some managed English oak available, making oak a far more sustainable option. But think about species like Ash, Beech, Birch, or maybe even Sweet Chestnut, all available from managed UK sources, but typically only from specialist suppliers. The website www.trada.co.uk/techinfo/tsg/ usefully lists timber species for various applications and lists suppliers of that timber.

RULES AROUND SUSTAINABLE MATERIALS

Find an architect that has knowledge of and enthusiasm for sustainability. Talk to them, visit some houses they have designed and be sure they are what you are looking for.

■ Research materials – what is appealing, what is available, what is local

■ Be costs conscious – find out what the material will cost before designing it in. Surprises can lead to hasty decisions in the construction phase.

■ Allow design to be an evolutionary process informed by the materials available for the elements that are to be sustainable.

■ Firm-up design decisions and select the best construction method for that design.

■ Find a contractor with enthusiasm for sustainability. A good contractor will help with sourcing materials and an unenthusiastic contractor will be a barrier.

■ Specify materials and work-up costs. Projects that come in on time and within budget are the exception rather than the rule.

This book is about sustainable building and renovation. It is not about greener homes. Some green products are not, per se, sustainable – cork is a case in point – where increasing demand has placed an insupportable burden on producers who are in some cases cropping too often and killing the trees.

The mantra for sustainable materials is re-used, recycled, renewable. But all of this is over-arched by the need for quality. Poor quality timber from a sustainable source will still need to be replaced sooner than good quality timber, and will ultimately lead to a less sustainable house.

3

The scope of the sustainable materials made available will be largely a product of the research and effort that the client puts in. Listed below are just a few of the many web sites selling sustainable materials.

- www.rounded-developments.org.uk
- www.greenconsumerguide.com
- www.greenshop.co.uk
- www.aecb.net

Some builder's merchants stock sustainable materials, notably Covers on the south coast and Burdens who have substantial ranges of sustainable products in each of their branches. Most builder's merchants will try and find particular materials if they are asked, so it is well worth finding the material you want and asking the local builder's merchant to supply it. The effect of this is to ease personal supply problems but also to make more sustainable materials available to more people. It may be just a bit of flag waving, but remember the people 10 or 15 years ago who brought us to where we are now.

SUSTAINABLE MATERIALS

3

4 INSULATION AND DRAUGHTPROOFING

This chapter has grown by about 50 per cent since the first edition, reflecting the idea that this is the most important issue for the sustainable builder – reducing energy consumption and consequently reducing CO_2 emissions. As a subject insulation is not sexy and not funny, but it is the single most important issue. The greatest environmental impact of a house is from the fossil fuels it burns for its energy. No amount of eco-certified, recycled bamboo flooring can compensate for the impact of a gas guzzling house. Conserving energy, minimising the energy needs of the house has to be the first priority.

In short, insulation is king. The money invested in insulation will go on repaying for the whole life of the building. Not only in financial terms but also in terms of reduced CO_2 emissions. And if it is sustainable insulation it will have minimal impact on natural resources and can be recycled into the next house.

Energy conservation does not start and end with insulation. There is also life-style and construction to consider. The Government tell us almost daily that switching off lights, TV's, phone chargers and turning the thermostat down a couple of degrees will save 20 per cent on the fuel bill. And they are right. How you live in your house is still a matter of personal choice, but increasingly how you build your house is being dictated by Government policy and the Building Regulations.

AIR TIGHTNESS

It is mandatory for all houses gaining planning consent after April 2010 to meet the Building Regulations Part L1A standard on air tightness. That standard is a permeability or leakage of not more than $10m^3/h/m^2@50pa$. That is, 10 cubic metres of air per hour escaping for every square metre of the envelope surface area with the air at a pressure of 50 Pascals – which is slightly lower than the air pressure in an aircraft cabin. What that actually means is a bit of a

INSULATION AND DRAUGHTPROOFING

mystery but in broad terms it is roughly equivalent to 1.5 air changes per hour, which has for many years been considered the optimum level to maintain a good, healthy internal atmosphere.

The 2005 building regulations stated that we had to have a maximum of 1.5 air changes per hour (ach). It was in the late 1980s that the standard changed from a minimum to a maximum. Until then 1.5ach was considered to be the minimum amount of air need to maintain oxygen levels, clear out exhalation CO_2, pollutants and smells.

When asked why $10m^3$ was chosen as the standard Mr Colin King, then head of BRE Wales, who was influential in drafting the standard, said it is 'an arbitrary figure. It has no direct relationship to air changes per hour.' But of course there has to be a relationship and the $10m^3$ standard is said to be around 1.5ach. And to put that in perspective, the German Passivhaus standard calls for less than $1m^3$/hr @ 50 Pascal.

At $10m^3$/h it is possible that the building will be 25 per cent more energy efficient than the 2002 standard. If we achieve the target standard of $5m^3$/h BRE say that we will save 40 per cent of the heating energy consumption. To make the standard work we need two things: a house that remains sealed, and a reliable mechanical ventilation system. To not put too fine a point on it, with permeability at even $5m^3$/h, a mechanical ventilation system is essential.

At a meeting of the Energy Efficiency Working Group at the Department for Communities and Local Government on May 5, 2006, the minutes show that the target permeability is actually $3m^3$/h/m^2@50pa. But there is a problem. To quote, "$7m^3$/h would be good but let's get $10m^3$/h first. Testing is still being ignored by many local authority building control officers.' It goes on to say that the standard will be increased to $5m^3$/h and eventually $3m^3$/h but that 'the

TYPICAL INSULATION LEVELS

Construction method	Loft mineral wool	Walls polyurethane	Floor EPS	Windows U-value
2006 Building Regs	270mm	70mm	75mm EPS	1.8
OMS – SIPS	350mm	120mm	100mm EPS	1.8
AECB Silver	300mm	70mm	70mm polyurethane	1.4
Passivhaus	350mm	300mm	110mm polyurethane	0.8
AECB Gold	350mm	300mm	110mm polyurethane	0.8

4

building industry just will not stand for it yet' Which begs the question why not? If it saves 40 per cent plus of the energy consumption and similarly reduces running costs, surely buyers would be queuing up for these massively energy efficient houses.

The answer is that the industry will have to change their long established building practices to produce a house with that level of air tightness. They will have to change the designs, the construction methods, their practices and the on-site management. All of that will cost money and the industry believes that the extra cost cannot be passed on. Which is fair enough. Why should we pay more for a house the same size, that looks the same and feels the same, and merely complies with building regulations?

We have a habit of enjoying the fresh air, of opening windows and moving freely in and out of the house. That habit has developed because we live in a temperate, relatively damp climate. There is no argument that increasing insulation and improving air tightness will reduce heat loss and produce a more energy efficient house. There is equally no argument that when air tightness gets below $7m^2/hr$ then we will need mechanical ventilation. But the idea that we are then living in a sealed house without the option of opening windows is a bit of a myth. To put it simply, if you want to open the window, open the window. If you want to leave the window open, switch the ventilation system off.

HOW MUCH IS ENOUGH?

The answer to that will be dealt with in some detail through this chapter. It is the 'super insulated' house that we consider here. Or, more accurately, the house describe to the client, by the architect as being 'super insulated', when in fact it is little, if any, better than required by Part L1A Building Regs.

The mantra through out this book is that the sustainable builder has to make their own way in the world. They need to arm themselves with the knowledge necessary to make good, well informed, decisions. And this is one of them.

In my day job as a sustainable building consultant I come across many, many clients who have had a 'super insulated' house designed by their architect which turns out to be nothing of the sort. The architect will be genuinely surprised when the idea of doubling the specified insulation is put forward and will often question the wisdom of such a course of action. But the fact remains that the house they designed has around a quarter of the thermal efficiency of a Passivhaus – the best standard we have – and about half of Energy Saving Trust best practice.

How much is too much? The truth is it is very difficult to get there.

INSULATION AND DRAUGHTPROOFING

4

DESIGN ENERGY CONSUMPTION

Each construction method or design standard has a consequential or imperative energy consumption rate for, at least, the space heating demands. For instance the Passivhaus standard has a fundamental requirement that energy consumption for space heating (and cooling!) be less than 15kWh per square metre, per year. If you don't do that, you can't have a certificate. The table below shows comparative energy consumption rates for each of the major design standards, and how that translates into insulation levels and running costs.

DESIGN ENERGY CONSUMPTION

Construction method	Average energy consumption	Typical insulation levels (1)	Air Tightness	Annual heat for 200m² house (2)
2006 Building Regs	55kWh/m²	Loft = 270mm mineral wool Walls = 70mm polyurethane Floor = 75mm EPS Windows = U-value 1.8	10m³/hr	£543
OMS – SIPS	25kWh/m² to 45kWh/m²	Loft = 350mm mineral wool Walls = 120mm polyurethane Floor = 100mm EPS Windows = U-value 1.8	7m³/hr	£247 to £445
AECB Silver	<40kWh/m²	Loft = 300mm mineral wool Walls = 70mm polyurethane Floor = 70mm EPS Windows = U-value 1.4	3m³/hr	£395
Passivhaus	<15kWh/m²	Loft = 350mm mineral wool Walls = 300mm polyurethane Floor = 110mm EPS Windows = U-value 0.8	<1m³/hr	£148 (3)
AECB Gold	<15kWh/m²	Loft = 350mm mineral wool Walls = 300mm polyurethane Floor = 110mm EPS Windows = U-value 0.8	<1m³/hr	£148 (3)

1 Assumes pitched roof, timber frame walls, solid concrete ground floor slab
2 Assumes oil-fired boiler as principle heat source
3 Assumes that heating is needed.

The point about Passivhaus (and AECB Gold) is that the house is passively heated, i.e. that the insulation levels are such that the heat generated by merely living in the house are all that is

4

needed. Therefore space heating cost should be zero.

The table on page 73 uses non-sustainable insulation for comparison purposes but of course, if sustainable materials were used they would have a similar impact.

INSULATION & U-VALUES

The U-value is essentially the rate at which heat passes through a fabric. So when the U-value for a wall, say, is discussed it includes everything that goes to make up that wall; from the internal plaster to the external brick. U-values are expressed in W/m²/degC, which is Watts per square metre per degree Centigrade (sometimes degrees Kelvin or K is used but it is exactly the

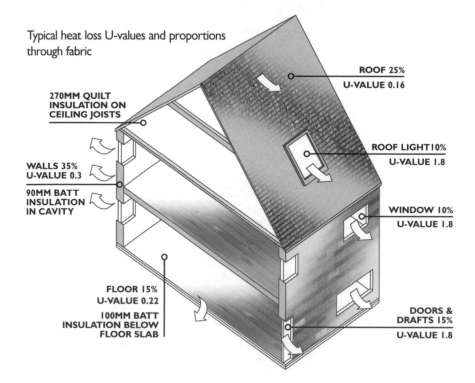

Typical heat loss U-values and proportions through fabric

270MM QUILT INSULATION ON CEILING JOISTS

WALLS 35%
U-VALUE 0.3

90MM BATT INSULATION IN CAVITY

FLOOR 15%
U-VALUE 0.22
100MM BATT INSULATION BELOW FLOOR SLAB

ROOF 25%
U-VALUE 0.16

ROOF LIGHT10%
U-VALUE 1.8

WINDOW 10%
U-VALUE 1.8

DOORS & DRAFTS 15%
U-VALUE 1.8

same). What that means is that the lower the figure the fewer Watts of heat are escaping through that material.

To calculate a specific U-value use one of the free calculators available on the web. A good and simple one to use is available from Build Desk at www.builddesk.co.uk It is free to download and will calculate

INSULATION AND DRAUGHTPROOFING

U-values for most common building materials.

The U-value is the reciprocal of the R-value, which is a material's thermal resistance. In this case the higher the figure the better. It is often used to express the thermal performance of a particular material. So in the case of our wall, each element – internal plaster, concrete block, insulation, cavity, external brick – will have an R-value and those R-values come together to enable the calculation of the U-value.

The R-value will be related to the thickness of the material; so 50mm of Isonat insulation has an R-value of 1.28 m².k/W and 100mm thickness = 2.56 m².k/W

The thermal conductivity (the K-value) on the other hand is an absolute figure for the material, irrespective of thickness. Isonat, for instance has a conductivity of 0.039 W/m.K and Kingspan has 0.021 W/m.K. What this does is allow direct comparison. From these two figures we know that Kingspan is about twice as good an insulator as Isonat or that we will need about twice the thickness of Isonat to achieve the same level of insulation. Bear in mind that these figures tell us nothing about the quality of the product as a whole, merely about its insulation characteristics.

Part L Building Regulations 2006 set a minimum standard for U-values. The table below compares these to U-values for other design standards.

DESIGN STANDARDS COMPARISON

	Part L1A Building Regs	AECB Silver	Passivhaus	AECB Gold
External walls	0.35W/m²C	0.25W/m²C	0.15W/m²C	0.15W/m²C
Ground floor	0.25W/m²C	0.20W/m²C	0.15W/m²C	0.15W/m²C
Pitched roof	0.16W/m²C	0.15W/m²C	0.1W/m²C	0.1W/m²C
Windows & doors	1.8W/m²C	1.4W/m²C	0.6W/m²C	0.6W/m²C
Air tightness	10m³/m²/hr	3m³/m²/hr	0.75m³/m²/hr	0.75m³/m²/hr

The U-values set in the 2010 Building Regulations are the same as those in the previous 2006 regulations. But the requirement under the 2010 regulatons is to achieve a 25 per cent improvement in CO_2 emissions over a similar house built to the 2006 regulations standard.

4

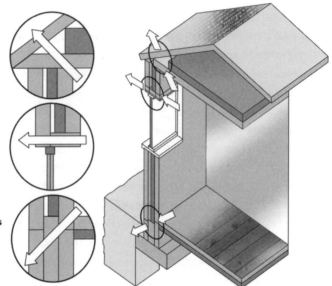

A thermal bridge is a straight line drawn from the interior to the exterior that does not pass through a full thickness of insulation

Merely hitting those U-values will not be enough. We have to do more in terms of insulation and airtightness merely to meet the standard.

THERMAL BRIDGING

The U-value is a measure of the thermal conductance of all the materials in a fabric or element. Therefore the design (of the wall, roof, whatever) and the workmanship will both impact on actual U-value.

A study for NASA in 2005 showed that a five per cent gap in the insulation (of a highly insulated building) accounted for 50 per cent of the heat loss. It is the basis of the reasoning for the air-tight house and shows that if the insulation is not installed properly a good deal of its benefit is lost. Heat will find the line of least resistance in its struggle to flee the building and thermal bridges are a good means of escape.

A thermal bridge is typically found where vertical and horizontal layers of insulation meet but don't overlap.

If you can draw a line from the interior of the property to the exterior without passing through a full thickness of insulation, you have a thermal bridge. They are very tricky to deal with in a retro-fit or renovation as finding them can be a problem, as can getting to the right spot to fix it.

INSULATION AND DRAUGHTPROOFING

They tend to occur over windows and doors, at the junction of the walls and roof and at the junction of the ground floor and walls.

Accurately calculating the effect of thermal bridges is a complicated business , on a project-specific basis. The result is that quoted U-values in the UK tend to be a bit optimistic. For instance a timber-frame wall U-value will often be quoted as 0.35 W/m²K, calculated to include the insulation. If the U-value is calculated through the studs (where there is no insulation) it could be 0.8 giving an overall U-value for the wall, including the thermal bridge of maybe 0.55 W/m²K. Most buildings contain design or construction defects, as a result of poor materials, poor workmanship or poor quality control, which further increase the buildings heat loss potential. As a result, the U-value which designers think they are meeting is not met in practice.

If you are building at 2006 Part L standard that probably does not matter too much but if you are aiming at a low-energy house or even only 2010 standard then you will need accurate figures if the house is going to work properly. U-values lead us to the peak heat load, which in turn leads us to the size of the boiler, heat pump, solar panels or whatever it is we choose to install. Get the U-value wrong and we end up with the wrong heat source. The best source of accurate guidance in this regard is probably Association of Environment Conscious Building – www.aecb.org.uk . Membership is cheap and they publish all sorts of useful information.

INSULATION MATERIALS
Non-Sustainable Materials

The non-sustainable market is covered by five market leaders; Kingspan, Celotex, Knauf, Jablite and Rockwool. Which are variously rigid polyurethane (PUR) and polyisocyanurate (PIR), expanded polystyrene and mineral wool. They all have good websites and loads of marketing that tell you all you need to know about the products. They are mass produced, relatively cheap and easily available through out the country. All are rated A or B on the Green Guide to Housing Specification.

These are all highly processed materials carrying a high overhead in terms of energy consumed in production, and the consequent CO_2 emissions. It has to be said that the manufacturers are taking steps to reduce their carbon footprint, by recycling energy and materials, and installing renewable energy systems. Which help, but also point at the high levels of energy they actually use. They also trumpet their sustainability credentials by pointing at up to 50 per cent material content being recycled. Even if that is true the other 50 per cent, as a minimum, is virgin material. They also claim that the insulation can itself be recycled, but in practice have these products ever come out of a building to be reused?

4

When these products are installed they are generally cut to fit between joist or rafters, resulting in a fair quantity of off-cuts. Most often those off-cuts are popped into a skip and sent to landfill where, because they are non-biodegradable, they will sit for eons.

Non-sustainable insulation products do the job they are intended to do, are cheap and readily available. But can they really form part of a sustainable build when there are so many options available?

Multi-Foil Insulation

There are now a couple of manufacturers of multi-foils, and they are pretty much the same and produce very similar products. They have a nominal thickness of 35mm made up of 19 separate layers, being a mixture of reflective films, flexible wading and closed cell foam. The separate layers are then stitched through to form a quilt-like sheet.

There is some controversy over the thermal performance of this product. The manufacturer commissioned a report from TRADA Technology Ltd, which states '"'...TRI-ISO SUPER 9 had insulating properties equivalent to mineral wool (glass) of 200 mm. This provides thermal performance to the equivalent of an overall thermal resistance (RT) of 5 m²K/W based on a recognised international thermal conductivity value for standard glass wool insulation of 0.04 W/m·K."

In 2004 Celotex Ltd commissioned the National Physical Laboratories, Teddington, to undertake a hot-box test (the standard test for all insulation materials sold in the UK), which gave a measured thermal resistance of 1.71 m²K/W, about one-third of that indicated by TRADA. This equates to a U-value of 0.58, which is not too good but close to what would be expected from a material 35mm to 40mm thick. It can be argued that the hot-box test is not appropriate for multi-foils, but it is what we have and what the rest of the insulation industry is content with.

In July 2005 the Building Research Establishment carried out in-situ measurement of the U-value of the product where Tri-Iso Super 9 is the principal or only insulation in walls, floor and roof constructions. The report provided to the ODPM runs to 12 pages but basically concludes by saying that the National Physical Laboratories is right.

Extract from circular number 06/2009 dated June 18, 2009 produced by Department for Communities and Local Government

"MULTI-FOIL THERMAL INSULATION PRODUCTS

1. Multi-foil insulation products consist of several layers of foil separated

INSULATION AND DRAUGHTPROOFING

4

by other materials, which inhibit heat loss by both providing a non-conductive barrier and by incorporating elements which reflect heat back towards its source. As you may be aware, there is a scientific dispute over the appropriate test method for measuring the thermal performance of multi-foil insulation products. Some multi-foil insulation manufacturers consider that the most appropriate method is comparative ('in situ') testing.

2. The Department maintains its previous view, based both on international scientific opinion and on new and previous scientific advice commissioned and published by it, that, currently, the only appropriate methods for measuring the thermal performance of materials and products are the "hot-box" test, which is a British Standard test based on Standardised European Norms, or tests that have been agreed at a European level, such as those which form part of an agreed ETA for a product or products. Consequently, at present, only results from hot-box or approved ETA tests carry a statutory presumption that they are correct. Therefore the references in the four Approved Documents L to measuring U-values using the methods and calculations set out in BR 443 (2006) 'Conventions for U-value calculations' apply.

3. The Department accepts that the scientific dispute over test methods for measuring the thermal performance of multi-foil insulation is likely to take some time to be resolved. However, as has always been the case, manufacturers of multi-foil insulation products can seek to persuade BCBs and Approved Inspectors that they should accept claims for their products' performance based on comparative ('in situ') testing, and BCBs and

Approved Inspectors are free to make their own judgements about compliance with the regulations based on their assessment of these claims."

What this all means is that regardless of who is right and who is wrong, Local Authority Building Control (the Building Inspector) will only allow multi-foils to be used in conjunction with another insulation material. So essentially if you have a real shortage-of-space problem then multi-foils might help, but otherwise stick to conventional insulation materials.

SUSTAINABLE INSULATION MATERIALS

Sustainable insulation comes in all shapes and sizes. There are many different types of material each with different properties, but they all have three things in common:-

■ I. They all come from a renewable source. Be it sheep's wool, wood fibre, hemp or whatever, one of the fundamental tenets of sustainable insulation is that it comes from a sustainable source. But this is not without its problems. There is an argument that growing the raw material for sustainable insulation takes land away from food production and that

4

that is not acceptable, not for this country and not globally. The counter argument is that a good proportion of these materials are by-products of other processes, e.g. sheep's wool is a result of meat production, wood fibre comes from waste wood, cellulose is (generally) recycled newspaper. There is no argument that insulating our houses is an absolute necessity. Certainly if all 22 million houses in the UK were to be insulated with hemp, we would have a food production problem. If even the 200,000 new houses it is said we need each year were to be insulated with flax, we would have a problem. But is it really beyond the wit of man or woman to make more and better use of the by-products and waste materials that we produce?

■ 2. All sustainable materials are, of necessity, natural and consequently have none of the problems in handling associated with non-sustainable materials. In essence, they don't make you itch.

■ 3. All sustainable insulation materials have low embodied energy. The amount of energy (and CO_2) used in the operation of the house will always far outweigh the energy embodied in its construction so the thermal properties of the insulating material are more important than its embodied energy. However, when we get to the higher levels of insulation the embodied energy can become a factor. Embodied energy is usually expressed in energy used per kilogram - but for any useful comparison to be made thermal performance and material density need to be included. For example, for 1 m² of surface to achieve a U-value of 0.2 W/m² K, the energy required would be thickness of material × material density × embodied energy value. For standard, non-sustainable, polyurethane that gives a figure of 424MJ. By comparison the two most popular sustainable materials are; Cellulose at 46 MJ/kg and Sheep's wool at 100 MJ/kg.

Price and Description

Provided here is a description of the characteristics of each of the principal insulation materials, together with the expected K-value and typical price. The price was accurate at the time of writing (summer 2011) but obviously will alter. The price of sheep's wool, for instance, is about five per cent down since the first edition.

So check the price, and that the material is manufactured in the UK.

SHEEP WOOL

Sheep's wool is available in slabs (batts) and rolls and are made from wool with a polyester binder and treated for fire and insect resistance. Sheep's wool has excellent hygroscopic properties that help to

4

moderate temperatures throughout the seasons.

As it is hydroscopic it helps to prevent condensation – wool absorbs 40 per cent of its dry weight in moisture. Because wool generates heat when it absorbs moisture, it produces 960kj of heat energy for every kg of dry wool. This warmth isn't noticeable inside the building but acts to prevent condensation in cavities by maintaining the temperature. It also helps keep moisture away from the timber frame, potentially increasing the life of the timber.

Sheep wool uses just 24 per cent of the energy used to produce glass fibre insulation so pays back manufacturing energy cost four times faster. The only additives to the wool are Boron to prevent insect and fungal attack and a small quantity of viscose (recycled) to aid binding. This also means that it is fully recyclable once it is removed.

Usage

Wool is suitable for use as insulation between rafters, joists and timber studs in timber 'breathing' wall construction. It adapts to the shape of the cavity that it fills but has a tendency to slump when used in walls so needs to be held in place properly. If properly installed it will have a life expectancy similar to that of the building.

Thermal Conductivity

Sheep's wool is comparable to mineral wool with a K-value of 0.038 to 0.040W/mdegK

THERMAFLEECE

Thickness of Batt	Coverage per pack	Price per pack	Price per m^2
50mm	20.16m^2	£112.75	£5.60
75mm	12.96m^2	£108.43	£8.37
100mm	10.08m^2	£112.52	£11.16

The product is available from many sources, including www.greenbuildingstore.co.uk and www.naturalinsulations.co.uk

ISOVLAS

Batt Size	Coverage per pack	Price per pack	Price per m^2
50mm x 600mm	7.2m^2	£27.15	£3.77
100mm x 600mm	3.6m^2	£30.89	£8.58
50mm x 400mm	4.8m^2	£20.60	£4.29
100mm x 400mm	2.4m^2	£18.09	£7.54

Isovlas is sold in packs of 10 batts. Each batt is 1200mm long and either 400mm or 600mm wide.

4

Price

The www.secondnatureuk.com website contains a list of suppliers throughout the UK. A new sheep's wool product on the market is Thermafleece PB20, designed specifically for use within confined loft spaces, this new development from Second Nature UK is available in roll form, each roll 5.3m in length, and available in widths of 370mm or 570mm to allow easy installation between joists. Aimed at DIY installation, each roll is compressed to form tightly compacted units to make it is easier to transport and store. In order to achieve this a lower quantity of wool is used than for standard sheep's wool insulation. To enable the insulation to return to its full thickness up to 35 per cent recycled polyester fibres have been included. Inevitably, this does slightly impact on the acoustic, thermal and moisture control properties.

Whilst Thermafleece PB20 is not as readily available as its older brother, there are a number of stockists across the country, and once again, a comprehensive list can be found of www.secondnature.co.uk.

FLAX

Flax has been produced as a plant material for hundreds of years, both for the fibre that is used to make linen and for the oil (linseed). The properties of flax are very similar to sheep wool and it is suitable for the same applications. The major difference is that the flax fibres are bound with potato starch and so the product is entirely natural.

Usage

Flax insulation is used in breathing wall construction, ventilated pitched roofs and in ceilings and floors. Like sheep wool it is non toxic and non irritant so no specialist equipment is required for installation which only needs a sharp knife and a keen eye.

FLAX 100

Thickness of Batt	Coverage per pack	Price per m^2
40mm	6.25m^2	£5.50
50mm	5m^2	£6.50
60mm	4.38m^2	£8.00
80mm	3.12m^2	£10.50
100mm	2.5m^2	£13.33
120mm	1.88m^2	£16.00
140mm	1.88m^2	£18.50
160mm	1.88m^2	£21.00
180mm	1.88m^2	£23.50
200mm	1.25m^2	£26.00

Flax 100 is sold in batts 1000mm long and 625mm wide. It is sold in a variety of thicknesses between 40mm and 200mm.

4

Thermal Conductivity

Flax is comparable to sheep's wool with a K-value of 0.038 to 0.040W/mdegK

Price

The two leading trade names are Isovlas Flax and Flax 100. More difficult to find than sheep wool but it is available through www.ecomerchant.co.uk and www.greenandeasy.co.uk or www.constructionresources.com.

Flax 100 is sold in batts 1000mm long and 625 mm wide. It is sold in a variety of thicknesses between 40mm and 200mm.

CLOTH

The only cloth insulation now available in the UK is Innotherm available from Recovery Insulation of Sheffield.

Innotherm is made from 100 per cent recycled industrial cotton waste, again with boron added as a fire retardant and insect repellent.

Usage

Their products comes in batt and in roll form and is very like sheep wool in its properties. It is suitable for use between rafters, joists and timber studs in timber 'breathing' wall construction. It also has a tendency to slump when used in walls so needs to be held in place properly.

Thermal Conductivity

Cloth is comparable to sheep's wool with a K-value of 0.039 to 0.041W/m°K

Price

All batts and rolls come in 1200mm lengths.

HEMP

Since 1996 the cultivation of low narcotic hemp has been allowed in the UK, but is still not

INNOTHERM

Batt/Roll size	Price per m²
75mm x 400mm	£6.40
100mm x 400mm	£8.50
100mm x 600mm	£8.50

All batts and rolls come in 1200mm lengths.

4

HEMP BATTS

Batt Size	Pack size (batts per pack)	Coverage per pack	Price per pack	Price per m²
50x385x1200mm	12	5.54m²	£44.38	£8.01
50x575x1200mm	12	8.28m²	£66.27	£8.00
75x385x1200mm	8	3.7m²	£42.63	£11.52
75x575x1200mm	8	5.52m²	£63.68	£11.54
100x385x1200mm	6	2.77m²	£38.55	£13.92
100x575x1200mm	6	4.14m²	£57.57	£13.91

permitted in the USA.

ThermoHemp was the 2006 Grand Designs winner for 'Best Eco Product' and hemp generally continues to grow in popularity. It is available primarily through an Irish company, Ecological Building Systems. Like all the organic insulation materials, hemp absorbs CO_2 while it is growing, which is held within the material. No herbicides or pesticides are needed during cultivation because it naturally repels pests and weeds. It has all the same advantages of sheep wool, flax and cotton but also has two properties that set it apart.

The first is that being stiffer than other fibres it is not prone to slump. This means that it does not form around pipes as well but also it will not drop in a wall to leave an insulation gap at the top. The second…? It smells nice.

Usage
Hemp comes in roll and batt form with various sizes available. The batts are available in either 580mm or 375 mm widths at 1200mm lengths and thicknesses of 30 mm to 180mm. The rolls are available in lengths of 6m or 8m and 375mm or 580mm widths, with thicknesses of 30mm to 80mm.

Thermal Conductivity
Again comparable to sheep's wool with a K-value of 0.038 to 0.040W/mdegK

Price
It is available through a number of outlets, including www. ecologicalbuildingsystems.com A second supplier of ThermoHemp

4

is Ty-Mawr Ecological Building Materials. Whilst there is a range of thicknesses available (according to ecologicalbuildingsystems.com), Ty-Mawr only provide two:

The prices below apply to Hemp Batts, produced by Natural Building Technologies, based in Buckinghamshire.

These hemp batts are slightly different in that the fibres are bound with a thermoplastic and are treated with inorganic salts to provide fire and pest resistance. This particular form of hemp insulation should not be used in cavity walls or under ground floors. In all other respects it is the same as Thermo Hemp and sells through a number of national and well known suppliers, including Travis Perkins and Jewson.

Isonat is another hemp trade name, this product being made from a mix of UK grown hemp and cotton waste although the final product is manufactured in France. It also contains 15 per cent polyester fibres as a binder. As with NBT Hemp it is treated with inorganic salts and prolonged exposure to water will cause it to decay. The product is available from Sustainable Building Supplies and Natural Insulations.

WOOD FIBRE

This is a huge area with a large number of different products, but essentially two types of product: Wood wool insulation which is made from forestry thinnings and saw mill residue with a binding of polyolefin fibres. The fire retardant in this is usually ammonium phosphate. Wood wool insulation is used in breathing wall construction, ventilated pitched roofs and in ceilings and floors – similar application to sheep's wool and hemp. Then there is wet-formed wood fibre board insulation, made from largely pre-consumer waste wood from saw mills. The wood is reduced to fine chips and then soaked in water before being pressed and dried without additional bonding agents. This process gives it slightly different characteristics and it can be used for things like sarking and external cladding. For these applications latex is usually added to provide some water-proofing. In some cases the board will accept plaster or render directly making it a useful external insulation material.

There are only a few main manufacturers of wood fibre insulation but each has a plethora of products as, unlike other sustainable insulation materials, wood fibre lends itself to many different applications. So in this case we deal with each manufacturer in turn and consider their main product lines.

STEICO

All of the wood fibre used in the production of Steico products is FSC certified, and are

4

available through www.ecomerchant.co.uk and www.burdensenvironmental.com.

Although Steico offer a range of good products with good provenance, the products perhaps need to be approached with caution as they are manufactured in Poland and transported to UK by lorry.

Steico Universal

Steico Universal is an insulated wall board that can be used as a sheathing board for timber frame walls, as a sarking board and as external insulation for roofs and floors. It has a tongue and groove profile which gives it good wind resistance and water proofing capabilities. It helps prevent thermal bridging and has a thermal conductivity of 0.048W/mdegK. It is fully recyclable with no specialist disposal costs. Like hemp, at the end of its life it can be composted or used for energy extraction.

Steico Special

Steico Special is intended for renovation work, specifically for external insulation. Once again it is multi-functional as a result of the double tongue and groove profile; wind tight, water resistant and heat insulating. It has been designed as a sarking or sheathing board, and has a thermal conductivity of 0.046W/Wk, and a fire class E rating.

Steico Protect

Protect has been designed specifically as a rigid, external sheathing board for timber frame walls, and can accept specialist 'direct render' systems. Again has a tongue and groove profile and a thermal conductivity 0.042W/mdegK.

It reduces the need for the addition of a façade to a timber frame building and therefore, to an extent, off-sets the extra cost of natural insulation. Prices are available on request from Burdens Environmental.

Steico Therm

Steico Therm is a rigid insulation board with high compressive strength and can be used as external insulation for roofs, internal insulation for floors or as sub screed insulation. This one does not have a tongue and groove profile but compressible edging strips are available. Thermal conductivity is 0.040W/mdegK.

Steico Flex

This is a flexible roof insulation, similar to hemp, specifically designed

4

for use within roofs, dry walls and ceiling applications, as well as cavity insulation for partition and external walls. It has good compression resistance and expands to fit adjoining components and, like all wood fibre products, it is hydroscopic but has a lower absorption rate than sheep's wool or hemp.

Further details of the Steico Product range can be found on www.ecomerchant.co.uk, along with contact details.

HOMATHERM

Homatherm WoodFlex Protect

A medium density semi rigid insulation in batt form. It is made from wood chippings with seven per cent to 10 per cent polyolefin fibres as a binder. It is suitable for timber frame constructions – walls, floors and roofs. The cellulose fibres enable absorption of 17 per cent moisture without losing thermal performance, which helps to protect the structural timbers. The polyolefin fibres are added as a binder and to provide a degree of flexibility.

The product is available from Construction Resource and Ecological Building Systems.

HOMATHERM WOODFLEX PROTECT

Thickness	Length and width (mm)	Coverage per pack	Price per pack	Price per m²
60mm	1250 x 570	3.6m²	£41.75	£11.72
80mm	1200 x 625	3m²	£42.75	£14.25
80mm	1250 x 570	2.85m²	£40.65	£14.26
100mm	1200 x 625	2.25m²	£40.08	£17.81
100mm	1250 x 570	2.14m²	£37.14	£17.38
120mm	1200 x 625	2.25m²	£45.86	£20.38
140mm	1200 x 625	1.5m²	£34.50	£23.00
140mm	1200 x 570	1.37m²	£31.50	£23.03
180mm	1200 x 625	1.5m²	£44.32	£29.55
200mm	1200 x 625	1.5m²	£48.65	£32.43
200mm	1250 x 570	1.425m²	£46.22	£32.44

The product is available from Construction Resources and Ecological Building Systems.

4

GUTEX

Gutex is a German company (again imported to UK by lorry) and all of their products are manufactured from the by-products of sawmills in southern Germany. Like most of these products it is a wet-formed fibre board but in the case of Thermowall, boards that are thicker than 20mm are made up of 20mm thick laminations. Durability is said to be 70 years plus (which sounds a long time but is probably less than the life of the building), the product has no chemical additives, no toxins or toxic emissions and is CO_2 zero rated.

THERMOWALL 040 & 045

Thickness	Length and Width	Coverage per pack	Price per pack	Price per m²
Standard size				
40mm	1190 x 590	70.21m²	£786.35	£11.20
60mm	1190 x 590	46.34m²	£967.58	£20.88
Large Size				
40mm	1250 x 2600	81.25m²	£1090.00	£38.81
60mm	1250 x 2600	52m²	£1055.00	£37.57

As with Homatherm, the main supplier of Thermowall is Construction Resources.

Thermowall

It is particularly useful as external cladding on timber frame as it is able to accept cement or lime render. It also displays slightly better thermal resistance than low density fibres (wool, flax, cotton, etc.) although it is a good deal more expensive. It is one to use for particular applications.

ThermoSafe 040

A rigid insulation board made in exactly the

THERMOSAFE 040

Board Size	Thickness	Price per pallet	Coverage per pallet
1200mm x 600mm	40mm	100	72m²
1200mm x 600mm	60mm	66	47.5m²
1200mm x 600mm	100mm	40	28.8m²

This product available from Construction Resources.

4

ULTRATHERM 045

Thickness	Coverage per board	Boards per pallet	Coverage per pack	Cost per pallet	Price per m²
All boards measure 1780mm in length and 600mm width					
50mm	0.84m²	40	42.72m2	£753	£17.63
60mm	0.84m²	34	36.31m2	£730	£20.51
100mm	0.84m²	20	21.36m2	£659	£30.28
120mm	0.84m²	18	19.22m2	£700	£36.42

This product available from Construction Resources.

same way as Thermowall and is suitable for flooring (below the screed), walls (internal and external) and roofs. It comprises of 97 per cent wood chippings, two per cent water and one per cent natural resin adhesive. All other properties are exactly the same as Thermowall.

UltraTherm 045

Another rigid insulation, although this comes in a tongue and groove format ideally suited for the thermal upgrading of existing roof structures. In effect a high performance sarking board that is also suitable for externally insulating timber frames or green oak framed buildings. It has a water-proof coating which makes it suitable as a temporary wall/roof covering, although it might be said to be too expensive for that.

All boards measure 1780mm in length and 600mm width.

As well as the main products listed above, Gutex also offer:

Multiplex-Top

A rain tight sub plate that is also suitable for interior applications. Thermal conductivity (W/mK) 0.044

ThermoSafe homogen

A single ply, universal insulating board with a thermal conductivity of (W/mdegK) 0.037

Thermoflex

A flexible wood fibre board for use with intermediate rafters and frameworks. Thermal conductivity (W/mdegK) 0.038

Thermoflat

A single ply board with compression proof instruction, suitable for flat wood, concrete and sheet metal roofs. Thermal conductivity (W/mdegK) 0.039

Thermoinstal

Single ply and compression resistant, this board is designed for the insulation of installation cavities, electrical power and plumbing lines. Thermal conductivity (W/mdegK) 0.039

Thermoroom

A single ply board suitable for the retrofit of interior walls within older buildings. Thermal conductivity (W/mK) 0.038 Thermoroom will be available through www.lime.org.uk.

Thermosafe-wd

Highly resistant to compressive forces, this single ply board provides insulation for any wall or floor. Thermal conductivity (W/mdegK) 0.039

Thermosafe-nf

Integrating tongue and groove joints, with spruce joint strips for easy installation, these boards are ideal for long and short plank flooring. Thermal conductivity (W/mdegK) 0.039

Thermofloor

Suitable for all floor applications, including wet and dry screed, and loads up to 5 nK/m2. Thermal conductivity (W/mdegK) 0.039

PAVATEX

Pavatex have been manufacturing wood fibre insulation boards in Switzerland since 1932 and in Fribourg, Germany since 1949.

Pavatex is exactly the same as all of the above in that it is produced from waste wood materials and is 100 per cent natural. All Pavatex boards are supplied with fully compatible fixings, renders and accessories. They consist of 99.5 per cent waste soft wood and 0.5 per cent inert water proofing. It can be used for new buildings, applied directly to timber or steel frames, and to all types of masonry. It can also be used for external and internal insulation and in renovations.

These products have an interlock system on all 4 sides which can

4

provide complete wind and water tightness. Comes in boards measuring 2500 mm in length and 770 mm in width. There are three thicknesses available – 22, 35 and 60 mm.

Diffutherm

This is an external wall insulation that can be used on timber frames and masonry walls as with all the Pavatex products. It is available through Calch Ty-Mawr Lime (www.lime.org.uk), NBT and Sustainable Building Supplies

It should be, and can be, sold together with a Bayosan thin mesh coat render. In timber frames it can be used as an external insulation in conjunction with a 'vapour open' insulation like sheep wool or hemp and again can only be installed by approved contractors who have been trained by NBT.

Diffutherm can also be used as an internal insulation for walls, floors and ceilings and for upgrading the insulation in existing buildings, both solid walls and brick-infilled traditional timber frames.

Isolair

A water resistant wood fibre board designed for use as underlay in roofs, and as a wind tight layer in ventilated facades. Isolair boards also have tongue and groove edging to provide a solid joint for placement between rafters and studs. It can be applied over rafter insulations to protect the insulation material or in inter rafter constructions onto the beams in place of underlays.

DIFFUTHERM

Thickness	Length and width	Number of boards	Coverage per pack	Price per m²	Price per board
20 mm	60mm x 120mm	8	5.8m²	£6.07	£4.40
40 mm	60mm x120mm	4	2.92m²	£12.26	£8.95
60 mm	1300mm x 790mm	30	30.19m²	£19.77	£19.90
80 mm	1300mm x 790mm	22	22.14m²	£26.43	£26.60
100 mm	1300mm x 790mm	18	8.11m²	£32.99	£33.20

This product is available through Calch Ty-Mawr Lime (www.lime.org.uk)

4

Pavatherm Plus

Pavatherm is made from 99.5 per cent waste soft wood and 0.5 per cent paraffin. When the boards are produced the wood fibres are pulped and mixed with water. The pulp is then heated to activate the natural lignin in order to glue the fibres together and the pulp is then mechanically pressed into boards. Pavatherm Plus can be used on walls but not on roofs. Isolair is roof specific and Pavatherm Plus is wall specific.

The boards are tongue and grooved on all four sides and it is typically used directly underneath external timber cladding and being hydroscopic means that a vapour permeable membrane is unnecessary.

The product itself keeps the building structure dry. Being air tight and rigid means that the insulation performance can be guaranteed for the life of the building. In timber frames it is suggested Pavatherm be used with another form of insulation such as Warmcel or hemp. On masonry constructions the Pavatherm boards can be attached directly to the masonry substrate.

The main UK supplier used by Pavatex is New Building Technologies and they in turn sell through the suppliers listed previously for the hemp batts.

Pavadentro

Pavadentro is a new product and is aimed specifically at the repair and refurbishment market. It has been designed to insulate external walls whilst reducing the chance of condensation build-up inside the building. These boards are good for refurbishment projects where the building cannot be insulated externally, such as listed or heritage buildings.

The boards include a mineral-based layer, sodium silica, which tends to protect the building fabric. The combination of the wood fibre and mineral regulates the passage of moisture by ensuring breathability (hygroscopicity), maintaining a healthy living environment.

RECYCLED PAPER OR CELLULOSE

Trade names for this material are Warmcel, Vital 040 and Termex, and stands along-side sheep wool in terms of its impact on the market.

WARMCEL

Produced by a company called Excel Building Solutions, based in Gwent, who supply across Europe. It is made from 100 per cent recycled paper and is available in a number of forms – Warmcel 100,

INSULATION AND DRAUGHTPROOFING

Warmcel 500, Warmcel 300, Warmcel RF.

Cellulose products are generally installed in one of three ways:

■ By hand – Usually when in pellet form, spread our by hand.

■ Turbo filling – a method used for closed panel structures. A hole is drilled into the wall, a hose is attached and the Warmcel is sprayed into the cavity.

■ Damp Spraying – use for open panels. The Warmcel is dampened, sprayed onto the wall and then levelled off to the depth of the studs. The moisture dries out naturally.

Warmcel 100

This is specifically for DIY loft insulation and can simply be emptied from the bag into the loft space, and spread by hand. It is non toxic and non irritant and uses inorganic salts to increase fire resistance. It is resistant to biological and fungal attack and unattractive to vermin.

Thermal conductivity of 0.036 W/m.K is the same as sheep wool, flax, hemp and cotton but performance is enhanced by its ability to create a high level of air tightness to prevent thermal convection currents if the insulation is firmly compacted.

Warmcel 500

This is used for Enhance Vapour Transfer (EVT) Technology applications, specifically EVT walls, roofs and floors. An EVT construction (used as a structural wall or roof) combines a high level of insulation with the ability to control the migration of any moisture that gets into the structure (which happens in any inhabited building) to the external side of the structure where it is harmlessly expelled to the atmosphere. This action, known as EVT, ensures that interstitial condensation does not occur, thereby protecting the timber structure throughout the lifetime of the building. The product is usually turbo-filled or damp spray installed. In essence this is a step up from simple hydroscopic material which just holds moisture until air movement dries it again.

The significance of this is that a major company in the home building industry, Excel Industries Ltd, are specifically using a natural insulation material because of the properties that it brings. As well as having the lowest embodied energy of sustainable insulation materials in this case they are using its hydroscopic qualities to provide a natural means of controlling and directing condensation.

Warmcel 300

As Warmcell 500 but specifically for new build lofts, floors or other open horizontal surfaces. It is dry blown to fill between and over joists.

4

Warmcel RF

Designed for retrofit installation into older properties for lofts and cavity walls. It is dry blown by specialists and can be used if there is no insulation at all or as a top up over existing insulation.

Warmcel is readily available with suppliers across the country through Pen Y Coed Construction (www.penycoes-warmcel.com) in Powys, Ecomerchant, the Low Impact Living Initiative (lowimpact.org.uk) and the South Yorkshire Energy Centre (syec.co.uk).

Vital 040

A cellulose insulation batt made from oxygen bleached wood pulp and viscose fibres. It also contains a food grade cellulose based binder and a ph neutral boron liquid to provide permanent protection against fire and mould. It can absorb 20 per cent of its weight in moisture without losing any significant thermal performance – seven times more than a mineral wool product of similar density. It is a semi-rigid product, manufactured in Finland (transport facilities to UK are not known).

Batts are 870mm by 565mm wide. Available from Construction Resources.

VITAL 040			
Batt Thickness	Coverage per pack	Price per pack	Price per m^2
Batts are 870mm by 565mm wide			
50mm	5.90m^2	£36.88	£6.25
100mm	2.95m^2	£36.88	£12.50
150mm	1.97m^2	£38.22	£19.40

This product available from Construction Resources

TERMEX

Another product from recycled newsprint produced in Finland from paper where vegetable oil based pigments are used exclusively for the ink. In all other respects the same as Warmcell and Vital but with a very slightly better thermal performance.

Available from Termex UK Ltd in York.

Homatherm flexCL

This product is from

TERMEX		
Depth of Termex	U Value	Price per m2
100mm	0.400	£5.19
150mm	0.267	£7.79
200mm	0.200	£10.37
250mm	0.160	£12.99
300mm	0.133	£15.57
350mm	0.114	£18.14
400mm	0.100	£20.75

Available from Termex UK Ltd in York.

HOMATHERM FLEXCL

Batt Thickness	Coverage per pack	Price per m²	Price per pack	Coverage per pallet	Price per m²	Price per pallet	Packs per pallet
Batts come in lengths of 1200mm and widths of 625mm							
30mm	7.5m²	£6.40	£48.00	105m²	£5.61	£589.23	14
40mm	6.0m²	£6.59	£39.56	84.0m²	£6.15	£516.89	14
50mm	4.5m²	£10.62	£47.81	63m²	£9.94	£626.06	14
60mm	3.75m²	£12.07	£45.28	52.5m²	£11.29	£592.72	14
80mm	3m²	£14.25	£42.75	42m²	£13.31	£559.13	14
100mm	2.25m²	£17.81	£40.08	31.5m²	£16.63	£523.69	14
120mm	2.25m²	£20.38	£45.86	27m²	£19.06	£514.62	12
140mm	1.5m²	£23.00	£34.50	24m²	£21.50	£516.00	12
160mm	1.5m²	£26.25	£39.38	21m²	£24.50	£514.50	12
180mm	1.5m²	£29.55	£44.32	18m²	£27.26	£490.70	12

This product available from Construction Resources.

recycled newspaper, with the addition of jute sacking. It comes in batt form with a slightly higher density than other cellulose products giving a better acoustic performance.

Batts come in lengths of 1200mm and widths of 625mm.

Again available from Construction Resources.

Homatherm flexCL 040

Homatherm is a high-density, semi-rigid batt, produced from recycled newsprint, with the addition of between seven and 10 per cent polyolefin fibres. It can absorb up to 17 per cent of its weight in moisture without affecting its thermal performance. The polyolefin fibres are added for flexibility. It has a thermal conductivity of 0.039W/mdegK. Homatherm flex is available through Construction Resources, and apparently, only through Construction Resources.

The sizes available are:

Non-Itch Masonry Wall Cavity Slabs

Made from 85 per cent recycled plastic, this insulation is designed specifically for use in masonry walls with a cavity thickness of 65, 75, 85 or 100mm. It is available in slab, or batt form and as such it is quick and easy to install. It is directly equivalent to glass fibre insulation, uses only recycled material, and once it has reached the end of its service it is recyclable once again. It is

4

unaffected by water (but not hydroscopic) and has good acoustic properties.

Information and prices available from www.naturalinsulations.co.uk

CORKBOARD

Cork works as an insulation material because slightly over 50 per cent of the volume is air trapped within the cell structure. It is normally supplied in board form which is manufactured from cork granules that are re-formed under heat and pressure and bonded together using natural cork resins. It displays very similar properties to wood fibre boards in terms of thermal performance, acoustics, fire resistance and processing energy. Cork is available in thinner sections than wood fibre boards, down to just 12mm, which makes it useful in renovations as floor and wall insulation.

The cork oak is a forest tree that grows in limited areas of Spain, Portugal and North Africa, but a huge proportion of the cork reaching the UK comes from Portugal. Cork bark is harvested from trees 20 to 30 years old with an optimum harvesting cycle of every 20 to 25 years. There is some concern that the stock of this slow growing tree is not able to meet the demands of the modern world. The temptation is to shorten the harvesting cycle, giving a higher annual output but damaging, and potentially killing, the tree. In addition the manufacturing process is quite tricky and embodied energy is around 26MJ/kg, about twice that of hemp, for example.

There are other materials that do everything that cork will do, but avoid the temptation to exploit a fading resource.

WHAT YOU DON'T GET FROM SUSTAINABLE INSULATION

Inarguably sustainable insulation will cost more. In terms of a whole house it could be 50 per cent to 100 per cent more. It is not produced in the same volumes as non-sustainable materials and has some way to go before those economies of scale start to kick in. However, considered as a proportion of the overall project cost this uplift can be said to pay for the things that you don't get from sustainable insulation:

■ Itchy hands
■ Sore eyes
■ Gassing-off
　■ A Health & Safety leaflet

DRAUGHT PROOFING

This is usually less of a problem with new build than renovation or

INSULATION AND DRAUGHTPROOFING

refurbishment. The DTI suggest that 10 per cent of the heat lost from a house is via draughts and this figure attributes to more modern properties rather than old draughty houses. In that case, especially when there is an unused fireplace, the figure can get to over 50 per cent.

It takes a person with dedication, persistence and without the burden of a full-time job to achieve a 100 per cent draught-free house. And in truth some air movement is necessary if for no other reason than to keep the oxygen refreshed. It is the unknown, uncontrollable draughts under doors, around windows, from disused flues that are the problem. The most overlooked draughts in older properties are those from the joint of the ground floor and the wall, especially where there is a suspended floor.

Sealing the obvious gaps is a fairly simple and cheap operation. There are many products available in the local DIY shed, from brush strips to mastics. It has been estimated that draught-proofing a three-bedroom Victorian house will cost £50 to £100. At that level it is the single most cost-effective way of reducing the energy consumption of your home.

RADIATOR REFLECTORS

It is obvious when you think about it that a proportion of the heat from a radiator is absorbed by the wall behind it. Which is not a wholly bad thing if the wall itself is well insulated as some of that heat will be leached back into the room when the radiator is turned off.

Once again your local DIY shed is likely to stock a sticky-back tin foil sheet, designed specifically for the purpose. It is tricky to fit as it entails moving the radiator from the wall but the DTI tell us that it will save another 5 per cent to 10 per cent heat loss.

INSULATING THE VICTORIAN TERRACED HOUSE

How to approach insulation in a renovation project will depend to a large extent on the scope of the renovation. Lifting floorboards may not be part of the plan if the renovation is more geared towards a quick lick of paint. But there are still things to do.

Roof

25 per cent of the heat lost from the building will be through the roof, and lofts generally benefit from a bit of extra insulation. Any of the hemp, cotton, wool or cellulose materials are great in the loft and extremely easy to work with, especially if the loft necessitates crawling about on hands and knees.

A minimum of 270mm should be installed but this should be increased if there is little opportunity to properly insulate walls and floor. 350mm or even 400mm is not unreasonable.

4

The point at which the energy used in the manufacturer of the insulation is outweighed by the energy saved by the insulation is 1m thick.

Walls

35 per cent of the heat lost from the building is through the walls and Victorian walls tend to be 9in solid brick. Adding just 40mm of insulation (internally or externally) will halve the heat loss. Older houses with cavity walls are easy to deal with, by getting in a cavity wall insulation specialist. It will cost a few thousand pounds, depending on the size of the house and will have a dramatic impact on the warmth of the property and the fuel bill. Whether sustainable materials can be used will depend on the situation but it is well worth asking, particularly for Warmcell.

Of the sustainable materials the wood fibre boards are probably the best option for internal insulation. Pavatherm and Thermosafe are both suitable for walls and can be plastered or wall-papered directly without the need for a plaster skim.

If there is insufficient room for a wood fibre board Sempatap wall lining may be an answer. It is a latex based product that can be glued to the wall and improves the thermal performance of the wall by about 20 per cent. It is just 5mm thick and therefore has little impact where it meets door or window frames. But a note of caution, Sempatap does not meet fire regulations for building with public access (holiday homes, B&B's, etc. would fall into this category).

Another similar product is Spacetherm which is available in a number of forms. It has a K-value of just 0.013W/mdegK and come bonded to Fermacell, plasterboard, chipboard or on its own. It is also available in strips as cold bridge insulation. An extremely handy product for the renovator.

Ground Floor

Another 20 per cent to 25 per cent of the heat will be lost through the ground floor. For a suspended timber floor there is no better option than taking up the floor-boards and installing a quilt or board insulation. Almost all of the sustainable materials will work well. At least 100mm quilt will be needed, 200mm would be better if space allows.

For a solid floor or where boards cannot be raised insulate on top with a wood fibre board or if thickness is an issue, Sempafloor.

Windows & Doors

In renovating older properties, style and appearance will be important factors. Replacing existing wooden windows with uPVC double

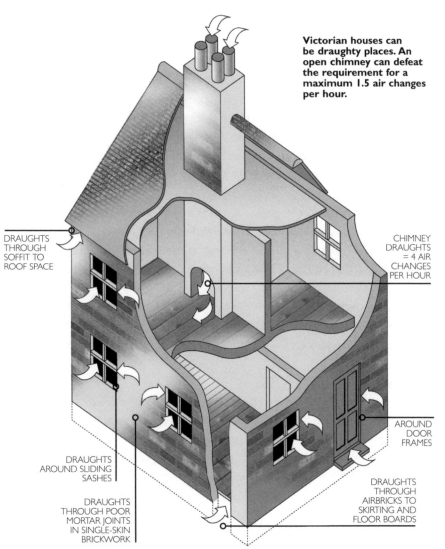

Victorian houses can be draughty places. An open chimney can defeat the requirement for a maximum 1.5 air changes per hour.

4

DRAUGHTS THROUGH SOFFIT TO ROOF SPACE

CHIMNEY DRAUGHTS = 4 AIR CHANGES PER HOUR

AROUND DOOR FRAMES

DRAUGHTS AROUND SLIDING SASHES

DRAUGHTS THROUGH AIRBRICKS TO SKIRTING AND FLOOR BOARDS

DRAUGHTS THROUGH POOR MORTAR JOINTS IN SINGLE-SKIN BRICKWORK

glazing will cost a lot of money and could be a stylistic disaster. The ubiquitous uPVC or PVCu frames that we see everywhere are an environmental nightmare (especially the wood-effect ones which even look like a nightmare). They use a huge amount of energy to produce and the production process releases high levels of dioxins and other carcinogenic chemicals.

On the other hand, Victorian sliding sashes are draughty and have a ridiculously high U-value,

4

usually over five (compared to 1.8 for modern double glazing). Having said that, the pay-back period on replacement double glazing is huge, around 94 years.

A 9in solid brick wall will have a U-value of 2.2 W/m²/degC. With 50mm of internal insulation that will come down to perhaps 0.4 – quite a bit better than a double-glazed window. So it is important to do something about those Victorian sliding sashes.

There are two possible answers. Retain the frames if they are in reasonable condition, draught-proof the sashes with brush strips and replace the glazing with double glazed units. The units will have a narrower gap than is usual, possibly 4mm or 6mm, but will still improve thermal performance.

Alternatively secondary double glazing may be the answer. There are lots of options available; from polythene film (from your local DIY store) held in place with double-sided tape and blown with a hair dryer to get the wrinkles out, to metal framed glass, held in place with magnets for easy cleaning. Both will eliminate drafts and significantly improve the U-value – at perhaps a tenth the cost of replacement double glazing.

A similar argument holds for doors. A solid timber door, typical in older properties, could have a U-value of 2.4, compared to around 1.8 for a uPVC door. Eliminating the draughts around the door will achieve a comparable U-value and retain the good looks of the original door.

Chimneys

If a fireplace is to be retained and used, there is no way of stopping the draughts when the fire is not lit. If the fireplace is not to be used, then blocking the flue with masonry will effectively block the draughts. But be aware that chimneys and chimney stacks tend to let in rain water and the flue is a natural means of keeping the chimney, and surrounding walls, dry. If the flue is blocked at the fireplace end then the stack end needs to be sealed as well to stop rainwater getting in.

Air Bricks

Air bricks are installed for one of two reasons; to vent a room with an open fire or boiler to make sure there is enough air to support the combustion, or to vent timber floors and cavities to prevent damp and rot. In either case the air brick is likely to cause draughts but those draughts are necessary if the air brick still has a function to fulfil.

IN SUMMARY
New Build

Improving air-tightness and reducing draughts is a requirement

INSULATION AND DRAUGHTPROOFING

4

under Building Regulations. Installing high levels of insulation is also a statutory requirement and makes good practical and commercial sense. Using sustainable insulation materials offers no benefit in terms of thermal performance, but the benefits in terms of their impact on the environment, the house and the people that live in it are many.

Insulation is about improving performance, and design is about determining how much you want to improve by – from current Building Regs to Passivhaus standard is the range of choice. As was stated at the outset of this chapter we seek to eliminate the gas-guzzling house and pragmatism, the available budget, may mean that choices have to be made. Sustainable insulation is a good option, but more insulation is the best option.

FOR THE RENOVATOR & REFURBISHER

Renovators start from a different place as the building already exists and they don't have the design freedom or, quite often, the access to install what might be the preferred insulation levels. In addition the design of the original building may mitigate against insulation. A barn with 500mm thick solid stone walls may work better in terms of breathability and removing moisture if the walls are left uninsulated.

There is often a balance between minimising energy consumption and allowing the building to function as it was designed to.

Beyond that the same rules apply; install as much insulation as you practically can, using the best materials the budget allows. And the order of play is:

■ Eliminate draughts, so far a possible

■ Deal with the big areas in order – roof, walls, floor

■ Deal with the little areas – windows and doors.

Bear is mind that at possibly £250 per m² double-glazing will take the bulk of the budget. Secondary double-glazing will certainly halve that figure and could get it down to

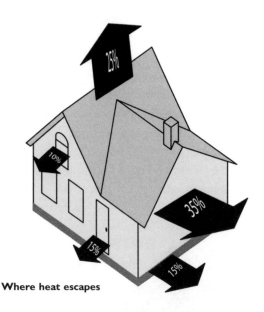

Where heat escapes

THE **SUSTAINABLE** BUILDING BIBLE

4

less than £25 per m², depending on style and quality. A single glazed window will have a U-value of 5.0W/m² and a double-glazed window will now be 1.8W/m2 or less. A secondary double-glazed window will be 2.5W/m² to 3.0W/m² but the older property is likely to have fewer windows, so the actual amount of heat energy lost through the windows will not be great.

Our mighty Government offers some help to the renovator with their CERT Scheme – check www.hvnplus.co.uk/files/cert.pdf for details. This provides substantial grants to insulate older properties. It will only pay for bringing the property to current Building Regs standard and if you want to go beyond that you will have to pay the difference.

Energy conservation is the key issue for the sustainable renovator and it is difficult to spend too much time, effort or money dealing with it. In capital cost terms it is far more effective than renewable energy, typically takes two to three years to return the investment and goes on repaying every year, for the life of the house, in terms of comfort and security as well as cash.

The illustration (right) shows how heat escapes from the house. As can be seen, 75 per cent gets our through the roof, walls and floor, 15 per cent attributes to draughts and just 10 per cent to windows and doors.

In money terms almost the reverse is true. A reasonable size house might need £20,000 for replacement double glazing but only £1,200 to £1,500 for full insulation and draught-proofing. Conversely, or even perversely, it is often the replacement double-glazing that is considered first. Which is largely due to the activities of the double-glazing industry's marketing department which has persuaded us that we cannot live without replacement u-PVC windows and doors and that secondary double-glazing is naf. At often less than £100 per window it is certainly cheaper than replacement windows, a good system will reduce the U-value of a single-glazed window from 5.0W/m² to less than 3.0W/m² (depending on the air gap between the panes), and will virtually eliminate any draughts around the sashes.

As an aside, triple-glazing will typically be 15 per cent to 20 per cent more expensive than double-glazing and will reduce the heat loss by around five per cent. Again, not cost effective for the UK climate. This sort of glazing springs from Northern Europe, Canada and the like where temperatures of -25degC are common and prolonged over winter. These temperatures mean that the heat loss through the windows is proportionately far greater than it is in the milder UK climate (U-value is actually expressed as W/m²/K or Watts of heat energy per m² area per degree of temperature difference – so the higher the temperature difference the more heat will escape through that material). In the truly super-insulated conditions of a Passivhaus

4

An inflatable bag is a simple way to stop draughts in an unused chimney

Sealing around draughty doors and windows is an essential first step

triple glazing will be necessary to get the overall U-values down to acceptable levels. In addition, with a super insulated wall with a U-value of less than 0.1, the windows become the weak spot, the prick in the balloon. So a better U-value is essential and only achievable with triple-glazing.

Draught-Proofing

There are many, effective draught-proofing systems available from your local DIY shed. From brushes to rubber profiles, and mastics. Most are fairly simple DIY installation and all are very cheap.

Sealing around draughty doors and windows is fairly obvious but also seal around skirting board to floor boards and make sure that loft insulation is below the draughts. Otherwise the insulation will merely push the cold air into the house.

Unused fireplaces can be very attractive, but draw huge amounts of heat from the house. Sealing these is important but not as easy as it looks. Draught-proofing at the room is easy with a simple inflatable bag, but the top of the flue needs to be sealed as well to prevent rainwater entering and gathering at the lower seal. Generally this is done with a slate and some mortar but you may need a scaffold to get to the chimney pot safely.

Bear in mind that if there are gas burning appliances or wood burning stoves in a room they need air! Over sealing these rooms is easy and dangerous.

4

Loft & Roof Insulation

Current building regulations call for 270mm quilt insulation in the loft. This will give a U-value of 0.16 and should be considered the absolute minimum. Upgrading to 450mm will halve the U-value to 0.08, and halve the heat loss. If space is an issue then switch to PUR or PIR insulation. These need about half the thickness to achieve the same U-value. Or, 100mm of sheep's wool or hemp with 150mm PUR on top will get a similar U-value and significantly reduce the gassing-off from the PUR into the house.

Ground Floor Insulation

The maximum U-value for a ground floor is 0.22W/m². That is achieved with 100mm of rigid foam but even that can be costly and difficult to install to a house with an existing solid floor. Without that insulation the U-value will be in the order of 4.0W/m². The only alternative is to insulate on top of the existing floor, and that, of necessity, will need to be thin. The only products available for this are Therma-Coat, an acrylic primer paint and Sempafloor, a neoprene-like material just 4.5mm to 12mm thick. Both reduce heat loss by around 20 per cent and if that is not enough then there is no reason not to use both.

Suspended timber floors are generally easier to deal with and there are a few proprietary products available, like Kingspan's Thermafloor. This is essentially Kingspan PUR insulation glued to an OSB board. It is fixed directly to the joist and a 50mm or 60mm thickness will achieve the desired U-value of 0.22. Of course any of the wood fibre insulation materials are just as good and do not require the sheet of OSB on

WARM ROOF CONSTRUCTION

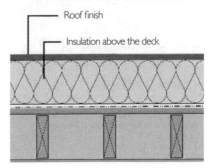

Roof finish

Insulation above the deck

Flat roofs can be insulated on the outside, often more easily than from the inside. And it will be just as effective.

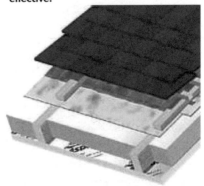

Insulating between rafters AND under rafters has the effect of improving the U-value and reducing the draughts. Cutting rigid insulation to fit between rafters tends to be less than perfectly accurate and leaves gaps, through which draughts can pass. The extra layer of insulation below tends to reduce this.

4

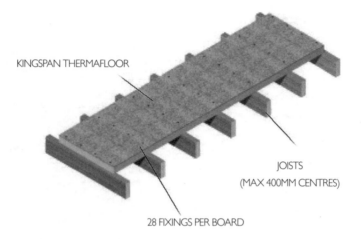

KINGSPAN THERMAFLOOR

JOISTS
(MAX 400MM CENTRES)

28 FIXINGS PER BOARD

top. These products tend to have a tongue-and-groove joint which also significantly reduces draughts.

Where space does not exist to insulate on top of the floor joists, the alternative is to insulate between the joist. The insulation is held in place using battens nailed to the joists or with wires laced across the underside of the joists. Either method allows the use of quilt insulation, hemp, sheep wool or similar, which can be cut slightly over-size and squeezed in to ensure a tight fit, again cutting down draughts.

But a note of caution. Suspended timber floors tend to have air-bricks in the walls to ensure air circulated around the joists to prevent rot. Care needs to be taken to ensure these air bricks are not blocked and that at least the bottom surface of the joist is exposed.

Intermediate Floor Insulation

Generally intermediate floors are only insulated for sound attenuation purposes. Ground floor rooms tend to want a slightly higher temperature than first floor rooms but this is only 2degC to 3degC and the necessary insulation can be achieved with the floor itself and the carpet on it.

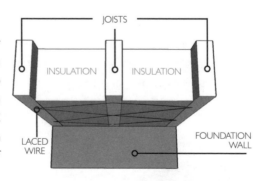

JOISTS

INSULATION INSULATION

LACED
WIRE

FOUNDATION
WALL

4

Internal Wall Insulation

Cavity wall insulation is a good idea if, and only if, the cavity is clean and especially the cavity ties are clean.

There are many cases of damp penetration after cavity walls have been filled with insulation. In most cases this is attributable to mortar sitting on the cavity ties. When the cavity is open the air moving through it is sufficient to remove any moisture being drawn to the mortar from the external brickwork. If the cavity is filled there is no more air movement and the moisture moves inexorably to the inside wall.

The rule is to get the cavity properly inspected before doing anything to it. If it is clean get it filled, if it is not, leave it alone.

It is important to have the cavity inspected before filling to avoid any problems with damp

If space allows, insulation can be fixed to the internal surface of the wall. Either directly to the wall with a vapour barrier on the internal surface of the insulation or with a timber stud frame constructed at least 25mm off the internal surface of the wall. Either will work very well and either can use sustainable insulation materials.

A 225mm (9in) solid brick wall will have a U-value of 2.23W/m². Installing just 40mm of insulation on the internal surface will reduce that to just 0.49W/m². Which sounds good but is still some way off the building regs maximum of 0.35W/m².

If space is a big issue then Sempatap or Therma-Coat (see Ground Floor insulation above) are a good alternative.

External Wall Insulation

External insulation is essentially the same as internal insulation, but on the outside. There are many proprietary systems available, using both sustainable and non-sustainable insulation materials. They all work in essentially the same way and give the same benefit over internal insulation. That is, the tea-cosy effect. Putting the insulation on the outside allows the wall to be used as thermal mass, storing heat and smoothing the daily heating cycle peaks and troughs. Which in turn saves energy. In addition, if the option for external insulation exists it is often easier

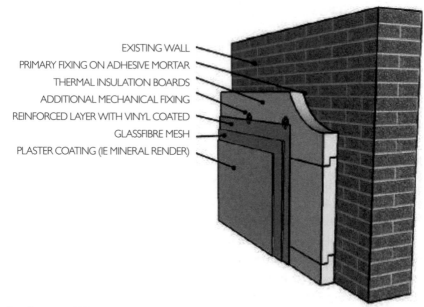

EXISTING WALL
PRIMARY FIXING ON ADHESIVE MORTAR
THERMAL INSULATION BOARDS
ADDITIONAL MECHANICAL FIXING
REINFORCED LAYER WITH VINYL COATED
GLASSFIBRE MESH
PLASTER COATING (IE MINERAL RENDER)

4

to install greater thickness.

Some systems come ready to render – the wood fibre ones, for instance – and some need a steel or glass fibre mesh to take render. Others need cladding with the preferred material – which could be bricks, brick slips, timber cladding or similar.

What comes out of this is that the opportunity exists for renovators to achieve similar levels of insulation as the self-builder. The process is a little more difficult and as a consequence may cost a little more. But that is the nature of renovation.

The idea that the renovator simply fits replacement double-glazing and calls that job-done no longer holds water, in terms of an insulated property. The mantra for the last few years has been 'Think about how much energy you want to buy in 10 years time' and applies equally to the renovator. And the products and methods are there to allow good results to be achieved.

5 RENEWABLE ENERGY: THE FACTS

omestic scale renewable energy, what is called micro generation, has been something of a shifting target in the past couple of years. There are still regular Governmental policy announcement on CO_2 emissions, sustainability and micro generation. Proposals for compulsory carbon emission targets in the Climate Change Bill are still in flux and likely to remain so for a year or two yet. But the prediction that they could have a significant impact on the way we design and run houses is coming true. As of 2009 increasing numbers of local authorities are demanding that new planning applications achieve at least Level 3 of Code for Sustainable Homes and 2010 saw that rise to Level 4 and the introduction of a new set of Building Regulations demanding at least a 25 per cent reduction in CO_2 emissions of 2006 levels.

The UK housing stock uses 27 per cent of the nations energy and it therefore presents a number of challenges. A high-proportion of the stock is old, poorly-insulated homes that have low-efficiency heating and lighting. In addition consumption of energy in the home is increasing, as greater personal wealth results in a growing list of appliances and gadgets. Also the density of the UK's occupation of housing is falling (high divorce rate = more sole-occupants), and small households produce disproportionately high carbon emissions.

The optimum strategy for cutting carbon emissions is reducing the need for energy in the first place. Changing occupant behaviour and improving the thermal performance of buildings are the most effective ways of reducing emissions, particularly as, in the case of building fabric, once an improvement is made, savings continue for the life of the building.

However, as carbon reductions of 60 per cent are needed to meet long-term targets, renewable energy sources are important too. There are basically three kinds of renewable energy technology; that which provides heat, that which provides electricity and that which provides both.

There is also that which provides none of the above. That we call eco-bling. Eco-bling is stuff, typically a solar panel or a wind turbine, that is bolted to a house with no real hope that it will achieve anything. People do it for the same reason that they wear bling – because it looks good and they want to be seen to be green without putting too much effort into establishing just how green they really are. The point of renewable energy is that it puts control of energy production in the hands of the home owner and limits the CO_2 emissions from that house. Eco-bling does not give control and merely adds to the CO_2 problem.

ENERGY USE IN THE HOME

We use energy as either heat or power – heat for keeping us warm, for hot water and cooking and power to run TV's, DVD's, kettles, computers etc.

The pie chart shows the spread of energy usage in a typical UK home in 2004. If we comply with 2006 building regulations on insulation 53 per cent of the energy we use will go in heating, 20 per cent on hot water, 16 per cent to power appliances, six per cent on lighting and five per

HOUSEHOLD ENERGY CONSUMPTION

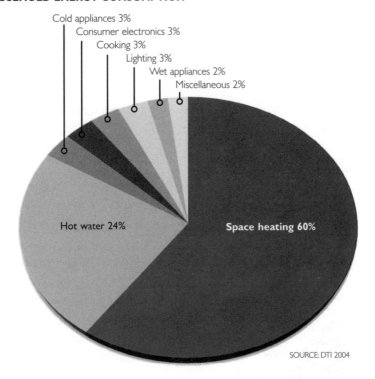

Cold appliances 3%
Consumer electronics 3%
Cooking 3%
Lighting 3%
Wet appliances 2%
Miscellaneous 2%

Hot water 24%

Space heating 60%

SOURCE: DTI 2004

5

cent on cooking (Figures from Energy Saving Trust – May 2007), or 73 per cent on heat and 27 per cent on power. If your house was built before 2004 and has not had the insulation upgraded then the proportion is more likely to be 84 per cent on heat and 16 per cent on power. What this shows is that the actual amount of energy only falls with insulation. The energy for power and hot water remains the same, or even increases. National statistics show that the electrical energy consumed by the average UK household has increased by a fairly steady four per cent year-on-year since 1950. Again this is to do with personal wealth and with the number of things we can use electricity for.

Installing renewable energy is one way of controlling this steadily increasing cost. Like everything else in the home, it will have a budget around it. Very few of us can throw enough money at the problem to make it go away and if you are thinking about how best to use a limited budget, think about heat first, hot water second and power last.

The well insulated home – up to Passivhaus or AECB Gold standard, perhaps – might have different priorities. In that case the proportions of energy use will be quite different. A 200m^2 house with four people in it is likely to use in the region of 5,000kWh of energy as power, 3,500kWh for hot water and, worst case, just 3,000kWh for space heating, the bulk of which will come from passive sources. In that case dealing with power and hot water are the priorities and producing electricity may be uppermost in people's minds.

PAY-BACK

One of the major issues around renewable energy is still its financial viability – i.e. does it make financial sense to generate what you could buy from a utility company? The advent of Feed-in Tariffs in April 2010 (see below) have changed this whole argument by giving renewable energy a level of financial viability it did not have before.

Looked at as individual components the pay-back on any renewable technology will still be in the region of five to 10 years. But a well-designed system meeting a high proportion of the household needs could now pay for itself in under seven years – in a really good location, in under 5 years.

For many, renewable energy remains a lifestyle choice. We do not calculate the pay-back on an Aga or Rayburn. We choose to install a £15,000 William Ball kitchen rather than one from MFI at £1,500 because we can afford it and it pleases us. We make choices about what to put in our homes for reasons of aesthetics, comfort, style, because they add value to the property and because they make us feel good. Why then do we demand that renewable energy, and only renewable energy, gives us a return on our investment?

If you are building or renovating your home, not installing some renewable energy would seem to be missing a trick. It will never be as cheap or so easy to install as when you have other works going on. And it is likely to become mandatory in the not too distant future. Currently, under Planning Policy Statement 22, or Technical Advice Note 8 in Wales, all developments of 10 properties or more must generate at least 10 per cent of the energy consumed on site, although these are guidelines rather than rules. The Westminster Government has stated that the aim is that ALL new buildings will be carbon neutral from 2016. The Welsh Assembly Government has given Wales until 2013 to achieve the same thing. The 2010 Building Regulations call for a 25 per cent improvement in CO_2 emissions on 2006 standard and that will be hard to achieve without at least some renewable energy.

Importantly for the individual, renewable energy gives us a degree more control. We are an oil based society and North Sea oil has been a boon to the whole of the UK. It has given us cheap fuel, relative to the rest of Europe, for 40 years and allowed us to become the fifth richest nation in the world. But natural gas from the North Sea has all but run out and the oil will follow soon. Oil is obviously a finite resource. The world is not making any more of it and the rate at which we can find and extract oil is, for the first time in history, being outstripped by the increase in demand. It now costs 0.8 barrels of oil (in equivalent energy terms) to produce one barrel of oil and production can no longer keep up with the rate at which developing countries are consuming it. To put it another way, as demand increases and supply falls oil is only going to get more expensive.

Renewable energy allows us to step aside from the oil economy. Producing energy by other means provides us with security, insurance perhaps, against whatever will occur in the energy market.

Pay-back will soon be a complete irrelevance. Not that long ago central heating increased the value of the property – it was considered an uncommon but desirable and saleable feature. Now not having central heating is odd and deflates the value of the house. In 2005 85 per cent of all new homes in Austria had wood pellet boilers fitted as standard (Austria does not have oil, but does have some trees). Wood, in the form of pellets, is now their de facto standard heating fuel. In Demark 'street heating' – where a whole street of houses is heated and powered by a single, central, often wood fuelled, combined heat and power system – is commonplace.

The UK will take its own spin on things but it is difficult to believe that in 20 years time there will be no change in the way UK houses are heated. People who install renewable energy

5

systems now will have that uncommon but desirable and saleable feature. They will sow the financial investment that their children will reap.

CAPITALISATION OF RUNNING COST

Perhaps more important than payback, or the lack of it, is the way we consider the investment we make in the house. In the UK we tend to want to buy our own home – getting on the property ladder. We tend to shun renting as it is considered giving money away with no possible return. When we buy a house we buy the responsibility for it, the maintenance, upkeep, refurbishment and likely improvement. But that is OK because we are on the property ladder.

Renewable energy can be considered in the same terms. By designing our house to be all-electric and investing in, say, a 5kW wind or hydro turbine, we are buying all the energy we will need for the next 20 or 30 years. As can be seen in the examples to follow, when we invest in that renewable energy we effectively fix the cost of our electricity at a bit below current retail prices – and almost certainly well below the price electricity will be in 20 years time.

Yes, we take on the responsibility for maintenance and repair, exactly as we do with a boiler or car, but we have the security of knowing that we are impervious to price fluctuations and will always be able to afford to run the house.

Add to that the idea that from 2016 (if current legislation is not changed) some 200,000 houses per year will be zero carbon (and therefore have low or zero running costs) and the notion of payback begins to evaporate. Within 10 years there will be close to one million homes in the UK with zero carbon emissions. If Government plans for upgrading existing housing stock come into being, there will be two to five million homes with low energy demands, some with renewable energy and consequently low running costs.

The question has to be asked, what price will a house with no renewable energy and high running costs command in that market?

FEED-IN TARIFFS & THE 2008 ENERGY ACT

The Energy Act came into force in November 2008 and led the way for the introduction of feed-in tariffs (FITs). It is considered by many that FITs will, in turn, lead the way for the proliferation of microgeneration systems.

FITs are a Government set rate for the electricity generated from renewable sources and exported to the grid. Essentially the purpose is to incentivise the installation of micro generation schemes (micro

5

generation being defined as less than 50kW capacity) and they have been used successfully across mainland Europe for many years.

In practice there are three elements to the UK FIT scheme:

■ Generation Tariff – a guaranteed sum paid for each kWh of electricity generated by renewable means

■ Export Tariff – a guaranteed sum paid for each kWh exported to the grid – the amount will track market rate and be inflated in line with RPI.

■ Import Tariff – users will pay the same rates and standing charges as everyone else, but use their own electricity at no cost.

The reality is that a home owner can generate electricity, use all of that electricity in their own home, and STILL get paid to do it. One of those rare occasions when something that sounds too good to be true is, in fact, true.

GENERATION RATES

The table below is an extract of the domestic scale rates. The scheme is guaranteed by the Government for 20 years, or 25 years in the case of PV. Year 1 is deemed to be April 2010 to March 2011, Year 2 April 2011 to March 2012, Year 3 April 2012 to March 2013. Rates are inflated annually in line with RPI but continue to degress for new entrants to the scheme on a

DOMESTIC SCALE RATES

Technology	Scale(kW)	Year 1 Tariff (p/kWh)	Year 2 Tariff (p/kWh)	Year 3 Tariff (p/kWh)	Tariff duration
Hydro	<15kW	19.9	19.9	19.9	20
Hydro	15 – 100kW	17.8	17.8	17.8	20
PV	<4kW (new build)	36.1	36.1	33.0	25
PV	<4kW (retrofit)	41.3	41.3	37.8	25
PV	4 – 10kW	36.1	36.1	33.0	25
Wind	<1.5kW	34.5	34.5	32.6	20
Wind	1.5 – 15kW	26.7	26.7	25.5	20
Wind	15 – 100kW	24.1	24.1	23.0	20
Existing schemes	Any	9.0	0		

5

EXAMPLES OF HYDRO AND WIND SCHEME COSTS

A 5kW hydro scheme

Capital cost, say	= £55,000
Output	= 30,000 kWh p.a.
System life	= 30 years
Maintenance cost	= £200 p.a.
Total life cost	= £61,000
Whole life output	= 900,000 kWh
Cost per kWh	= 6.78p per kWh

Value at today's prices;
Assume 5,000kWh used on site

Electricity used on site = 5000kWh @ 14.5p/kWh	= £725 p.a.
Generation Tariff – 30,000kWh @ 19.9p/kWh	= £5,970 p.a.
Export Tariff – 25,000kWh @ 3p/kWh	= £750 p.a.

Total Value

Electricity used on site	= £725 p.a.
Income from FiTs scheme	= £6,720 p.a.
Total	= £7,445 p.a.
Return on investment	= 12.2 per cent

A 5kW Evance Iskra R9000 wind turbine
Assume an annual average wind speed of 5.5m/s

Capital cost, say	= £25,000
Output	= 9,300 kWh p.a.
System life	= 25 years
Maintenance cost	= £200 p.a.
Total life cost	= £30,000
Whole life output	= 232,500 kWh
Cost per kWh	= 12.93p per kWh

Value at today's prices;
Assume 5,000kWh used on site

Electricity used on site = 5000kWh @ 14.5p/kWh	= £725 p.a.
Generation Tariff – 9,300kWh @ 26.7p/kWh	= £2,483 p.a.
Export Tariff – 4,300kWh @ 3p/kWh	= £129 p.a.

Total Value

Electricity used on site	= £725 p.a.
Income from FiTs scheme	= £2,612 p.a.
Total	= £3,337 p.a.
Return on investment	= 11.1 per cent

5

A 11kW Gaia wind turbine
Assume annual average wind speed of 5.0m/s

Capital cost, say	= £55,000
Output	= 31,000 kWh p.a.
System life	= 25 years
Maintenance cost	= £500 p.a.
Total life cost	= £67,500
Whole life output	= 775,000 kWh
Cost per kWh	= 8.71p per kWh

Value at today's prices;
Assume 5,000kWh used on site

Electricity used on site = 5000kWh @ 14.5p/kWh	= £725 p.a.
Generation Tariff – 31,000kWh @ 26.7p/kWh	= £8,277 p.a.
Export Tariff – 26,000kWh @ 3p/kWh	= £780 p.a.

Total Value

Electricity used on site	= £725 p.a.
Income from Feed-in Tariffs	= £9,057 p.a.
Total	= £9,782 p.a.
Return on investment	= 14.5 per cent

A 6kW Solar PV scheme

Capital cost, say	= £30,000
Output	= 4,500 kWh p.a.
System life	= 30 years
Maintenance cost	= £50 p.a.
Total life cost	= £31,500
Whole life output	= 135,000 kWh
Cost per kWh	= 23.34p per kWh

Value at today's prices;
Assume 3,000kWh used on site

Electricity used on site = 3,000kWh @ 14.5p/kWh	= £435 p.a.
Generation Tariff – 4,500kWh @ 36.1p/kWh	= £1,624 p.a.
Export Tariff – 1,500kWh @ 3p/kWh	= £45 p.a.

Total Value

Electricity used on site	= £435 p.a.
Income from Feed-in Tariffs	= £1,669 p.a.
Total	= £2,104 p.a.
Return on investment	= 6.7 per cent

5

three-year.ly cycle The thinking behind this is that as more people take up renewable energy systems competition will increase and the capital cost will fall. The scheme aims at an average eight per cent return on investment which means that the rate or payment can fall in line with capital cost. In practice achieving 10 per cent or 12 per cent return is entirely feasible for all but PV technology.

The problem with this is that the fall in the tariff rate is pre-determined but the fall in capital cost is not.

These figures are paid for the generation of electricity. In addition, the scheme owner will be paid an extra 3p for each kWh of electricity exported to the grid. The scheme owner will have the opportunity to opt out of the export tariff every year, and opt back in again the following year should they choose to do so. This reflects the idea that the wholesale price of electricity is likely to rise and the scheme owner may be able to get a better price on the open market. The 3p offered under the scheme can be considered as a minimum guaranteed price. A backstop figure, if you will.

It should be recognised that the figures for solar PV systems improve with size and time, as the capital cost falls and the return on investment increases. In 2011 it may be possible to get this system installed for under £25,000 as technology improves and competition increase.

Obviously none of the figures given in the examples can be accurate. The capital cost will vary with the site, the value of the electricity exported will vary, the generation tariff will be inflated with RPI and maintenance costs are likely to change over the life of the system. But, they serve to illustrate the point.

TARIFF LEVELS FOR RENEWABLE HEAT INCENTIVES

Technology	Scale	Tariffs (pence/kWh)	Tariff lifetime (years)
Small installations			
Solid biomass	Up to 45kW	9	15
Biodiesel	Up to 45kW	6.5	15
Ground source heat pumps	Up to 45kW	7	23
Air source heat pumps	Up to 45kW	7.5	18
Solar thermal	Up to 20kW	8.5	20

In addition to Feed-in Tariffs, there is also a proposal for a Renewable Heat Incentive scheme due to come into effect in October 2012.

It has to be said that the rates currently being considered are far higher than previously suggested, so some downward adjustment might not be a surprise. For small, i.e. domestic, scale installations the payment due will be based on the SAP assessment for a new build or an Energy Performance Certificate for an existing property. The property will be deemed to have an energy need for space heating and hot water and the payment will be based on that deemed requirement.

It should also be noted that the payment is for the renewable energy proportion of the heat produced. For example; if the house is deemed to need 10,000kWh per year and a ground source heat pump with a COP of 4 is used to produce that heat then the heat pump will use 2,500kWh of grid electricity to produce the 10,000kWh of heat. So RHI will be paid on the difference, i.e. 7,500kWh.

CALCULATING HEAT LOSS

Whether you're installing a heat pump or a gas boiler, you need to know how much heat you need to produce. Standard gas or oil-fired boilers have a wide modulation range. That is the amount of heat they produce at any moment can vary within a range – which could be as wide as 4kW to 24kW. Renewable energy technologies tend to impose tighter limits and it is important to be sure you are in the right range.

On the next page is a simple method of calculating the heat loss from your property. It does NOT replace a full SAP calculation but is quick, easy and reasonably accurate.

Accuracy will be improved by doing this calculation for each room and totalling the result.

The calculation is based on our standard house and Area is simply the measured area of the element (floor, wall, window, etc.) in square metres, as is the Volume. The U-value is explained in Chapter 4. The Temperature Difference is for a (increasingly less common) winter day; so an outside air temperature of –2degC with an inside temperature of 21degC in main areas will give a temperature difference of 23degC.

Heat loss is a simple multiplication of area x U-value x temperature difference and the corrected heat loss applies a coefficient of broadly 21 per cent to allow for system inefficiencies.

The U-value is obviously an important part of the calculation and is not always easy to get at. There are a number of free U-value calculators on the internet, Build Desk at www.builddeskonline.com/sw56237.asp is a pretty good one. A simpler, but slightly less accurate one is at www.vesma.com/tutorial/uvalue01/uvalue01.htm

5

TARIFF LEVELS FOR RENEWABLE HEAT INCENTIVES

Element	Area	Volume	U-value	Temp diff	Heat loss	Corrected Heat loss
Doors	8		1.8	23	331.20	401
Windows	14.78		1.8	22	585.29	709
Rooflights	4.32		1.8	23	178.85	217
Ground Floor	117		0.16	23	430.56	521
First Floor	135		0.5	3	202.50	245
Walls type 1	124.16		0.35	22	956.03	1158
Roof type 1 (net)	187.44		0.16	23	689.78	835
Roof type 2			0.16	23	0.00	0
Ventilation		605	0.4	23	5566.00	6741
Total Heat Loss					8940.21	
Total Corrected Heat Loss - Watts						**10828**
Solar Gains						**0**
Casual Gains						**600**
Heating load					**Watts**	**10228**

In this calculation we assume a standard level of insulation and produce a peak heat load of 10.2kW. That means that your principal heat source must have a rated output of at least that amount to meet the space heating requirement (there will be an additional requirement for domestic hot water – DHW – but this is dealt with later) .

Calculating the actual annual energy consumption from this figure is a fairly complex process and tricky software (and expensive) has been developed to do it. For a very rough estimate we can assume that the heating will be on from 7:00 a.m. to 8:30 a.m., while we have breakfast and get ready for work or school, and again from 4:30 p.m. to 10:30 p.m. then we have a total running time of seven hours per day. If we also assume a 'heating season' of 220 days per year (effectively October to May) then we have (7 × 220) 1540 running hours per year. At 10.2kW this equals

5

15,708kWh per year. But 10.2kW is the peak load, only needed when the outside temperature is -2degC. Typically the house will need less than this so round down to 14,000kWh.

That is the amount of energy needed to heat the house, not necessarily the heat energy needed from the boiler as the boiler will not be 100 per cent efficient. We also need to factor in heat gains from living in the house (casual gains) and heat from the sun (solar gains). Solar is just the sun warming the house from time to time. Casual gains are those heat gains from things like the cooker, TV, shower, toaster, anything that uses electricity to produce heat as well as power. Around 15 per cent of the heat needed for the house will come from the casual and solar gains, reducing the demand on our example boiler to about 12,000kWh. But generally, unless the house is super-insulated, or there is a particularly large glazed area to the house, these gains are ignored . Which, in the case of the example calculation, brings us back in line with 2006 building regulations requirement of 55kWh/m^2 floor area/year.

In Chapter 2, Design Right, we discuss the idea of putting energy consumption at the centre of the design. If we do that we start from the point of knowing what the energy consumption will be, for each m^2 of floor area, and calculating annual consumption is then easy – simply multiply floor area by the energy consumption figure.

In addition the house will need hot water. Assuming four people in occupation and a normal hot water demand of 50 litres per person per day, the energy requirement is for a further 4,234kWh per year.

RUNNING COST COMPARISON

To produce that same amount of heat will cost :

RUNNING COST COMPARISON

To produce that same amount of heat will cost :-

Fuel	Equipment	Efficiency	Price per KWh	Annual cost
Natural Gas	Condensing boiler	85%	5.2p	£1,223
Air source heat pump		COP 3	15p	£1,176
Oil	Condensing boiler	85%	4.8p	£1,129
LPG	Condensing boiler	85%	4.7p	£1,106
Ground source heat pump	Horizontal array	COP 4	15p	£ 882
Wood Pellet	Boiler	90%	4.8p	£ 844
Water Source heat pump	From borehole	COP 5	15p	£ 706
Wood Chip	Boiler	80%	2.8p	£ 550

5

The figures assume newish, condensing type boilers. Non-condensing and older boilers can have efficiency levels as low as 65 per cent. It should also be noted that the prices for heating oil and LPG are correct at end 2009, after a record dip in wholesale prices. It is highly likely to be higher at the time of reading.

The price per kWh will vary with the supplier and it has to be borne in mind that the price of oil, gas (including LPG) and electricity have increased by between 80 per cent and 100 per cent in the past three years. Biomass in the form of wood pellet has increased by about 10 per cent and wood chip has fallen in price.

It should be borne in mind that the oil-fired boiler will be nearing the end of its life at 12 to 15 years. Efficiency will have fallen below acceptable levels, causing fuel consumption to increase as well as CO_2 emissions. The heat pump and wood pellet boiler will have a life of 20 to 30 years without any noticeable reduction in efficiency.

HEATING DISTRIBUTION

Before plumping for a particular heat source, decide on your distribution system. Basically this comes down to radiators, underfloor heating or skirting board heaters. There are other options like forced air and even hot ceilings or heated windows, but these have a very small proportion of the market and that proportion has not grown significantly so we focus only on the three main options.

The issue is the optimum temperature at which the delivery system will operate. As will be seen, different heat sources also operate best at different temperatures and matching the two – heat source and distribution system – is essential to an efficient system.

Optimum operating temperatures for the main methods are:

■ Underfloor heating   30 - 45degC
■ Skirting heating   40 – 65degC
■ Low temperature radiators   45 - 55degC
■ Conventional radiators   65 - 75degC

There are other factors that will affect the choice of heating distribution system, like comfort, aesthetics, available wall space and these are all a matter of personal choice. In sustainability terms because underfloor and skirting heaters operate at lower temperatures they uses less energy. If you want sustainable credentials you have to have a good reason to use anything else.

Essentially, heat pumps need underfloor or skirting heating. This technology needs to operate at a low flow temperature so is best

5

suited to those heating distribution systems. Skirting heating, particularly Climaboard products, has the advantage of flexibility in that it can operate effectively at a wider range of flow temperatures. The other main heat sources – biomass, solar, gas or oil boilers – all produce high temperature water and can effectively use any of the distribution systems.

RENEWABLE TECHNOLOGIES

I. COMBINED HEAT AND POWER

Often referred to as micro-CHP, it is essentially an engine that powers a small generator. It is called combined heat and power because it produces both heat and electricity. In this way it is a very efficient use of the fuel consumed.

Micro-CHP, i.e. domestic scale, is still a rarity in the UK and CHP tends to be associated with large installations, hotels, hospitals, leisure centres and the like. As at the end of 2005 about 1,500 CHP engines were in operation in the UK, only a few hundred of which are domestic scale.

Set against that are the assertions of the industry and the DTI that some 12 million homes in the UK are suitable candidates for micro-CHP. Which perhaps answers why the technology is moving to the forefront.

At the end of 2009, when this book is being revised, there are significantly more CHP machines available and major companies, notably Baxi and Worcester Bosch have moved into the market. Baxi now has three machines available, compared to only one in 2005. This includes a fuel cell CHP unit, said to be the most efficient type of machine. Although some of these machines are not actually due on the market until 2011, the Baxi Ecogen unit is due out in 2010 and looks like being a good option.

In its simplest form a CHP plant is a standard internal combustion engine driving a largish alternator – just like you would have in your car. The heat from the engine is captured (sometimes exhaust heat is also captured) and the alternator will produce 240v or 440v electricity rather than 12v. These tend to be fairly large machines, like the Baxi Dachs unit (previously the Dachs Zenertec), suited to large buildings.

Smaller machines use a Stirling Engine, an external combustion engine invented in the nineteenth century by Rev Robert Stirling. At the domestic scale the attraction of this engine is its higher energy conversion efficiency and its lower noise levels.

Fuel cell technology is still at the development stage, but likely to be the final answer to CHP technology. It is quiet, efficient and easy to install. When it finally comes to market it is likely to

5

be comparable in price to a standard gas boiler and seems destined to take over the market.

CHP units will run on gas (natural or LPG), oil (diesel or kerosene) or wood. Fuel cell technology is also being developed to run on hydrogen but there are still a number of question marks over this technology. Wood pellet or wood chip fuel machines tend to be large – 100KW plus – although there are a couple of domestic scale machines emerging.

The cost per kWh for CHP machines is generally a little over the price of the gas used to drive it. Meaning that the electricity is being produced at broadly the same price as gas – or about one third of the retail price of electricity from the grid. The reason being that CHP produces electricity with around 90 per cent efficiency, compared to just 27 per cent efficiency for electricity from a power station.

In summary :

■ CHP is still best suited to larger houses, often in combination with a suplementary heat source, although it is likely that smaller machines like Baxi's Ecogen will soon provide an answer for the standard house. It is easy to install and operate, achieves high levels of efficiency and some reductions in CO_2 emissions. But it cannot realistically make a big contribution to large-scale reductions in carbon emissions.

■ CHP is now "known" technology so exporting excess electricity to National Grid is easy, but it is still within a pilot scheme so far as the Government's Feed-in Tariff scheme is concerned and owners may have to negotiate with energy companies for a good price.

■ CHP is not renewable energy as it runs on gas or oil. This also means that it inherently produces carbon emissions, although these are lower than the alternatives. It is being touted as "tomorrow's technology" but it raises the obvious question, why develop technology to run on fossil fuel?

2. GENERATING ELECTRICITY

Wind Turbines

There are only two issues related to selecting a wind turbine; size and location.

If you want to work out the size of the wind turbine you need from base principles then you may want to read 'The Green Building Bible, Volume 2' or 'The 40 per cent House'. They have all the information you need to carry out a reasonably accurate calculation on wind speed and swept diameter to probable power output. In the real world there is limited choice available to

5

the domestic user and you may as well limit your calculations to those that you can actually buy.

To decide on the size of your wind turbine you will need to know your actual annual electrical consumption. The simplest way is to look at your electricity bill. It will show the number of units or kWh you use. Alternatively read the meter and measure what you actually use in the course of the year – don't calculate and don't rely on estimated bills.

Electricity consumption tends to attribute to the people in the house, rather than the house itself. So even if you are moving to a spanking new house, your electricity consumption will be broadly the same.

To give a view as to the margin of difference, a typical three to four bedroom house with four people in occupation, using all incandescent light fittings and ageing electrical appliances will use 7,000kWh to 8,000kWh per year. Move those same people into a new house with all low energy lighting and A+ rated appliances and the consumption could fall to 5,000kWh to 6,000kWh. A substantial reduction in consumption and CO_2 emissions but not enough to materially affect the selection of the wind turbine.

You also need to decide on the proportion that you wish to generate. Again this can vary from, realistically, 30 per cent to as much as your site will allow. Once you have done that calculation you will find that you are limited to a choice of two or three wind turbines,, or at most four.

WIND

Wind force	Metres / second	MPH	Description	Effect
0	0 to 0.5	0 to 1	Calm	Smoke rises vertically
1	0.5 to 1.2	1 to 3	Light air	Smoke drifts but wind vanes not moved
2	1.2 to 3	4 to 7	Light breeze	Wind felt on face, leaves rustle
3	3 to 5	8 to 12	Gentle breeze	Leaves and twigs in motion, wind extends flags
4	5 to 8	13 to 18	Moderate breeze	Raises dust and paper; small branches move
5	8 to 10	19 to 24	Fresh breeze	Small trees in leaf sway, crested wavelets in inland water
6	10 to 13	15 to 31	Strong breeze	Branches in motion, whistling in telephone wires, umbrella used with difficulty
7	13 to 16	32 to 38	Near gale	Whole trees in motion; difficulty walking against the wind

The highlighted figures show the band within which wind turbines are typically rated and it is clear that it is not a common situation.

5

Manufacturer's power output figures are usually based on a wind speed of 12 metres per second (m/s) or around 30mph. And while they are not inaccurate, they may be a bit misleading. Drive your car at 30mph and pop your hand out of the window to see the affect. 30mph is a strong wind, much stronger than the UK experiences on a daily basis. A more common average wind speed is 5 m/s to 6 m/s or 10 mph.

As an example a 1kW rated wind turbine (similar to the one sold in your local DIY shed) will produce 1kW at 12m/s but at 6m/s it will produce just 125W – one eighth of its rated output. In urban locations the wind speed is slowed by all the roof tops and becomes more turbulent. The affect of this is that a wind that starts out at 6m/s will slow to 4m/s or even 3m/s by the time it gets to the town centre and our 1kW wind turbine will be producing next to nothing.

The figures highlighted in white in the 'Wind' table on the previous page show the band within which wind turbines are typically rated and it is clear that it is not a common situation. The figures highlighted in blue are nearer the national annual average windspeed.

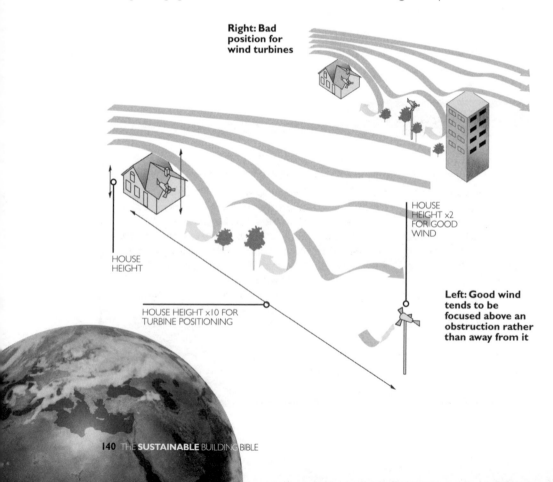

Right: Bad position for wind turbines

HOUSE HEIGHT x2 FOR GOOD WIND

HOUSE HEIGHT

HOUSE HEIGHT x10 FOR TURBINE POSITIONING

Left: Good wind tends to be focused above an obstruction rather than away from it

5

The DTI provide a wind speed database (at http://www.decc.gov.uk/en/windspeed/default.aspx). This will indicate the annual average wind speed in a 1Km square around your property at various heights above ground level. It is a good place to start and will indicate whether it is worth going any further. A general rule is that if the DTI database indicates an average wind speed of less than 5 m/s it is unlikely to be productive. Less than 4 m/s it definitely won't. Over 5 m/s and it is looking good for a turbine.

But beware. The database is based on a postcode and there can be a significant difference from one end of the postcode area to another. And the wind speed on any site can vary across very small distances. As little as 10m can bring the turbine out of the wind-shadow of a tree or building and into clean air. Raising the turbine on a taller mast can have the same effect.

An effective wind turbine will cost between £5,000 and £50,000. Investing £300 and perhaps six months in testing the wind speed and finding the best location would seem to

WIND TURBINE COMPARITIVE COSTS

	Kestrel E300	Skystream 3.7	Evance Iskra 9000	Gaia 11kW
Installed cost	£7,000	£9,000	£25,000	£45-£55K
Capacity	1kW	2.4kW	5kW	11kW
Tower height	10m	10 or 18m	9, 12, or 15m	18m
Rotor Diameter	3m	3.7m	5.4m	13m
Annual production (1)	2,200kWh	3,600kWh	9,000kWh	31,000kWh
Unit cost per kWh over 20 years	15.9p per kWh	12.5p	10p	8.06p
Annual return from FIT (2)	£759	£1,069	£2,673	£9,207

Kestrel E300   Skystream 3.7   Evance Iskra 9000   Gaia 11kW

The turbines shown are typical for a domestic installation. Others are available and which is best will depend on location, wind-speed and budget

5

make sense, even if the DTI database is indicating strong potential. A wind monitoring system like 'Wind Prospector' from Windandsun Ltd (www.windandsun.co.uk) or the Power Predictor from better Generation (www.bettergeneration.com) will indicate wind speed and direction across time and give an almost definitive guide as to the potential power.

Planning Consent

Wind turbines always need planning permission. The legislation is changing to make it easier (and cheaper) to obtain, but it is still needed. Some suppliers provide all the technical information – noise data, sizes, schematic drawings etc. – that are needed for a planning application. But some don't. A good supplier can also provide information on other installations to support an application. These can significantly shorten the application process and reduce the cost.

The turbines illustrated on the previous page are typical for a domestic installation. There are many other available and which is best will depend on location, wind speed and budget.

Possible Return on Investment

From the comparison table opposite it can be seen that, so far as wind turbines are concerned, size matters. It is probably no surprise that bigger machines are more productive than smaller machines – it is why wind farms go for very big machines.

What this table does not take into account is the value of electricity used on site. It needs to be remembered that organising things so that the house uses as much of the generated electricity as possible as this is the most efficient and generates the best financial return.

In summary

■ Check before you buy. Wind is fickle and a small investment in checking speed and direction can save huge sums.

■ If you have neighbours, you need their approval. A single objector is often enough to kill a planning application (although the legislation is changing to help overcome this).

■ Wind turbines in urban locations do not justify their cost or their embodied CO_2

■ Wind turbines fixed to the house are less efficient than a wind turbine on a mast. In addition it is becoming increasingly difficult to insure a house with a wind turbine bolted to it.

■ The bigger the turbine the better the return

■ Wind turbines are not as noisy as you think. What is an

RETURN ON INVESTMENT

5

	Kestrel E300	Skystream 3.7	Evance Iskra 9000	Gaia 11kW
Installed cost	£7,000	£9,000	£25,000	£55K to £65K
Capacity	1kW	2.4kW	5kW	11kW
Tower height	10m	10 or 18m	9, 12, or 15m	18m
Rotor Diameter	3m	3.7m	5.4m	13m
Annual production (1)	2,200kWh	3,600kWh	9,000kWh	31,000kWh
Unit cost per kWh over 20 years	15.9p per kWh	12.5p	10p	8.06p
Annual return from FIT (2)	£759	£1,069	£2,673	£9,207

Notes:
Assumes an annual average wind speed of 5m/s
Assumes Feed-in Tariff of 26.7p per kWh generation plus 3p per kWh export tariff and that 100 per cent of energy generated is exported.

acceptable noise level is a very personal matter and the only way to check if it is acceptable to you is to go and see one.

■ 'Flicker' is often a bigger problem than noise. That is when the turbine blades either pass across the sun or reflect the sunlight, causing a flickering effect which may not be noticeable to the owner but may annoy neighbours. Again, location is the key and relating the prevailing wind to the path of the sun will indicate if flicker is likely to be a problem.

■ Equipment tends to have a long life – 20-plus years – but needs maintenance

Note on bird and bat strike

There is some concern that the proliferation of wind turbines will decimate the bird and bat population of the UK. Birds and bats do come into contact with wind turbines, as they have with overhead power cables ever since we invented the grid. And whilst it is not to be denigrated or dismissed, the numbers are not great. We nonetheless have a responsibility to position turbines in such a way as to minimise the potential for bird and bat strike. Generally this means staying at least 25m away from known flight-lines.

Research carried out recently at Manchester University has shown that white is the second

5

most attractive colour to insects (after yellow) and purple the least attractive. Birds and bats follow the insects. So the answer might be to paint your wind turbine purple.

PHOTOVOLTAIC CELLS

Sometimes called solar panels and easily confused with solar thermal panels. Solar thermal panels produce hot water and a PV cell generates electricty by allowing light to pass through a silicon crystal. Because of its atomic structure an electronic charge naturally moves around inside the crystal, but in a random manner. Arsenic and boron are added to the silicon and these impurities cause negative and positive molecules to join and encourage the flow of an electric charge in a single direction. Bombarding the molecules with sunlight causes electrons to be released, increasing the electric current which can be harvested. If you need to know more details of how they work and how they are made, read Richard J Komp's Practical Photovoltaics.

They have been produced on a large scale for over 50 years and benefited from a significant amount of research and development, R&D that continues today. Sharp, one of the world's largest manufacturers, recently released a product that achieves a four per cent improvement in conversion rates. This may not sound much but overall efficiency is only about 18 per cent.

Taking our standard house, we need to generate 5,000kWh p.a. to power it. Using PV alone we would need an array of nearly 6.7kW rating to do it. In the UK a 1kW rated PV array will generate between 750kWh and 850kWh per year depending on location and installation efficiencies. Therefore divide 5,000 by 750 and you get to 6.7kW.

That equates to 0.75kWh per 1kW rating for the UK. By comparison, in Arizona they get around 5kWh per year per 1kW rating. Where you are in the world has a huge impact on the viablity of PV.

PV is the most expensive renewable energy option. Current prices for PV vary from £2,500 to £4,000 per kW installed. Our standard house will need to spend around £20,000 to generate the power they need.

The introduction of the feed-in tariff scheme in April 2010 sets a generation tariff for PV of 36.1p/kWh for this size of system, plus 3p export tariff. That means that our 6.7kWp system will produce an income of £1,955 p.a. assuming that 100 per cent is exported. That reduces the payback period to slightly under14 years.

There are three basic types of PV cells, monocrystaline, polycrystaline and amorphous crystal. As the name suggest the monocrystaline is made from a single silicon crystal, polycrystalline from many

PV technology is changing. As well as standard silicon cells, now we have PV arrays that look like roof slates and thick-film systems that replace the roof covering.

crystals, amorphous cells being made from thousands of silicon crystals.

Essentially, mono-crystalline are more efficient and most expensive. Poly-crystalline are less efficient and less expensive, amorphous are very inefficient and very cheap. Amorphous are the ones used in calculators, watches and the like and are cheaper to produce than the batteries they replace. But with efficiency ratings of around five per cent they offer no practical solution at domestic or commercial scale. A lot of research is being done in this area, especially by the Chinese and efficiency is said to be up to 7.5 per cent now. The word is that they are waiting until they break the 10 per cent barrier before launching products on the market.

These may sound like very low efficiency rates but the best monocrystalline are only achieving efficiencies of 18 per cent. The industry has been saying for many years that the price of moncrystalline cells will not fall unless and until there is a significantly higher take-up of product. Which rather flies in the face of actuality which shows prices falling by up to 30 per cent over the past three to four years. This fall in price is largely due to the incursion of Chinese manufacturers into the market and has not prevented BP, Kyocera, Sony, Sharp and other huge multi-national companies investing millions in R&D.

PV systems are seeing a better take-up in commercial buildings where the extra cost of PV is considerably lower. A 1kW array at £4,000 equates to a cost of £500 per m². If a prestige wall covering costs £300 per m² then the on-cost is only £200 per m² or £1,600 per kW. The simple payback falls from 46 years to under 18 years. Add in the feed-in tariff payment and the payback is less than 10 years. If and when these same economics can be applied to houses, PV will become a viable option for the home owner.

PV arrays, as in the first illustration, are typically fitted on top of the roof covering as they need freely circulating air to keep them cool. Conversion efficiency falls as the temperature of

5

PV (photovoltaic solar panels generate electricity by the Photovoltaic Effect, discovered in 1839 by the 19yr old Edmund Becquerel. The photovoltaic effect is the phenomenon that certain materials produce electric current when they are exposed to light. For traditional PV solar panels a semiconductor PN junction is manufactured in which two halves of one pure silicon crystal are coated with two different materials (eg. arsenic, boron, aluminium, phosphorus). One half of the crystal is left electron deficient (the positive-type layer), and one half is left with an excess of electron (the negative-type layer). The coating on the silicon lead to an electric field across the junction between the two halves of the crystal with electrons able to travel in one direction only – from the electron rich half to the electron poor half.

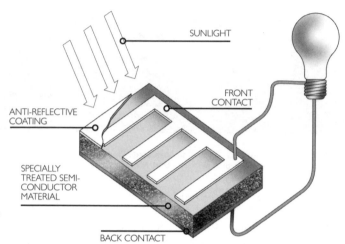

the cell rises above 25degC. New products are emerging, like the second photo which shows PV cells formed to match roof tiles or the third, which is a glass free PV panel which makes it very thin and very flexible. These work well in low light conditions inherent to cloudy climates and low pitch roof angles.

PV systems tend to produce 12v DC electricity which has to pass through an inverter and control panel to convert it to 240v AC electricity for use in the home. All the reputable installers deal with this at the time of the installation and the cost is included in the rate per kW. Many suppliers will quote a diminishing price per kW for larger systems. This is because the fixed costs for the likes of control systems, scaffolding to get on the roof, turning up on site, remain the same for a 1kW system or 10kW system. So the bigger the system you buy, the cheaper it gets.

In Summary

■ Once the system is installed it is maintenance free and will produce a consistent amount of electricity throughout its life.

■ Systems are supplied as modular panels and are easily scaleable to the electrical demand.

■ High capital cost can be off-set if panels are used to substitute roofing or cladding materials.

■ Grid export is easy but necessary as generation is typically not usually coincidental with use.

■ It should be noted that this area of technology benefits more from R&D investment, and increasing volume of sales to commercial buildings than any other. As a consequence prices tend to fall and efficiency rise more quickly than other technologies. A cautious approach would be to spread investment in PV over time to allow some of the benefits to come through.

Photovoltaic-Thermal

Otherwise known as PV-T, this is a hybrid system producing both electricity and heat (in the form of hot water). The technology combines mono-crystalline photovoltaics with a solar thermal collector which is said to give 25 per cent higher output efficiency than equivalent PV.

PV cells are semiconductors and performance degrades outside a specific temperature range. The optimum operating temperature for PV is 25degC. In the UK on a sunny summer's day, when you hope to be making the most of your PV, panel temperatures can reach over 100degC. At that temperature the system will produce less than 10 per cent of its maximum output.

PV-T technology regulates the panel temperature using a fluid cooling system to maintain a constant 25degC. This allows a higher electrical yield compared to the equivalent area of mono-crystalline PV and a significant amount of free heat.

The problem is using or storing that heat. A system will typically be sized to meet an electricity demand and the heat produced taken as a bonus. PV-T panels produce heat at a ratio of either 1:1 (electricity to heat) or 1:3, depending on type. Assuming that the system is designed to produce 5,000kWh of electricity per year, to meet a typical domestic demand, it could produce 15,000kWh of heat. That should be more than enough to meet the total heating and hot water demand of a well insulated house. The problem is that it produces the heat at the wrong time.

Across a day, or even two or three days this does not really matter as the heat produced in sunny times can be stored in hot water. But about 50 per cent of the total annual production will be in summer, 20 per cent in spring and autumn and just 10 per cent in winter, when it is most needed. To make PV-T effective means storing heat available in summer for use in winter.

Research started in the USA in the early 1940s has come up with two distinct ways of doing it; phase change materials (PCM) and ground or geothermal storage.

5

Phase change materials absorb, store, and release heat when they change state, typically from a solid to a liquid and back again. When the temperature rises above a PCM's transition temperature (the point at which the material changes phase), the PCM absorbs heat and melts. As the temperature decreases, the PCM releases the stored heat and returns to a solid state. Think about water - heat water and it will change to steam, cool it and it changes to ice. That is phase changing.

Large temperature variations and long term storage is provided by seasonal storage devices. As the name suggests these systems will store large quantities of heat from summer to winter, with little appreciable loss.

Cost is a factor and these systems are not cheap, but what they do is unlock the potential for the entirely solar powered house, providing effectively thermal mass in light-weight construction.

The argument between the two principal construction systems – light-and-tight or mass-and-glass – has been going on for some time. Essentially the argument is that light-and-tight construction may give better insulation levels but to utilise passive solar energy – and be truly energy efficient – needs mass. It needs masonry or concrete to absorb solar heat and release it after the sun has set. The result of the argument is that energy efficient houses tend to be a compromise between the two construction methods.

By way of comparison concrete has a heat storage capacity of 0.784 kWh/m^3 while a PCM will hold between 38 to 105 kWh/m^3.

The alternative for seasonal heat storage is ground, or geothermal, storage, a technology developed in Canada, Sweden and Germany. Essentially this technology amounts to a borehole (maybe 100m to 150m deep) and some solar panels. Water is heated in the summer months and that heat conveyed down the borehole, raising the temperature of (typically) the rock at the bottom of the borehole. The rock is raised to something like 85degC and although the heat storage capacity of rock is not great, the cost of getting the heat there makes it a practical proposition. On a £'s per kWh stored it is usually more economical than PCM.

Both seasonal PCM and geothermal systems store energy in the form of heat, so the technology can be used to raise or lower temperatures. If needed the technology can store winter cold to provide summer coolness, just as well as summer heat for winter warmth.

An alternative solution put forward by the Italian manufacturer, Anaf Solar, is to link the PV-T to a water source heat pump. The

5

PV-T effectively pre-heats the water and significantly raises the effective COP, which can get to over 6.5. Obviously the system also provides at least some of the electricity needed to run the heat pump. Altogether a fairly neat solution.

In the UK at least the technology has hardly raised its head above the parapet. As usual, Germany and Canada are well in front and the technology is becoming reasonably well regarded, if still experimental. But there seems a happy inevitability about it. The sun is the ultimate source of all renewable energy but all solar technology is plagued by the same problem – the sun always sets. A sensible storage system would seem to be a natural, essential and welcome development.

Hydro Power

Hydro is the granddaddy and if you have a stream with some head you really need to think about it. Modern Pelton wheel and Turgo turbines can trace their antecedence to Roman times. The physics has not changed although the technology has moved on a bit. They still work in basically the same way – water passes over a wheel, producing torque (rotation) energy 24 hours a day, seven days a week. Nowadays that energy is used to drive a generator which then produces electricity.

The key issues are head – the vertical distance between the highest and lowest points of the stream – and flow – the amount of water passing a point, measured in litres per second.

Measuring the stream to assess the potential is a complicated business and experts charge a lot of money to do it for you. It is quite possible to measure it yourself and get accurate enough to decide if it is worth investing in an expert to do it properly.

The first thing is to establish if you own both banks of the stream. If not you will need the express, legal consent of the person who owns the other bank. You will be making a substantial investment in a hydro turbine that is likely to generate an annual income. The existing owner of the other bank may be a perfectly nice person and happy for you to do what you want. The person he sells his property to may not be so nice.

If you own both banks, start with measuring the head. Head is the vertical distance from the top of the stream to the bottom. Typically you will not own the whole of the stream so only measure the bit you own.

The easiest way is to buy a large scale OS map and find your bit of the stream on it. The contour lines will then tell you the height the stream falls.

Alternatively invest in a little altimeter.

5

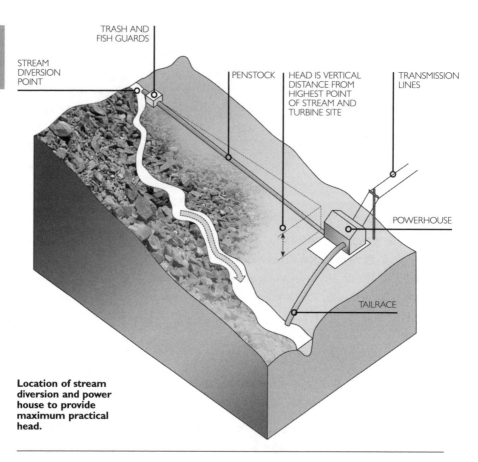

STREAM
DIVERSION
POINT

TRASH AND
FISH GUARDS

PENSTOCK

HEAD IS VERTICAL
DISTANCE FROM
HIGHEST POINT
OF STREAM AND
TURBINE SITE

TRANSMISSION
LINES

POWERHOUSE

TAILRACE

**Location of stream
diversion and power
house to provide
maximum practical
head.**

We are ideally looking for head of more than 10m. With a fairly small flow 10m head will generate a reasonable amount of power. It is quite possible to use streams with lower heads – down to as little as 2m – but the more head the more power to be obtained from it.

Measuring flow is a more complex business if it is to be done accurately. The time of year and the recent rainfall are likely to affect the amount of water in the stream and therefore the flow rate. The flow rate is likely to be different in January to June. It is possible to estimate the flow rate across the year, and hydro experts typically have access to the necessary data and software to do it accurately.

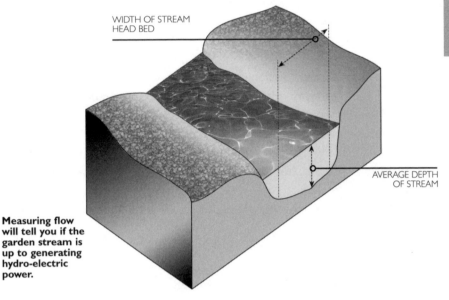

WIDTH OF STREAM
HEAD BED

AVERAGE DEPTH
OF STREAM

**Measuring flow
will tell you if the
garden stream is
up to generating
hydro-electric
power.**

There are two methods of getting a rough estimate of the flow rate.

The first was set out by A.A Milne in House at Pooh Corner – playing Pooh sticks. Find a reasonably clear stretch of the stream, the longer the better but at least a 2m long stretch. Ideally it needs to be free of stones, logs or anything that will interrupt the flow. Place two markers on the bank of the stream at a known (and convenient) distance apart, drop a stick in the stream at the upstream marker and time how long the stick takes to reach the downstream marker. Repeat until bored. Average out the results and that will give a figure in metres per second.

> **To calculate the stream flow rate:**
> 600mm x 75mm = 0.045m^2
> 0.045 x 0.5 (m/sec) = 0.0225 m^3 per second
> 1m^3 = 1000 litres, therefore 0.0225m^3 = 22.5 litres per second flow rate in the sample stream.

5

Next measure the size of the stream, which may involve wellies. Measure the width of the stream (at the point you played Pooh sticks) and its average depth. These figures do not have to be spot on, but the more accurate the better.

Illustration of stream cross section

Lets assume that a sample stream is 600mm wide and 75mm average depth. And that it flows at a rate of 0.5m per second.

An alternative method, if there is any sort of waterfall in the stream, is to find a container (bucket, tub, barrel – bigger the better), measure its capacity in litres, place it under the fall and time how long it takes to fill. That will also give a figure in litres per second. Again, repeat until bored and average the results.

With those two figures – head and flow rate it is possible to calculate the potential power in the stream.

The calculations is:

Head x flow rate x gravity x 0.7 system inefficiencies

For our sample stream the calculation is :

$10 \times 22.5 \times 9.81 \times 0.7 = 1545$ watts of power.

1.5kW may not sound much compared to, say, a 5kW wind turbine but a 1.5kW hydro turbine will produce 1.5kW 24 hours per day, every day. It will generate around 12,000kWh per year where a 5kW wind turbine might produce 75 per cent of that. Our standard house needs just 5,000kWh per year, leaving 7,000 to be sold to the grid.

In reality the flow rates of most streams are likely to vary across the year – more rain in winter, more water in the stream. Well designed hydro systems will account for this by building in different nozzles to optimise the power potential to the flow of the stream.

Another factor is that it is unwise, as well as unlawful, to use all the water in the stream. The stream is an ecosystem that relies on the water. Removing it will kill the ecosystem. In all cases the Environment Agency needs to be contacted to advise as to what is a reasonable amount to extract but it is unlikely to be more than half. So in our sample case we would be thinking of installing a 0.75kW turbine which will generate enough power to meet the demands of our standard house.

Typical Hydro Installation

A typical installation needs:

■ Water intake – to divert the flow from the water course to the turbine. This will also incorporate a trash guard and a fish guard. Both essential elements of the system.

■ A penstock – which is usually a pipe to carry the water from the intake to the turbine. The diameter and material are critical to ensure head pressure is maintained and contained.

■ A powerhouse – a grand name for what is usually little more than a shed, although often constructed from concrete blocks.

■ An outflow – to ensure the water gets back to the stream with no pressure build-up in the turbine.

■ Control system to get the electricity generated to the point of use.

Types of turbine installation

There are two types of water turbines; Impulse and Reaction. The best way to understand the basic difference is to imagine yourself on roller skates and someone turned a fire hose on you. Your movement under this condition would be "impulse". Now suppose that you were handed the fire hose. Your movement under this condition would be "reaction" The Pelton, Turgo, crossflow and Kaplan are impulse turbines, deriving their power from turning, slowing or stopping the flow of water striking their blades. The Francis, Leffel; and Fourneyron are reaction turbines, deriving their power from the reactive force of the water passing between their blades.

Impulse Turbines

The Pelton Turbine is common for micro-hydro and is made up of a wheel with a series of blades, each of which is a split bucket. A high pressure jet of water is directed at the blades and as the jet hits each blade it is split in half, so that each half is turned and deflected back almost 180deg. Up to 90 per cent of the energy of the water goes into propelling the blade and the deflected water falls out of a discharge channel.

The Turgo turbine is equally common and very similar to the Pelton. In this case the jet strikes the plane of the blade at typically 20deg angle so that the water enters the runner on one side and exits on the other. In this way the flow rate is not limited by the discharged fluid interfering with the incoming jet (as is the case with Pelton turbines). As a consequence, a Turgo turbine will have a smaller diameter rotor than a Pelton for an equivalent power.

Both Pelton and Turgo turbines need a reasonably good head to produce the pressure necessary to generate power. In both cases the diameter of the jet nozzle can be varied to cope with different rates of flow to accommodate variations across the year. This can be a manual change of the nozzle, or more sophisticated systems can automate the switch.

5

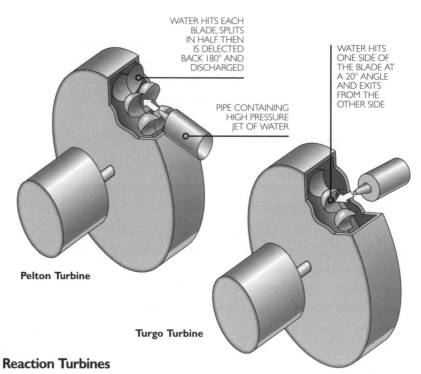

WATER HITS EACH
BLADE, SPLITS
IN HALF THEN
IS DELECTED
BACK 180° AND
DISCHARGED

WATER HITS
ONE SIDE OF
THE BLADE AT
A 20° ANGLE
AND EXITS
FROM THE
OTHER SIDE

PIPE CONTAINING
HIGH PRESSURE
JET OF WATER

Pelton Turbine

Turgo Turbine

Reaction Turbines

The most common reaction turbine in micro-hydro installation is the Francis turbine which is a good option for low-head schemes. In this case the water changes pressure as it moves through the turbine, releasing energy. The turbine inlet is spiral shaped to get the water spinning before it hits the runner vanes. Guide vanes direct the water tangentially to the turbine wheel. This radial flow acts on the runner's vanes, causing the runner to spin. The guide vanes can be adjustable to allow efficient turbine operation for a range of water flow conditions.

As the water moves through the runner its spinning radius decreases, further acting on the runner. For an analogy, imagine swinging a ball on a string around in a circle; if the string is pulled short, the ball spins faster. This property, in addition to the water's pressure, helps Francis and other inward-flow turbines harness the energy in the water energy efficiently.

Spiral-case Francis

Typical Francis-type installation

To work well the water needs to be given a spin as it enters the turbine, this is done either in the casing or in the intake.

5

Kaplan Turbine

The Kaplan turbine is an inward flow reaction turbine, very similar in many respects to the Francis. Its basic operation is the same in that the water changes pressure as it moves through the turbine and gives up its energy. In the case of the Kaplan, the runner is a propeller shape. The inlet is again a scroll-shaped tube and water is directed tangentially through the inlet and spirals on to a propeller shaped runner, causing it to spin. The outlet is a specially shaped draft tube that helps decelerate the water and recover kinetic energy.

The best source of information on all types of hydro turbines – large and small – is the British Hydro Association at www.british-hydro.org

Costs

The down side of hydro power is that the cost can vary from the sublime to the ridiculous. For our sample stream a 0.75kW turbine alone can vary in price from £600 to £6,000 depending on supplier, manufacturer and type of turbine. The generator and control equipment can similarly vary from £2,500 to £5,000. These are the known elements. The unknown elements are the costs associated with capturing the water and delivering it to the turbine. These vary with every installation as every stream is different. And some suppliers charge considerably more for this element than others.

The good news is that there are few "big players" in the domestic scale hydro market. It is

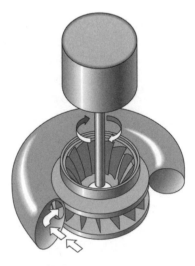

The Francis Spiral-case turbine

5

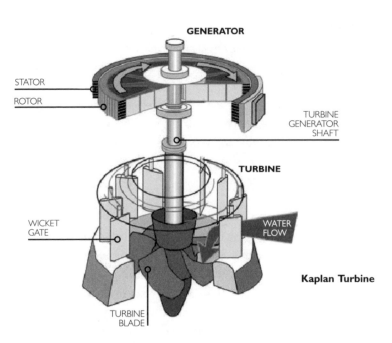

Kaplan Turbine

serviced largely by an increasing number of small businesses run by enthusiasts.

By way of illustration, if we assume that the capital cost of our example 0.75kW system is £20,000 a cost analysis would show:

Capital cost	= £20,000
Output	= 6,525 kWh p.a.
System life	= 30 years
Maintenance cost	= £200 p.a.
Total life cost	= £26,000
Whole life output	= 195,750 kWh
Cost per kWh	= 13.3p per kWh
Value of Production	
Generation Tariff on 6,525kWh @ 19.9p/kWh	= £1,298
Electricity used on site 3,000kWh @ 14.5p/kWh	= £435
Exported to the grid 3,525 @ 3p/kWh	= £106
Total Value	= £1,839 p.a.
Return on Investment	= 7 per cent

Of course all these figures can vary and are illustrative only, but the return on investment is not untypical, and better than can be obtained at most banks. A point to bear in mind is that a 7.5kW system might cost twice as much to install but will produce 10 times the revenue.

The unit cost of 13.3p per unit may not sound much better than the 14.5p price from the grid, bear in mind that the 13.3p is fixed for 30 years and that the 14.5p is quite likely to rise. In addition the 30 year life is entirely notional. A hydro scheme is made up of a large number of relatively low cost components. As a single component comes to the end of its life it can be replaced.

The Environment Agency is, together with the National Rivers Agency, responsible for every river and stream in the country. It is essential that the EA is contacted in every case. There is a legal requirement to obtain an Abstraction Licence and pay the necessary fee (although you may well ask why you need to pay a fee to use the water in a stream you already own!) which will vary with the size of the scheme but will be in the order of hundreds of pounds. The total cost of obtaining an Abstraction Licence will be £1,500 to £3,000 depending on the size of the scheme, followed by an annual fee of £140 upwards, again depending on the size of the scheme.

There is also a moral obligation to ensure that the scheme does not damage the ecology and the EA are the right people to advise on this and generally their advice is good, well intentioned and free.

Noise can be an issue with hydro power, more so than wind. Water is moving at relatively high pressure across a spinning wheel of some sort. It is bound to generate noise. Unlike wind, however, the hydro turbine will be contained in a plant room. This may be as small as 1.5m x 1.5m x 1m but is sufficient to contain most of the noise as well as the kit.

Planning consent will be an issue. Hydro-electric schemes are considered in the same way as a mine or a quarry and the local planning authority must always be consulted. Once they understand that this is a MICRO generation scheme they are typically only interested in the plant room and if that is small, they are usually happy to grant consent to allow the project.

In Summary
■ Pound for pound a good hydro scheme will produce more electricity than any other technology.
■ The cost will vary hugely with the scheme but should always be a worthwhile investment – if the water and head are there.

5

■ Modern equipment is highly resilient and should comfortably have a life of 30 years plus.
■ Designing and installing hydro schemes is expert work, but establishing if it is worthwhile can be done by the amateur.

Electricity Storage

Electricity will be produced on sunny days, cloudy days (just not so much.), when the wind blows or the stream flows. We want most of the electricity in the evening when conditions may not be right and our system is not generating. In addition our hyrdro turbine may be 0.75kW output, or the wind turbine 2.5kW and if we have just a few appliances running, there is just not enough power available. But the hydro turbine will run 24-7 and the wind turbine all the time the wind blows and either will produce enough energy across the year for the demands of the house.

So we need to store the electricity we generate until we want to use it. The most practical option is to use the electricity in the house when you can and export to the grid when you can't. This is the cheapest option and the connection needed (called a G83 connection) is well known and recognised through out the grid generating industry. It should be noted that G83 is limited to an export capacity of 16 amps per phase, or 3.8kW maximum capacity. This is a fairly arbitary figure and can usually be extended to 5kW. Generators above that capacity tend to produce 3-phase electricity and need a different connection system, called G59, which tends to be purpose built and consequently more expensive.

A metering system will be needed and is usually supplied by the company installing your system. Typically this will amount to two extra meters; one to measure the amount of electricity generated and another to measure the electricity exported to the grid. Under the Feed-in Tariff, both produce a payment. The meter already in the house will measure the electricity purchased from the grid.

Batteries are sometimes used for storage when grid connection is not available. These need to be deep-cycle batteries to be able to put up with the charge and discharge cycle typical in micro generation. Deep-cycle batteries are expensive and will add significantly to the cost of the installation. They will have a life of perhaps 10 years, and a disposal problem.

There is a notion that the 'autonomous' house, unconnected to the grid, is somehow more eco-friendly than a connected house. The reality in this country is that the grid exists and will continue to exist whatever an individual chooses to do. Denying access to the grid will increase the cost of the system by the price of the batteries, will remove any potential to share excess production and places a further burden on the environment from the production of batteries and their eventual disposal. So not a good idea.

3. GENERATING HEAT

In a house built to 2006 Building Regs standard up to 70 per cent of the energy used in the house will be in the form of heat, for space heating and domestic hot water. In a better insulated house the proportions will change, up to Passivhaus standard where the proportions can be reversed.

Considering the preferred heating system is first a matter of considering the amount of heat needed. In a house that needs a lot of heat biomass might be a good answer as, although capital cost is high, running cost is very low. In a Passivhaus with very low heat demands an air source heat pump would be a better answer. Capital cost is relatively low and although efficiency is not great it won't be doing too much work so efficiency is not a major factor.

In addition, the ability to generate energy may come into the equation. If the option exists to grow your own wood then investing in a log boiler makes sense. If electricity (in the quantities delivered by a wind or hydro turbine) is available then a heat pump needs thinking about. As does the option for solar thermal energy.

Along with the Feed-in Tariff (FIT), the Government is also proposing to introduce a Renewable Heat Incentive scheme (RHI) to come into effect from April 2011 – see page (133) in this chapter. Note that installations commissioned before June 2009 will not qualify for RHI payments.

All of this probably only serves to confuse the issues around which heating system is best. The answer is to start at the other end: design the house to have a minimum heating requirement and then the question of which system or which fuel to use almost answers itself.

Biomass

By biomass we mean anything that was grown and can be used as fuel. It is most often wood, in the form of logs, chips or pellets, but also includes wood dust briquettes, straw bale or pellet, rape seed pellets, wheat and miscanthus pellets. It is still something of an emerging technology in the UK, but is well established across central and northern Europe. In 2005, 85 per cent of all new homes built in Austria had wood pellet boilers installed as standard. Austria does not have oil, but it does have some trees.

5

Biomass is virtually carbon neutral, the CO_2 produced as a result of combustion being no more than the CO_2 absorbed while it was growing. There is an issue to do with harvesting, processing and transport which all add to the carbon footprint, but it still has the lowest real-terms affect on CO_2 emissions.

Efficiencies in modern biomass boilers can be high, up to 92 per cent, but care has to be taken with selecting boilers to match the fuel. A few boilers will burn multiple fuels but most are designed specifically for a particular fuel type. Some are capable of burning multiple fuels but are set-up at the time of installation to burn a particular fuel or to burn that fuel most efficiently.

Most of the biomass boilers you bump up against are wood pellet boilers, but that doesn't necessarily mean that wood pellet is the best idea. Fuel supply is still a local issue as there is no nationwide network of supply. There are an increasing number of companies supplying wood pellets and a few that deliver to a wide area, if not nationwide. There are also a small number of companies supplying pellets from other materials – rape seed, straw, miscanthus. What is available in your area, reliably and at a good price, will influence which system you buy. Rape seed pellet may look like a good idea – cheaper than wood with a better calorific value – but if the supply is not reliable or from some distance it could be risky to invest in a boiler that is set up to burn only that fuel.

A point to consider is that the Government has decreed that as of 2008 five per cent of diesel road fuel must come from a renewable source. The automotive fuels industry has decided that will be prinicpally rape-seed oil because they can mix five per cent rape oil with diesel without any noticeable change to the performace of the engine. When oil is extracted from rape seed, it leaves a residue called 'cake', which is a biomass fuel with a good calorific value (you gets lots of heat from it). A mix of five per cent may not seem much, but spread across the nation (and the whole of Europe) it is a lot of rape seed cake. What effect that will have on the price of rape seed pellet is yet to be seen, but it will at least put a lot more potential fuel on the market.

In addition, that five per cent mix is set to rise to 20 per cent over the next few years, meaning there is likely to be a lot of rape seed cake about. Whether that gets turned into pellet is yet to be seen, but it might.

The manual labour involved in biomass can have an impact. Biomass boiler systems can be highly automated, but none of them are free of some labour input. At the lowest level the user will have to empty ash from the boiler, perhaps as infrequently as every three months. At

5

the other end of the scale the batch log boilers require the user to load logs and empty the ash, usually on a daily basis. There are various steps in between and when you are buying a biomass boiler you need a clear understanding of the work you will have to put in.

There is also a relationship between work and fuel price. A log harvested from your own land, chopped, stored, dried and loaded to your boiler by hand will give 'free' heat. Free, that is, if the cost of that labour is ignored. Logs, pre-cut and delivered to your home might cost £45 per tonne, but still need loading to the boiler. Wood pellets delivered in bulk, direct to a silo is virtually labour-free, but will cost up to £230 per tonne.

Essentially, you-pay-your-money-and-take-your-choice.

The Biomass Fuel Market

A Royal Commission report in 2006 into the potential UK Biomass Market stated that biomass already provides approximately 60 per cent of total EU renewable energy utilisation and is therefore the most mature and commercially viable renewable technology in the EU.

The Forestry Commission estimates that the sawmill co-product (dust and off-cuts) available in Britain totals around 859,000 oven-dried tones per year, 20 per cent of which is sawdust, available for pelleting. There are existing markets for most of this resource but the Forestry Commission estimates that around half the sawdust could be made available for fuel without serious disruption to existing industries. In addition, some 2 million tonnes of timber go to UK landfill every year. A huge proportion of that could be used as fuel.

The only figures we have on biomass prices comparisons are produced by Strathclyde University (not surprisingly, Scotland is very interested in wood fuels).

Price Comparison (As at November 2006)

Electricity	4.5 to 12.6p/kWh
Heating oil (in condensing boiler)	5.2p/kWh
LPG (in condensing boiler)	6.7p/kWh
Coal (anthracite grains)	3.5p/kWh
Natural gas	3.5p/kWh
Logs in stove	0 to 5.1p/kWh
Wood chips	2 to 2.5p/kWh
Wood pellet	3.2 to 3.8p/kWh

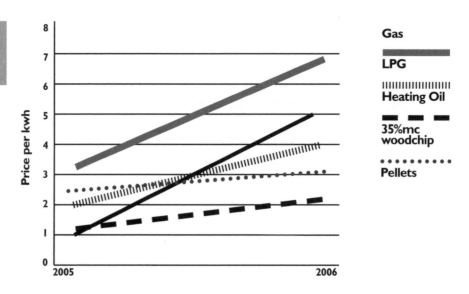

Price Changes 2005 – 2006 Compared to Fossil Fuels

The graph above shows that while wood chip and wood pellet prices have both risen, the rise is much slower than fossil fuels and that in fact the rise can be attributed to the increased transport cost brought about by the rise in road fuel prices.

Fuel Storage

Unlike other renewable energy technologies, biomass fuel has to be stored on site. And it can be quite bulky. Our standard house (i.e. 200m² built to 2006 building regs) will require about 3 tonnes of wood pellet a year, or 5 tonnes of logs. For a well insulated house the figure could drop to around 1 tonne of wood pellets. The storage capacity needed will vary with the fuel (wood chip is a lot bulkier than wood pellet) and the frequency of delivery. For guidance 6 tonnes of wood pellet is around 10m³ which could easily double or even treble for wood chip.

A typical delivery would be 2 or 3 tonnes so a bulk storage of 3m³ or 4m³ would be typical if you are using pellet. That can be either a proprietary system, like the one below, or a purpose built store. In either case a delivery system is also be needed to move the fuel from the store to the boiler.

Most biomass boilers have an on-board fuel hopper that can be loaded by hand. These can be just a few litres capacity or up to several hundred litres, depending on the boiler.

5

For full automation (or as close as can be got) a fuel store is necessary. Okofen and KWB machines shown are the more automated options and a complete system, including fuel store, fuel delivery system and installation could cost £12,000. But taking on the burden of loading by hand makes major cost savings. The illustration below shows an Extraflame pellet stove with back boiler, and the on-board hopper being loaded.

The hopper will hold around 20kg of wood pellet, which is handily delivered in 18kg or 20kg bags. Depending on the time of year and the level of use, one hopper load could last three or four days. This system would cost around £3,000.

The UK biomass boiler market is changing rapidly as more machines come in from central and northern Europe. The high-price machines are still there but there is an increasing range of lower-price machines. These cheaper machines tend to look a bit more industrial and may not have all the bells-and-whistles, but they are robust and they do the job. Well worth checking just what is available and what will suit your application.

Grow Your Own Fuel

For the more energetic among us the potential exists to grow your own fuel. You will need around two hectares or five acres of land and the will power and energy to plant, harvest and process the crop.

A good plantation will have a mix of coppice and short rotation crops, so a mix of willow, hazel, alder, ash and possibly miscanthus. This will not only encourage all sorts of flora and fauna but will give a crop every year from year two.

The cheapest and most effective use of home grown fuel is as logs. Wood chip can also be

**Above: two types of pellet-storage system.
Right: Extraflame pellet stove with back boiler, and the on-board hopper being loaded.**

5

an option as the process equipment needed is just a shredder. The crop needs to be dried before it is processed or burnt and typically the wood is cut, left to dry for three to six months, shredded and left a further six to twelve months. This will get moisture content below 30 per cent and this regime of dry-shred-dry is used for a couple of reasons. If the wood is shredded wet it will have to be turned regularly to avoid it composting. Shredding the wood dry puts more strain on the shredder and shortens the life of the blades. Partial drying first is a happy compromise.

Storage becomes even more of a issue but if you have five acres of spare land then you probably have room for a fuel store.

In Summary
- Biomass is a direct replacement to oil or gas-fired boilers.
- It is effectively carbon neutral
- The cost of fuel is rising on a much flatter curve than fossil fuels
- The availability of biomass fuels is still not good, but is improving every year
- Local availability of a reliable source of fuel is key to a reliable installation
- Biomass fuel has to be stored on site and fuel stores can be big and expensive.

HEAT PUMPS
Heat pumps have been big news but in 2008 only 14,000 units were installed across the UK. This compares to 1.6 million gas boilers, of which 1.2 million were condensing.

There are three different types of heat pumps – air source, ground source and water source – but they all use compressor technology identical in all but size to that used in refrigerators to move heat from one place to another. They do not, or should not, generate heat. Heat pumps work by collecting heat from air, water or the ground, using compression and expansion to, in effect, magnify the heat and transfer it to water or air.

Because the technology "magnifies" the heat, the less they have to magnify the more efficient they are. That is, the closer the source temperature and the required temperature are the more efficient the heat pump. The ground below 1m deep remains at a failry constant 7degC to 12degC through out the year. We want a temperature of 21degC in the house. That is a temperature difference of 14degC to 9degC. What that presents are known and quantifiable limits for heat pump manufacturers to work with. Machinery can be designed to optimum levels to work extremely efficiently within those relatively close parameters. External air, on the other hand,

5

can vary in temperature from -5degC to 25degC giving a potential temperature difference of 26⁰C when we need heat most, in winter.

Manufacturers of heat pumps advertise their wares as having a Coefficient Of Performance (COP) that will typically be 3, 4 or 5. This means that for every 1kW of electricity you put in, you will get 3, 4 or 5 kWs of heat out. It is calculated by the manufacturer based on the optimum input and output temperatures. The output temperature is the critical factor and will generally be between 30deg and 40degC. This is to minimise the temperature difference and achieve a reasonable COP. It is not accidental that 30deg and 40degC are good operating temperatures for underfloor heating. Radiators need temperatures over 55degC and hot water needs to be stored at 65degC to avoid Legionnaires disease.

Forcing air and ground source heat pumps up to 50degC or 60degC significantly reduces efficiency. To overcome this some manufacturers install what are effectively immersion heaters in the machine. So a heat pump rated at 12kW may actually be a 6kW heat pump with 6kW of immersion heaters. The manufacturer can then, in all honesty, claim that it has 12kW output and a COP of 4. The fact that the two don't come together need not be said.

Irrespective of whether the heating distribution is underfloor or radiators the fact is that domestic hot water needs to be stored at 65degC. How that temperature is achieved is a different question but so far as the heat pump is concerned, buyers need to ask sellers what the COP will be at 65degC. And if the buyer is told that the COP is the same at 65degC as at 45degC they probably need to look for another seller.

The most effective option is to have two separate systems, one for space heating and another for hot water. The heat pump driving underfloor heating will be working at relatively low temperatures and at peak efficiency. The hot water system can be heated by solar panels or, if budget doesn't allow, by immersion heaters on off-peak electricity tariff (Economy 7), or a small gas or oil boiler.

Mixing heat pumps and immersion heaters in the same machine means that at times of peak heat load (winter) the immersion heaters will be used as a primary heat source, with the consequent impact on the electricity bill. To return to the opening statement, heat pumps move heat from one place to another. They should not generate heat.

The big questions around heat pumps are:

■ Do they work? Yes, is the short answer. Fridges work, have done for years and no one questions it. Heat pumps are the same technology. A better question is, how well do they work, and the answer is, it depends on how well they are installed. This is dealt with for each type of heat pump, below.

5

■ Which type is best? Depends on the situation. Where the insulation levels are high and the heat load low, then the lower capital cost of air source makes sense. If the heat demand is higher then the better COP inherent in ground source is preferred. If there is a source of water available or the cost of a borehole is low, then water source will be best.

■ How big are they? Again it varies. In broad terms from the size of an under-counter domestic fridge to a 4-draw filing cabinet.

■ Do they make much noise? Once again it varies with manufacturer, model and type. Noise output will vary from 40dB to 55dB (at 1m distance), where a library is reckoned to be around 30dB, a fridge about 50dB and normal conversation about 65dB.

Ground Source Heat Pumps

The first ground source heat pump (GSHP) installed in the UK went into the Royal Festival Hall in 1951 and it is by far the most popular form of heat pump. It is about to become even more so with manufacturers like Worcester-Bosch and Dimplex entering the market in a big way.

GSHP's utilise an array of pipes in a closed loop burried in the ground as heat collectors. Pipes can be either straight or slinky and both operate by pumping a cooled fluid through the pipes, absorbing the heat in the ground and extracting the collected heat via a heat exchanger.

There is no material difference in whether straight or slinky pipes are used as the machine will be configured to work best with that type of pipe.

Horror stories abound of large sums of money spent on heat pumps that don't work. In 99 case out of 100 there is one of two reasons, sometimes both.

The heat pump is too small for the house. The effect of this is magnified if the house is poorly insulated as well. The heat pump is working flat-out, trying to meet a heat demand is was not designed to achieve and consequently it it working longer and at a far lower COP than anticipated. The consequence is that the electricity bill goes through the roof.

The garden is too small to accommodate the ground array. The ground, any ground anywhere, is capable of rendering-up a maximum of 20W per sq metre, depending on the quality of the ground. This figure can drop to 10W per sq metre in very dry sandy soils. Therefore a heat pump using moist cohesive soil (clay or similar) needs 50m² of ground area per 1kW heat output. Those are hard figures. They cannot be squeezed or modified. A 10kW heat pump must have a minimum of 500m² of ground to accommodate the ground array. Any less and the heat pump is trying to take too much heat from the ground, that will eventually

5

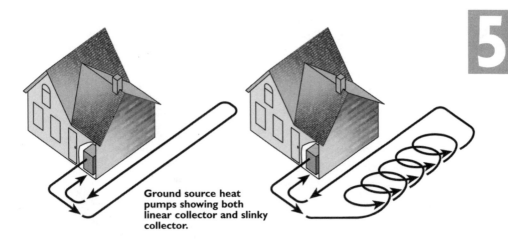

Ground source heat pumps showing both linear collector and slinky collector.

chill the ground and significantly reduce the COP. Again, the affect is that the electricity bill goes through the roof.

In neither case is it the fault of the technology. More likely the fault of the salesman.

Pipes need to be buried in trenches 1m to 1.5m deep. Different machines require different minimum depths. In all cases 1 to 1.5m deep ensures a more constant source temperature. But new health and safety regulations stipulate that trenches over 1.2m must have trench shuttering to prevent trench collapse, increasing the cost of the installation.

The pipes also need to be spaced apart properly to ensure that each pipe is not robbing heat from the pipe next to it. In the case of straight pipe this will be not less than 3m apart and slinkies not less than 5m apart. A 10kW heat pump using a slinky array will need 500m² of ground to accommodate it.

Which is where the real impact of the heat pumps that incorporate immersion heaters is felt. If this type of system is undersized or squeezed into too small a ground area the immersion heaters take over sooner as the heat pump is unable to delive the expected heat. The system is then running on a COP of 1 for a proportion of its output and electricty bills will spiral out of control.

There are compact collectors available where the necessary ground area is not available and pipes can be arranged in multiple boreholes but these options add significantly to the capital cost, to the point where other technologies may offer a better option. Having said that, new products and ways of collecting heat pop up now and again and it is worth keeping an eye on the market.

Water Source Heat Pumps

The same basic idea as GSHP but uses an open loop of pipes that take water from a source (stream, lake or borehole), extracts heat from it and returns the water to another stream, lake or borehole. (It can't go back to the same source as it will chill the water already there.)

The illustration shows water being extracted from a borehole, passing through the heat pump and returned to a stream. This illustrates that the return water is as clean as it was when it came out of the borehole. If there is a good size stream that close it would make more sense to take the water from the stream and return it slightly downstream.

Lakes can be used but the feed to the lake must be at least as much as the water being extracted or there is the potential to drain the lake.

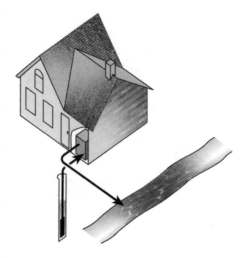

A water-source heat pump in action. Water is taken from a borehole, it passes through a pump in the house, the heat is extracted and then the water is returned to the stream.

The amount of water required is usually 1.5litres per kW per minute. So our 10kW heat pump will need 15 litres of water each minute that it runs. Typical running time will be six hours per day so the system needs 5400litres of water per day.

Water source heat pumps tend to operate at better COP than ground source, typically five instead of four, due to the high volume of source material. They are also use superheat heat exchangers to raise the output temperature of a small volume of water over 65degC.

Water source heat pumps most commonly use boreholes as the water source but this can add considerably to the capital cost.

The cost of a borehole will vary enormously with the ground conditions, the depth to the water table and the amount of water needed. They are never cheap. The cost of mobilising borehole drilling equipment is high and remains the same whatever the depth of hole needed. Minimum cost will be £4,000 and it could be five times that much.

Power Supply

Both ground and water source heat pumps impose a heavy start-up load on the electricty supply. This load is for less than a second and has no implications in terms of the bill but usually has implications in terms of the supply itself.

The start-up load varies with the size of the heat pump and with the manufacturer but can reach 65amp or 70amp. Normal domestic supply is 80amp which means that if there is normal domestic activity going on in the house when the heat pump starts up, it will pop the fuse. Many manufacturers are installing soft start motors to reduce the start-up load but buyers should always check what the start-up load for the particular model is, and if their existing supply can cope. If not, upgrading the supply can be expensive and a quote from the electricty supply company needs to be obtained before ordering the heat pump. Larger heat pumps, over 15kW, often require a 3-phase supply, and again, quotes should be obtained from the electricity supplier before committing to the purchase of the heat pump. Installing a 3-phase supply can cost from a few thousand pounds to several thousands of pounds.

Air Source Heat Pumps

These in turn breakdown into air-to-air and air-to-water.

Air-to-air are basically air conditioning machines operating the other way round. They have very low COP, maybe as little as 1.5 in winter, and tend to be small output, 1.5kW or 2kW is common. They are best used in small, isolated areas that have high solar heat gains so that they can serve the double function of heating and cooling. At either end of the scale the COP is low and they are really only efficient in spring and autumn when the inside and outside air temperatures are closer. On the upside they are low capital cost items, £250 to £300 would be usual with DIY fitting quite practical.

Air-to-water heat pumps have made the biggest strides in the market in recent years, with big companies like Sanyo and Mitsubishi entering the UK market. Technology has improved so that they now offer a COP of 3 to 4 (the COP will vary through the year as the air temperture varies). Machines range from 3kW output to 17kW and although the COP tends to be lower than GSHP, so is the price.

But COP figures are the key and must be treated with caution. The COP may be quoted as annual or seasonally adjusted or simply based on optimum operating conditions. For air source it will often be given as A7/W35 = COP 3. This means that when the outside Air temperature is 7degC and the flow temperature of the Water is 35degC then the COP is 3. Further, if the assertion is that the COP is still 3 when the water temperature is, say, 55degC then clearly that

5

cannot be true. The only thing that has changed is the flow temperature. The source temperature is the same and the machine is the same, so efficiency must be lower.

But even that figure can be misleading as the British Standard only requires the compression and condensation elements of the heat pump to be included in the calculation. The manufacturer can opt to exclude things like circulation pumps or de-icing from the COP calculation. There is no accurate way to calculate actual annual energy consumption based on the COP figure alone. In reality it is no more than a guide.

The Mitsubishi Ecodan is a relatively recent entrant to the UK and has taken a significant share of the market. It has been independently tested to BS EN 14511 by the BRE (Building & Research Establishment - Watford) in its HVAC test facility, as have all heat pumps. These tests showed that the Ecodan's average overall seasonal COP is 3.45. That sounds good but we don't know how the average is arrived at. It could be 4.9 in summer and 2 in winter. That gives an average of 3.45 but means that the heat pump will cost more to run and emit more CO_2 than a gas boiler. We need a winter COP over 2.5 to compete with natural gas on any level. And getting that information from manufacturers is proving tricky.

But let's be clear. Air source heat pumps are good machines, used in the right way in the right location. The problem is that they are sold by people who generally have little understanding, and less interest, of what the right conditions are. Horror stories abound because we accept what the salesman says. And why should we not? We are in no position to argue and the supply companies have a responsibility to ensure their staff are properly informed and properly trained. Unfortunately the supply companies do not always discharge their responsibility properly.

In Summary

Heat pumps are good, reliable technology, used in the right way. A properly designed and sized system needs no back-up system (gas or oil boiler) and, with proper servicing, will last 15 to 20 years. Heat pumps can meet all the space heating demands, and deliver domestic hot water, and reduce energy consumption, but they can't do all three at once. The best system will be a combination of a heat pump for space heating and solar thermal panels for domestic hot water.

Heat pumps are good at delivering low temperature heat very efficiently, so good for underfloor heating. As the delivery temperature rises so efficiency falls. What this usually means is that a second heat source is needed – solar panels, small biomass, gas or oil boiler – to deliver the domestic hot water. As consumers we have got used to a single piece of kit meeting all the

5

heat demands, and we are unwilling to invest in two pieces of kit to do what we see as one job. The heat pump industry are trying to meet that expectation by incorporating equipment within the box to boost the output temperature. It satisfies the expectation at the time of purchase but not the long term objective of reducing energy consumption.

Heat pumps are not stricly renewable energy as they run on electricity (unless you generate the electricty from a renewable source) but they are the most efficient way of using non-renewable energy to heat the home.

If they are run on mains electricity they may in fact increase the CO_2 emissions.

Sharp selling practices and insufficient ground space can lead to poorly designed systems that become remarkably inefficient.

Water source is best, but only if there is a supply of water available. The need to drill a borehole can make the project too expensive.

Air source needs to be treated with caution. There are good air-to-water machines available but there are also very poor air-to-air machines.

With ground source the cost and disturbance of the trench should not be overlooked.

Heat pumps still cost more than a comparable gas or oil fired boiler but the price is falling and over the life of the machine heat pumps will always save money.

Solar Hot Water

A solar hot water system comprises a solar thermal collector (flat panel or evacuated tubes – explained later), a fluid system to move the heat from the collector to its point of usage, a pump, a control system and a hot water storage tank. The systems can be used to heat water for a variety of purposes, but typically for domestic (or sanitary) hot water, swimming pools, and as a supplement to a primary heating system.

A typical domestic solar hot water system of 3m² to 4m² flat panels or 20 to 30 evacuated tubes will deliver 1,500 to 1,800kWh p.a., providing 60 per cent to 70 per cent of annual hot water needs, saving about 0.2 to 0.4 tonnes of CO_2 per annum. Which is all a bit wishy-washy as there are so many variables – type of flat panel, type of tube, angle of inclination, angle of orientation, size of hot water storage tank. What is right for any situation depends on the situation and there is no easy way to calculate it.

Once the system is installed there are no maintenance charges and no running costs. It will go on producing hot water for up to 40 years, maybe more. This is an area where there is most excitement about pay-back. A typical domestic system will cost £4,500 to £5,500 installed and will repay its cost in around 16 years, compared to generating the same heat from a gas boiler.

5

That may seem like a long time, but double glazing will cost in excess of £20,000 and pay-back will be more than 90 years in terms of the energy they save. If energy prices continue to rise at the same rate they have over the past four to five years then the payback period starts to fall dramatically. The advent of the Renewable Heat Incentive means that (when the legislation comes in) an average system will generate an annual payment of around £350, reducing the simple payback to under seven years.

All solar panels work on the same principal of light passing through glass being refracted and generating heat. The heat is captured in a collector, usually water, brine or glycol, and stored in a hot water cylinder. The cylinder needs to be bigger than the normal 80 litre copper cylinder as the system needs to store as much heat as possible while the sun shines. Although in fact solar panels don't actually need sunshine. So long as there is light they produce heat. The more light, the more heat. Balancing the size of the hot water cylinder to the size of the array of panels or tubes, and to the daily hot water consumption is important as it impacts on the efficiency of the system. If the cylinder is too small the water will get hotter, but there may not be enough of it. Too big a cylinder and the water will not get hot enough to kill legionella.

There are two kinds of solar panel, flat plate and evacuated tube.

Flat plate is a box with pipes running through it covered by a flat glass or polycarbide plate. These can be used for roof integration (where they are mounted in the roof in place of the roof covering) as well as roof mounting (where they are mounted on top of the roof covering). On a hot, sunny day, flat plate panels will produce the same amount of heat, more or less, as evacuated tubes of the same area. Under all other conditions, the vacuum tube panel will outperform flat plate panels. Flat plate panels perform badly during windy weather, in cold conditions, in overcast conditions etc. Some of the very best flat plate collectors can compensate for this with more advanced design, but even then, they still do not perform as well as vacuum tube panels. But they are cheaper, and it may be better to invest in more flat panels.

Evacuated tube are, as the name implies, a glass tube carrying a vacuum, similar to a thermos flask. They usually have a copper pipe running down the middle carrying the fluid in it to collect the heat and carry it to the hot water store. Tube system can only be roof mounted and are more fragile than flat plate. They are therefore not suited to mounting in places where they could come into contact with a cricket ball or falling branch.

Evacuated tubes come in two types – essentially either single-wall and double wall. The difference relates to the design of the solar tubes. The standard tubes are double-walled, with a vacuum between the two

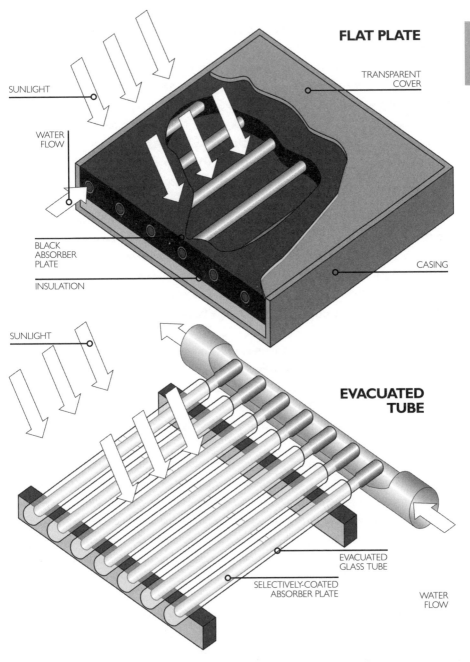

FLAT PLATE

SUNLIGHT

TRANSPARENT
COVER

WATER
FLOW

BLACK
ABSORBER
PLATE

INSULATION

CASING

**EVACUATED
TUBE**

SUNLIGHT

EVACUATED
GLASS TUBE

SELECTIVELY-COATED
ABSORBER PLATE

WATER
FLOW

5

walls of the glass. The centre is filled with air and a copper pipe runs up through the centre. The single walled tube is entirely filled with vacuum, and the vacuum is sealed by a glass-metal weld sealing the pipe to the glass. This is technically much more difficult to do, and consequently they cost much more. The single walled tube has a marginal advantage over the double-walled tube in that it reacts much quicker to sunlight (eg in winter it starts to heat water within 5-10 minutes rather than 10-15) – so it is slightly more efficient in marginal conditions. However, it also cools down quicker, whereas the standard tube will continue to heat for 10-15minutes after the sun goes in. A 10 tube single walled panel (70mm diameter tubes) produces about 10 per cent less heat than a standard 20 tube double-walled panel (47mm diameter tubes), but they cost about the same.

The standard tubes are 47mm diameter,1.5m long, and are of twin wall construction. There are also 58mm twin-walled tubes 1.8m long. This means that for a given number of tubes the 58mm tubes will produce 50 per cent more heat than the same number of 47mm tubes (but the cost is 50 per cent higher too!). The 47mm tubes are easier to transport, and are less fragile in handling due to their shorter length. Single-walled tubes are usually 70mm diameter and 1.8m long. They are more expensive to manufacture but provide better performance in cold conditions.

There are lots of figures about on the relative efficiencies of the two types. Manufacturers of each can prove conclusively that their product is more efficient than the other. Evacuated tubes are a bit more expensive and in some situations, notably when the roof is some degrees off south, can be more efficient. Flat panel are the only option for roof integration and should be used if there is any danger of breakage. The cost of repair is extremely high as it involves at least two people and scaffolding.

The reality is that it does not make much difference which system you choose. The more important decision is choosing a good supplier. An evacuated tube system will cost a bit more but will produce a bit more energy. On a like-for-like basis the cost per kWh of energy produced is broadly the same. A good supplier will make the difference between a good system and a poor system. A good supplier will properly design the system, professionally mount and install it, make sure it is set-up and commissioned properly so that it works to its maximum potential for the whole of its life. And if there are any problems (they do occur!) a good supplier will be swift in their response.

Solar panels are well known technology and there is no reason for big variations in price, but nonetheless there are big variations. It is being seen as a 'quick-fix' for people who want to seem green and is being high-pressure sold in the same way that double glazing was 25 years ago. A 4m² flat panel installed on-roof, including a 200litre tank, all labour, peripheral parts and control systems should cost no more than £5,500. An evacuated tube system will be 20 per cent to 25 per cent more. If the price you are quoted is significantly above that, find another supplier.

New Solar Technology

The Energie thermodynamic solar energy system being marketed by Thermal Reflections Ltd is the first genuinely new product in the solar energy market for many years. It uses a refrigerant gas in the panels rather than water with the gas at -20degC. If the outside air is anything above that temperature they can effectively extract heat. The system uses a lightweight solar panels which are usually roof mounted but because they operate on temperature difference rather than light collection they can be mounted horizontally, vertically on walls or pretty much wherever you want. A heat exchanger is incorporated and connected to an air source heat pump compressor unit, making it effectively a hybrid system.

Planning Consent

In general consent is no longer needed but if it is it will always be granted except in conservation areas and on listed buildings. In these cases normal planning restrictions will apply and a case must be made for the grant of consent.

Swimming Pools

Solar thermal systems are increasingly becoming the heating method of choice for swimming pools. The size of system you need depends what area of pool you need to heat, how well insulated it is, whether it has a pool cover, if it is above/below ground, how many weeks of the year you need to use it etc. As a rule of thumb generally the area of solar panels needed is equivalent to 50 per cent of the pools surface area. As panels are modular, it is easy to upgrade at a later date so it may make sense to reduce to, say, 25 per cent, and add more as the need arises. A pool cover is essential, whether the pool is heated or not, when the pool is not in use, as it dramatically reduces heat loss through evaporation.

If you are considering a natural pool, as discussed in the next chapter (The World Outside), care needs to be taken over heating. Many of the plants and animals responsible for cleaning the pool water do not take kindly to being heated. Speak to the pool designer and obtain specific guidance as to the amount of heat that can be introduced, when and if it is acceptable to heat the pool.

5

In Summary
■ A good solar system will provide all the hot water in spring and summer and can contribute to space heating.
■ Solar thermal systems are simple, robust technology with extremely long life.
■ They are maintenance free and have extremely low running costs.
■ Siting to be south facing and to avoid shading is important to effectiveness
■ Every home should have one.

FUEL COST COMPARISON

	Part LIA Standard = 55kWh/m²/yr	Best Practice Standard = 35kWh/m²/yr	Passivhaus Standard = 15kWh/m²/yr	Zero Carbon Standard = 10kWh/m²/yr
2009	£540 p.a. Oil-fired boiler	£340 p.a. Oil fired boiler	£90 p.a. Heat pump	£80 p.a. Wood pellets
2010 20% price rise	£648	£408 p.a.	£108 p.a.	£96 p.a.
2011 20% price rise	£778 p.a.	£490 p.a.	£130 p.a.	£115 p.a.
2012 25% price rise	£972 p.a.	£612 p.a.	£162 p.a.	£144 p.a.
2013 25% price rise	£1,215 p.a.	£765 p.a.	£202 p.a.	£180 p.a.
2014 30% price rise	£1,579	£994 p.a.	£262 p.a.	£234 p.a.

Fuel cost comparison for 200m² house for space heating only

GRANTS FOR RENEWABLE ENERGY
As of 2010 the situation is confused. Put simply, there are none in England or Wales. The Low Carbon Build Program in England & Wales was superseded by Feed-in Tariffs in April 2010 and the grant program shut down. There is controversy over people who installed systems and obtained a grant after June 2009 and before may 2010. Notionally these people qualify for Feed-in Tariff as well but are being refused registration for Feed-in Tariff unless they refund the grant. The argument is on-going. Grants in Scotland are still available for some technologies in some areas

5

but exclude the owner from registering for Feed-in Tariff.

They may still be local authorities offering grants, as may rural development agencies, although these tend to be for farms, community projects and the like.

At the turn of the millennium the idea of petrol costing more than £1 per litre was unthinkable. In 2003, when petrol and diesel first went over £1 per litre, there were demonstrations, rolling convoys and refinery blockades across the country. In 2010, petrol was typically around £1.15 is the norm. We now get distressed as it goes higher, but we live with it.

The price rises discussed in the table above may seem unreasonable but consider that the average price of electricity in 1999, now averaging 14.5p per kWh, was just 4.7p per kWh. In 1999 it was impossible to predict a three-fold rise in the price of electricity. The idea was unimaginable, but it happened.

The questions before the sustainable builder are where and how much to invest in renewable heat technology, not whether to do it.

6 WATER MANAGEMENT

D id you know that the UK has less available water per person than most other European countries and that technically, London is drier than Istanbul whilst the whole of the South East has less water available than the Sudan and Syria? This is according to Waterwise, who are a UK NGO responsible for improving water efficiency and are considered to be the leading authority on water use in the UK.

According to DEFRA (Department for Environment, Food, and Rural Affairs) and Waterwise, the average person uses approximately 150 litres of water a day. This has been steadily increasing at a rate if one per cent per year since 1930. Around 45 litres (30 per cent) of this is used for flushing the toilet and only 37 litres is for washing and bathing.

In a paper produced by the DTI entitled 'Strategy for Sustainable Construction: Water Use', it is suggested that a maximum consumption of 120 litres per person per day should be the target for a good sustainability level, and 100 litres in areas where water is scarce. Under the Code for Sustainable Homes there are six code levels and achieving a higher code rating means improving the water efficiency.

Summer 2006 brought one of the worst droughts this country has experienced and summer 2007 one of the worst floods. Autumn 2009 brought the highest rainfall ever recorded in the UK in a single day – Cumbria received 370mm of rain in 24 hours. Floods bring a lot of water, the trouble is that it is not water that can used in the mains supply. In the 2007 flood large parts of Gloucester and Tewkesbury were under water but it was weeks after the flood receded before the unhappy residents were able to safely use the mains water supply.

Hose-pipe bans

WATER CODES

Code Level	Litres per day
1	120
2	120
3	105
4	105
5	80
6	80

are routine across most of the south of England, in some areas they are permanent. Waterwise maintain that the current levels of water consumption cannot be maintained in the medium to long term (their goal is to significantly reduce consumption by 2020 – which feels more like short term).

In the same way that oil is being recognised as a scarce resource that has to be used with circumspection, ironically (in this country at least) water is becoming an equally scarce resource. It is therefore necessary for the sustainable builder to give the same consideration to water use as they do to energy use and recycling. And as we look at energy in and CO_2 out, we need to look at water in and waste out.

WATER IN

There are two issues to consider; the source of the water we use and how efficiently we use it. Looking first at what we take in there are a couple of options to mains water.

Rainwater Butts

The simplest and cheapest form of rainwater harvesting is the traditional water butt. Used correctly and with careful gardening, a water butt will provide all the water you need for your garden throughout those long hot summer months that we all remember.

Even without a hosepipe ban it doesn't make sense to be using high quality drinking water in your garden. Careful gardening means using rainwater from a water butt on your plants, delivering it with a watering can or drip irrigation system and mulching your soil. This way you can have a beautiful, living garden which uses the minimum amount of water.

You'll also reduce your carbon footprint as each household has half a tonne of water delivered to their door every day. The energy costs associated with treating and pumping this water are huge.

If every household in the UK got a standard water butt this would save about 30billion litres of water each summer – that's enough to fill Bewl Water reservoir! (That was the one that was running on empty all through the summer 2006).

Outdoor water use accounts for around seven per cent of the total water use, but in the summer this can rise to over 50 per cent of peak demand. However, this is one of the easiest areas to save water as we don't need to waste valuable tapwater on our plants. Plus, plants actually prefer rainwater – it is better for them!

Rainwater can generally be stored for long-periods without problems. There are products that can be added to water butts to ensure no odour, algea or bacterial build-up but generally

6

the turnover of water use is quick enough to deal with these problems. Mosquitoes can pose a problem, but that can be solved by fitting a lid or placing a layer of polystyrene balls (you can use waste packaging) on top of the water. Alternatively, and a bit controversially, pop a couple of goldfish or ghost coy in the butt. They will enjoy eating the mosquito eggs (and any algae) and are more interesting than polystyrene, balls or otherwise.

There are now quite a variety of water butts available. These can range from a few hundred to a few thousand litres.

■ Standard water butt - A standard water butt is between 100 to 300 litres in size. Generally plastic, but can be wood, normally barrel shaped with a tap near the base.

■ Ornamental tanks - these are above ground and can generally store between 50 and 300 litres and can be in the shape of boulders, fences, benches etc.

■ Large above ground tanks - these are large rectangular tanks and are normally placed next to a garage or somewhere they can be hidden, they will require a level, firm base (slabs or tarmac) and can hold up to 2000 litres of water.

The size and style of water butt will vary with the situation and is largely a matter of personal choice – and maybe budget. Clearly they have to be in a position where rainwater can drain from the gutters to them They are ideal for the renovator where installing a full-blown rainwater harvesting system would be impractical and too expensive.

Rainwater Harvesting

Rainwater butts exclusively provide water for use in the garden. Rainwater harvesting extends the idea, making water available for use in the house as well . It is the most obvious way of countering our dependence on mains water and making better, and cheaper, use of the water that is available. It is a practice that has been followed for thousands of years and archaeologists have found evidence of its use in the Negev desert from 4000 years ago, and in ancient Roman, Greece and Turkey.

The British Standard for rainwater harvesting, BS8515 which sets standards for rainwater harvesting equipment manufactured in this country was published in early 2009. BS8515 sets the minimum standards for suppliers and manufacturers. It also addresses the possibility of cross-contamination of mains drinking water with rainwater.

Calculating how much water is potentially available is relatively easy, as we have a good idea as to average rainfall. The calculation is :

Roof area x annual rain fall x run-off coefficient x filter coefficient

The roof area is the horizontal area covered by the roof in

square metres, not the surface area (usually slightly larger than the foot print). The annual rain fall varies across the country but a figure of 900mm is a good average. Having said that, climate change is making the difference across the country greater than it once was. It is probably worth checking for your region at the Met Office web site or Weather Online.

The run-off coefficient relates to the type of roof covering and amount of water that will be held on the roof, or lost to wind and evaporation. The filter coefficient relates to the harvesting system itself, but again in both cases the figures given are good averages.

So for our 200m² house the footprint will be 100m² and the roof area 110m² This gives:

110 x 900 x 0.75 x 0.9 = 66,825 litres p.a.

Note: This same calculation applies to water butt collection – which is why water butts are generally associated with sheds or garages.

By way of comparison, a house with four people in occupation will use water at a rate of 150 litres per person per day (the UK average). That is 219,000 litres per year for each household. At a rate of 80 litres per day (the Code for Sustainable Homes and Waterwise targets) consumption drops to 116,800 litres per year.

The figure of 150 litres per person per day includes all types of use – from drinking water to washing the car. It might seem obvious but we don't actually need water of the same quality for all those activities. Unfiltered, un-disinfected rainwater is perfectly good enough to flush the toilet, water the garden or wash the car.

All rainwater harvesting systems operate using standard roof drainage layouts. Rainwater runs down the roof and into the guttering and down pipes in the normal way, passing through a course filter, which removes leaves and other debris. The rainwater is then stored in a tank, under or above ground, containing a pump and filter.

The water is filtered again as it is pumped from the tank to the house and can be used, with or without the addition of a header tank, for a variety of non-potable uses. These include flushing toilets, washing vehicles, gardening and washing clothes.

However, this type of system is not usually fitted to existing properties because of the extensive internal plumbing work required. They are more suited for new-build, where the only on-cost is the tank and associated equipment.

A more typical 'retro-fit' rainwater harvesting system would be one designed for watering the garden. Garden systems use a filter attached to the guttering downpipes and filter the water into a free standing above-ground tank. The garden can consume up to 50 per cent of peak demand in the summer, so keen gardeners that harvest rainwater could save thousands of litres of tap water each year, as well as cutting bills.

6

For example, the Kingspan Raintrap system. The water is pumped from the tank to a hose or sprinkler, which means gardeners no longer have to trudge back and forth to the water butt, filling and refilling a watering can. And, as an added bonus, plants will thrive on the warm, soft, chlorine-free rainwater. It can easily be installed by the property owner because no internal plumbing work is required.

Basic Components

■ Tank – Either above ground or below ground, the tank will be sized to the roof area (the potential collection). Typical domestic sizes are 2,500 litres to 10,000 litres. They are typically plastic – polyethylene – but sometimes concrete. Some of the manufacturers offer recycled polyethylene, notably Wisy tanks. The design and installation of the tank is important as an empty tank will tend to 'float' in a high water table and tanks have been known to break through the surface. It is worth checking what the installation requirements are. Some underground tanks are fitted with wide flanges around the centre line so that the surrounding soil will hold them down when they are empty. Others need to be surrounded in concrete.

■ Filters – Typically there are up to four filters in a domestic system. An initial filter sifts out the larger items of debris, leaves, twigs, sweet wrappers, etc., followed by the calming inlet filter which ensures that when the water enters the base of the tank it doesn't disturb any silt on the bottom. Next is the overflow filter positioned near the top of the tank that skims the surface for any lighter particles. Finally comes the pump inlet floating filter, just beneath the surface of the water.

Harvested rainwater is normally used for 'grey water' applications – flushing the toilet, washing machines, cleaning the car – as the water is not clean enough to be used as drinking water (and there is generally not enough of it). Cleaning the water to potable standards can be done and just needs two extra filters; a mechanical filter – typically stainless steel or glass granules – which filters particles down to five microns, and an ultra-violet light filter which kills bacteria. A potable water filter system will add around £650 to £900 to the price of the system.

■ Pumps – either a submersible or suction pump is needed to convey the water from the tank to the house. The submersible pumps are mounted in the tank and have a floating inlet that draws water from 200mm below the surface of the water to avoid picking up any floating debris. Being in the tank they are practically silent in operation but more tricky to get at for servicing

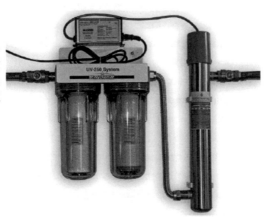

UV filters which kill bacteria are one of two essential stages needed to create drinkable water

or maintenance. Suction pumps are mounted above the tank or in the house. They are therefore slightly more noisy, easier to maintain, but prone to sucking in air.

■ Rainwater Collection System – essentially pipework from the guttering downpipes, through the initial filter, to the tank. Usually these are supplied as part of the overall system.

Rainwater harvesting systems are now widely available, and becoming increasingly popular. A typical domestic system will cost between £2,500 and £4,500. The price is falling as popularity increases and it is easy to see that they will become a standard feature of new builds in the not too distant future.

Below is a list of companies able to supply individual components or complete systems:

■ Stormsaver Ltd
■ Ecovision Systems Ltd
■ EcoFirst Ltd
■ Source Control Systems Ltd
■ Hydro International
■ Rainwater Harvesting Systems Ltd.

BOREHOLES

Essentially drilling a 150mm to 200mm diameter hole in the ground deep enough to hit the water table (as it will vary from winter to summer), inserting a pipe and pumping out water. Similar to an artesian well. A number of water authorities take some or all of their water from

6

aquifers or the water table so a borehole may not actually reduce the drain on the natural resource. What it does do is significantly reduce the energy and infrastructure needed to convey the water from the aquifer to the house.

The practicality, depth and cost of a borehole will be entirely dependent on the location. The aquifer or water table may be 10m below ground level or 100m and this obviously has a direct impact on the potential cost and the suitability. As a guide, a borehole capped with a manhole with a suitable pump installed will cost not less than £2,500 and could get over £20,000 – dependent entirely on location and ground conditions.

The big advantage of a borehole is that it will meet 100 per cent of the water needs of the house. But that is no reason to be profligate with the resource.

As with rainwater, borehole water is technically not clean enough to drink and a fine particle filter and UV disinfection will be needed, which will cost £650 to £900. What you get is water without added fluoride, chlorine or aluminium sulphate, the chemicals that water companies insist we need – and about which the home owner must make their own decision.

WATER USE

Whatever the scarcity or otherwise of water, it is difficult to deny it is becoming an increasingly expensive resource. In the north of England the average unmetered bill is around £229 while across southern England the average bill is £324. In the west of England the average unmetered customer pays £650 per year. The national average for 2008 to 2009 was £330 and Ofwat has agree price rises of five per cent to eight per cent for different parts of the country.

If we assume that a rainwater harvesting system has a life of 20 years, the capital cost of an installed system of £4,500 looks fairly cheap at £225 per year. That cost is fixed for 20 years, unlike water charges that have been given approval to rise by 18 per cent over the next five years. But It has to be accepted that there is little commercial benefit in rainwater harvesting or boreholes. The main benefits lie in the comfort of 'doing-your-bit' and having a water supply for the garden when others have a hosepipe ban.

An issue to bear in mind is that it is becoming mandatory in an increasing number of water utility areas to install water meters in all new housing, or where there is any change to the existing supply. Notionally this is so that water companies can reduce the amount they charge by only charging for what is actually consumed. If that policy is fully implemented it will result in a substantial reduction in water company profits – a trend that is not immediately recognisable in any utility company. What it does do is make us aware of the amount of water we actually consume.

6

That is at least a first step on the way to reducing our consumption.

However the water gets to the house, and whatever its source, it needs to be used efficiently – or to put it another way, sparingly – and there is a plethora of equipment available to help. Here we deal with each of the four main means of water use in turn:

Machines

Taken together, dishwashers and washing machines account for about 28 per cent of the domestic water consumption. Washing machines used to use as much water per wash as a person now uses in an entire day – up to 150 litres. Advances in technology over the past 20 years, however, have succeeded in reducing the average water consumption to about 50 litres per wash. Washing machines vary tremendously in how much water they use per wash: when adjusted for capacity, some use as much as 20 litres per kilogram while others as little as six litres per kilogram.

A common misconception is that dishwashers use more water than hand washing the dishes; in fact, these machines can be water savers. In the 1970s, dishwashers used as much as 50 litres per cycle and some modern models can use as little as 10 litres – less than washing up by hand.

The Waterwise web site at waterwise.org.uk/reducing_water_wastage_in_the_uk/house_ and_garden ranks all the most water efficient machines currently available on the UK market.

Taps

There are a number of different types of taps, and fittings for taps, that can save water. Proximity detection taps that only operate when a hand is near (and because you don't need to touch the tap they are said to be more hygienic). There are aerated taps that use less water than they appear to, and there are taps that have two pressure settings, a low pressure in the first position and a higher pressure in the second. There are also products that can be fitted to existing taps to make them more economic, for example water reducing valves, which can be fitted to all appliances to reduce the flow. Also bear in mind the costs incurred from leaking and dripping taps; a dripping tap can waste enough water in a day to run a shower for five minutes.

■ Flow restrictor valves – can be fitted to all taps and limit the flow rate to the required minimum. They are DIY to fit and apparently will save up to 70 per cent of the water used, at a cost of as little as £3.79.

■ Spray Taps – the basic spray taps are widely available and are very reasonably priced, e.g. a pair of standard bathroom taps can cost as little as £30. By spraying water they achieve a larger wetted area with a lower flow rate.

■ Push taps – these can be added to existing taps by replacing the top of the tap with a push

THE **SUSTAINABLE** BUILDING BIBLE

6

tap conversion. Cost is around £24 per unit and they save water by shutting-off the flow after a few seconds.

■ Sensor Taps – The main selling point of these products, in addition to the water saving benefits of course, seems to be that it is the most hygienic tap on the market. Mains or battery operated will cost around £400 the pair.

Bear in mind that reduced flow taps may not be appropriate for main kitchen and bath taps as they simply increase the time needed to fill the sink or bath – consider using a variable flow rate tap in this case instead.

The single best option is to change separate hot and cold taps for a single mixer tap. This not only save about 20 per cent of the water used, but also saves energy as you only use the hot water you need.

Devatap at www.deva.org.uk have a good range of low water use taps and shower heads and Tap Magic Ltd (www.tapmagic.co.uk) sell a range of spray adapters for existing taps. Alternatively check out the Waterwise site at www.waterwise.org.uk for a whole range of water saving devices.

Toilets

The toilet is the single largest user of water in the home – 30 to 35 per cent of total consumption. Reducing the amount of water used can be achieved by simply putting a brick in the cistern.

For those wishing to be a little more discerning they could try a Hippo Bag. A pack of 10 bags will cost £10.00 from Ecoptopia, and by simply inserting them into your cistern (of 9 litres capacity) you could save between 2.5 and 3.5 litres of water per flush. Some water authorities give them out for free, one of which is Welsh Water.

For the even more discerning is the Interflush. It is a kit that fits onto the siphon and connects to the front mounted flush handle. It works by ensuring the toilet only flushes when the handle is held down. Once the handle is released the flush stops. It could save up to 30 litres of water per person per day and will only cost around £20.

■ Delayed Action Inlet Valves – although toilets are rated with 9, 7 or 6 litre cisterns they actually use more water than this. As soon as the cistern is flushed it starts refilling, and goes on trying to refill the cistern until there is insufficient water to maintain the siphon and the flush stops. That extra water is more than was needed and is lost. A valve is available that remains shut when the flush has started and only opens to refill the cistern once the flushed water has drained away.

■ Dual flush and low flush toilets – these cut household water use

6

by up to 20 per cent (so says the Environment Agency) and save more than half the water used to flush the toilet. The standard flow for a dual-flush cistern is 2 and 4 litres per flush. Ultra-Low flush toilets will use about a third less water than a standard cistern – 2 to 3 litres per flush. In a study carried out at St Leonards Primary School in Hastings there was a saving of nearly 40 per cent in the water used to flush the toilets.

■ Dry Toilets – For the really committed among us is the dry toilet. They work by providing an enclosed environment to collect the waste and provide aerobic decomposition. They can be installed in the home just like normal toilets and use little or no water. They are not connected to the sewerage system so that you can recycle your own waste for use in the garden (but hopefully this is not compulsory!). They are expensive, comparatively speaking, and will cost around £1000 installed.

Showers

Having a shower rather than a bath is a good step towards saving water. A five minute shower uses 35 litres whilst a bath can use around 80 litres. Below are a few examples of the type of shower available, although they are all similar in principal to the water saving taps on the market.

As with taps one way of saving water in shower-heads is by reducing the flow. A typical flow will be 15 to 20 litres per minute and restricted flow heads cut this to around eight litres per minute. They are relatively cheap at around £25 and can be used with power-showers and shower pumps.

Some shower heads accelerate the water flow, energising and oxygenating it. This increases the pressure of the shower and gives the impression that more water is being providing than there actually is.

There are also electronic showers on the market, like the sensor taps, that only operate when movement is detected. They have an in-built flow regulator at six litres per minute, although it can be deactivated to give 15 l/m. It is available as a mains operated device as well as battery operated, and retails at around £750.

Generally water saving showers seem to have exactly the same effect on water savings as taps but with generally less customer satisfaction, probably for obvious reasons.

GREY WATER RECYCLING

The quality and purity of greywater has been address by another new British Standard BS8525 for greywater introduced late in 2009.

Grey Water is water that has been used specifically for washing, from laundry, dishwashers,

6

baths, showers and hand-washing, which could be reused for toilet flushing or watering the garden. The three grades of water are clean (or potable), grey and black. Black is that from toilets, or with other pollutants that need a high level of treatment to be reusable, potable is clean water than needs no treatment, and grey water is somewhere between. It needs a bit of treatment, but not too much.

A grey water system does not rely on any specific kind of building or level of rainfall and can therefore be used in any type of household. The amount of grey water available is largely dependent on whether baths or showers are used, but in all cases make a significant contribution to the overall water consumption.

The price of grey water recycling system varies from £20 to £3,000, compared to £2,500 to £4,500 for rainwater harvesting, and saves nearly as much water. The average rainwater harvesting system will produce between 30 per cent and 50 per cent of the overall consumption, compared to 20 per cent to 40 per cent for grey water. They also tend to be a lot easier to install as they do not always require a large capacity tank buried in the garden, although some of the larger, more complex systems do.

Where rainwater harvesting really falls in the remit of the self-builder, greywater recycling can easily be part of the renovator's scheme. The larger, more complex systems need space and, for best operation, a basement. But the smaller systems can be easily retro-fitted.

The Water Green Siphon Pump

At the lower end of the market, this is basically a siphon for emptying the bath. It is merely a tube with a built in siphon primer bulb and a standard hose pipe fitting. One end of the tube is placed into the bath or sink that is to be emptied and the other end is fed through the window and connected to a hosepipe. The siphon primer pump is then squeezed a few times and the water is drawn up through the pipe. Providing that the 'water out end' of the pipe is below the height of the bottom of the bath the water will continue to be sucked out.

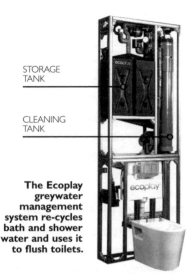

STORAGE TANK

CLEANING TANK

The Ecoplay greywater management system re-cycles bath and shower water and uses it to flush toilets.

This is most suitable if the grey water is for immediate reuse for, e.g. garden watering. The water should not to be used on any edible crops and if it is to be stored for use later on then it should be disinfected.

The WaterGreen Pump is available at £19.99.

Ecoplay System

This may be considered a more typical and more complete system in that it automatically collects grey water and prepares it specifically for toilet flushing. As such it replaces the need for clean water for flushing and therefore directly saves 30 per cent of the overall consumption.

The system comprises a cleaning tank, where the water is collected and cleaned, a storage tank, with a capacity of 100 litres, and a control unit. This has a built in computer that monitors the quality of the stored water, how long the water is stored for, how often the toilet is flushed and how often water is taken from baths and showers. Water that is stored too long is drained off to the sewerage system. It also ensures that water is immediately drained off to prevent stagnation if there is a power failure.

There are a number of systems like this that are designed specifically for recycling water solely for flushing the toilet. Costs tend to be in the £900 to £1000 bracket.

Brac Systems W-200

This technology is a step up from the Ecoplay in that it collects greywater and makes it available for all the toilets in the house, rather than just one. It consists of a compartmented tank (a wet area, and a mechanical area) with 200litre capacity, a pump with pressure tank, a filter, an automatic water valve system, and various pipes and fittings. The greywater passes through a 100micron filter, and into the holding tank. The option exists to add chlorine tablets for disinfection, but as the water can only be used for toilet flushing this seems an unnecessary extra. It has all the expected control systems to prevent overflowing and in case of failure and is considerably less expensive than the Aquacycle, but less versatile.

The AquaCycle 900

This type of system is further up the scale again, possibly at the top. It is a biomechanical process that takes water from baths, showers, washing machine, dishwasher and treats it for use to flush toilets, re-use in the washing machine or in the garden for irrigation or washing the car. It can treat up to 600 litres of water per day, which is equivalent to the average daily consumption for a four person household.

6

 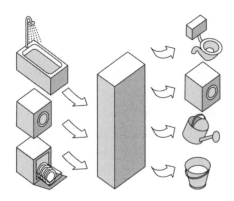

The AquaCycle® 900 cleans and stores water from the shower, bath, washing machine allowing you to use it for your toilet, garden, laundry or domestic cleaning.

The system comprises three tanks in which the water is filtered, treated and UV disinfected so that the outflow water is as close to being potable as can be without actually being potable.

The system can also accept harvested rainwater in an optional extra tank and the price, at around £3,000 installed, is close to a rainwater harvesting system.

The reason that grey water is not used in baths and showers is the same as why it is not used as drinking water. In a bath or shower there is the potential for water to get in the bather's mouth, together with any pollutants that may lurk in the grey water after it has been filtered. Some of the systems clean the water so well that it is indistinguishable from drinking water, but as responsibility for the cleaning rests with the user, the manufacturer is, wisely, not prepared to advertise it as drinking quality water.

WATER OUT

There are four ways of dealing with the waste water leaving the building; direct it to the main sewer, direct it to a septic tank, use a micro treatment plant (a bio-digester) or construct a reed bed.

In terms of sustainability there is very little to choose between the first three options. With the exception of reed beds the process is largely the same and it is a matter of where the treatment takes place rather than improving the treatment. The processes (except reed beds) all leave a highly polluting sludge and the question is always ultimately how to dispose of it.

Reed Beds

Only reed beds provide a sustainable solution in that they take no energy, are self-sustaining, produce a useful by-product – reeds – and have no resulting sludge. The outflow water can be from grey to very pale grey, depending on the extent of the reed bed. At the lowest level it produces water that is clean enough to maintain a healthy ecology in a pond or stream.

The majority of constructed reed beds for water treatment and sewage treatment are refinements of an original design by Professor Kilkuth, a German who developed the original system in the 1970s. The principles remain largely the same and are fairly simple. The common reed (Phragmites Australis) has the ability to transfer oxygen from its leaves, down the stem and out via the root system. As a result of this oxygenation a high population of micro-organisms flourish in the root system. Essentially the reeds provide a surface on which other organisms can grow and proliferate. These organisms (fungi, algae, mosses and aquatic invertebrates) have the ability to remove contaminant from the incoming water. For example, certain species of fungi have the ability to remove a range of synthetic chemicals including pesticides and chlorinated hydrocarbons. Reed beds can be constructed to remove specific contaminants either biologically or by chemical or physical filtration, sedimentation and absorption.

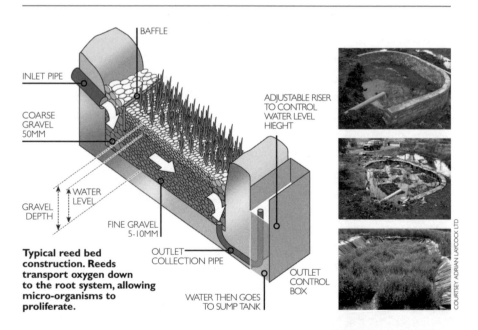

BAFFLE

INLET PIPE

COARSE GRAVEL 50MM

ADJUSTABLE RISER TO CONTROL WATER LEVEL HIEGHT

WATER LEVEL

GRAVEL DEPTH

FINE GRAVEL 5-10MM

OUTLET COLLECTION PIPE

OUTLET CONTROL BOX

WATER THEN GOES TO SUMP TANK

Typical reed bed construction. Reeds transport oxygen down to the root system, allowing micro-organisms to proliferate.

COURTSEY ADRIAN LAYCOCK LTD

6

Construction

Reed beds normally have an impermeable liner (usually high density polyethylene) to ensure that the effluent material is contained until it has been fully treated. On this will be a gravel bed which can be made up of different grades of gravel or sand. The type of gravel used will depend on the intended use of the bed and the quality of material entering it. For example, iron rich sands or a soil and seashell mixture are used specifically to remove phosphorous. Most reed beds are constructed to have a subsurface flow and for these the gravel layer is constructed with a coarser layer at the bottom with a lighter support material on top.

Flow System

There are three kinds of reed bed:

■ Horizontal flow systems are the most popular type for domestic purposes and systems usually have a gradient of 1 in 100, and a depth of 0.6m to 0.7m. The flow of waste water into a horizontal bed is a continuous one, with a designated inlet and outlet. The horizontal beds stay full most of the time and rely on the reeds pulling oxygen down into their roots to feed the aerobic micro-organisms that keep the water smelling fresh.

■ Subsurface Horizontal Flow. This design allows water to flow below the surface of the reed bed through gravel media. The reeds are planted in the gravel and there is no water visible in the bed. It therefore presents no public safety or odour problems. The reed plants are allowed to die back in winter and form a warm composted layer which protects the biofilm below. This design is effective in reducing contaminants and partial ammonia removal. It is also effective in removal of hydrocarbons, some heavy metals and nitrates.

■ Vertical flow systems are similar to horizontal beds in their materials. The principal difference is that the reed bed is flooded and the waste water is allowed to drain down through the system and then out again. Once it is dry oxygen will refill the voids left within the system, replenishing the supply. In some vertical flow systems perforated pipes are added to increase oxygen levels still further.

Beds can be set up separately or with interconnecting beds that may run in series or in parallel. In each of these cases it is wise to rotate the beds to ensure that those receiving untreated waste water are swapped for those receiving partially treated waste water. This will ensure that beds aren't exhausted.

The water coming out of a well designed and maintained reed bed is virtually drinking quality so you can do pretty much whatever you like with it. Typically the outflow is directed to a land drain or soak-away

6

and allowed to permeate into the water table. It could also be directed to a pond or to a watercourse – or back to the house for all the uses you might use rainwater or recycled greywater for.

A good installer (and YES Reed Beds (www.yes-reedbeds.co.uk) is one) will design and construct the right bed, sort out all the Environment Agency paperwork and re-visit the bed after construction to ensure it is working properly. The price of a reed bed will depend on size and a normal domestic size bed will be 4m² to 6m² and cost in the order of £1,500 to £2,000.

Conclusion

At this moment we know that we need to reduce the amount of water we use but we don't know how much water we need to save. Waterwise suggest 20 per cent but it is difficult to see the science behind this as we still do not know what the true effects of global warming will be. James Lovelock, the man who developed the Gaia principle and first brought global warming to our attention in the 1970s, was asked what we should expect from global warming. His answer was 'Surprises'. Cool wet summers; warm wet winters; hot dry summers; cold dry winters. They all seem to be on the cards and all come as a surprise, so maybe he is right.

What we know is that the existing water and sewage infrastructure needs around £46 billion spending on it to meet the demand expected between now and 2050. But when did this great Government of ours last get the expected demand right and who is volunteering to stump up the £46 billion?

7 THE WORLD OUTSIDE

I n dealing with sustainability we are talking about lifestyle choices as well as hard financial decisions and so sustainable landscaping is as much a part of a sustainable home as natural insulation. And possibly a lot easier to deal with.

As with the house itself, forethought and design are the keys. Landscaping is a significant element in completing the home. It can consume 10 per cent to 20 per cent of the budget, can be a resource, add interest, potentially extend the living space, encourage biodiversity and can make or break the kerbside appeal of the house.

We are not dealing with biodiversity to any extent as it is a specialist subject, beyond saying that an interesting garden will have more of it than a boring garden. We are also not dealing with landscaping, per se, as that is another specialist subject with way too many variables.

One of the principal, and increasing, problems with an interesting garden is its demand for water. Hosepipe bans are now common place in the UK, and in some areas they seem permanent. Rainwater harvesting and grey water recycling are dealt with in Chapter 6 but here, in the garden, is the principal reason for installing them. Put simply, the luxury of being able to maintain a healthy garden legally and with a clear conscience.

PERMEABLE SURFACE TREATMENTS

A publication produced by The Environment Agency in September 2008, entitled 'Guidance on the permeable surfacing of front gardens', sets out changes brought into practice from October 2008. This details the need for planning permission for hard-standing parking areas in the garden. If the surface to be covered measures more than five square meters, and the intention is to use traditional, impermeable driveways, it is now necessary to obtain planning permission, clocking up another fee of £150, as well as the palaver of completing application forms and professional plans. However, you will not need planning permission if it is your intention to use a permeable treatment, or if you direct the rainwater to a lawn or border to enable natural drainage.

7

Limiting surface water run-off, principally by using permeable treatments, form an integral part of both Ecohomes and the Code for Sustainable Homes. Beyond the new legislation the motivation to take on the 10 per cent to 15 per cent increase in cost over standard surface treatments if not easy to grasp. The direct effect of efficient energy use in the house is a reduction in running costs. A supplementary effect is a reduction in CO_2 emissions, which has little affect on the individual emitting the CO_2 but a potentially massive effect if everyone does it. Limiting surface water run-off follows the same argument but without the reduction in running costs.

Typically gentle rain produces 90 litres of water per hour on any one driveway, while a summer storm might produce 630 litres. It is estimated (by Acheson-Glover) that rainfall will increase in volume by up to 40 per cent in the next 50 years, and that the incidence of summer storms will also increase. Add to that the increasing rate of building and, to put it simply, the existing system of sewers cannot be extended or enlarged quickly enough to cope.

Surface water run-off hitting the sewer system increases the amount of pollutants carried into watercourses, reduces the amount of water recharging aquifers and increases the risk of flash-flooding. Using a permeable treatment could reduce the amount of water entering a sewer by up to 80 per cent.

The simple answers for homes and gardens would be mulches. These are best used in infrequently used areas, but barks and pebbles could be the cheapest and most effective solutions, closely followed by crushed rocks and gravel. For something a little sturdier consider the following.

PERMEABLE CONCRETE & ASPHALT

Essentially the same as standard concrete or asphalt but made with a single size aggregate. The effect of this is to leave gaps between each piece of aggregate, through which water can penetrate.

As with all permeable surface treatments, it requires special treatment to the sub-strata to maintain stability and to allow the water to drain into the soil, and eventually find the water table.

The product itself is no more difficult to find than standard concrete or asphalt but may be a little more expensive. Constructing a suitable substrate takes more time and thought but also should not be too much more expensive.

TARMACDRY

The product that we all know and refer to as 'Tarmac' should more correctly be termed bituminous macadam, or tar macadam. Tarmac is the title of the publicly listed company that

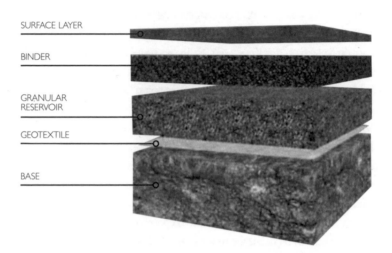

SURFACE LAYER

BINDER

GRANULAR RESERVOIR

GEOTEXTILE

BASE

more popularly produces this widely used surfacing. But now they have a permeable creation, TarmacDry.

The top layer is a coarse, surface layer, designed to remove contaminants, and can be tinted to achieve a more aesthetically pleasing finish. The second layer is the binder layer providing structural support and allowing water to pass easily to the third layer, the granular reservoir. The thickness of this layer depends on the requirements of the project and the nature of the soil beneath as it can provide water storage within the system. The fourth layer is the geotextile layer, included to provide additional filtration before water is allowed to pass into underlying layers. It also serves to prevent material lying underneath it from being pumped into the granular reservoir.

TarmacDry is produced, supplied and installed by Tarmac's own national contracting teams, details of whom can be found through their website, www.tarmacdry.co.uk.

SELF BINDING GRAVEL

Gravel is possibly the simplest surfacing to construct and the availability of wide range of gravels, in varying colours and sizes, means that it can be a very attractive option. All of the materials required are readily available and relatively cheap. However, gravel does have the tendency to shift, being easily scattered and misplaced. It is not ideal for use in sloping locations, and can be problematic for wheelchair or pushchair access. Self binding gravel limits these negative points.

7

On the whole, gravel usually has all of the fines (or dust) removed, ensuring that the product that you are provided with are essentially clean pebbles. Self binding gravel is designed to keep (and at times, even add to) the levels of fines in order to capitalise and improve upon self binding properties.

During installation of self binding gravel, the path or driveway is prepared with a granular sub-base, which is compacted before the self binding gravel is applied. This top layer is then also compacted (usually using a heavy-duty roller), before being dampened and rolled once more. This enables the gravel to stick or 'bind' together, reducing the opportunities for displacement.

When the gravel is bound, affording a more stable surface than traditional gravel, it retains the permeable properties. In addition, in contrast to hard surfaces such as permeable macadam, self binding gravel can be dug up and removed and re-used relatively easily.

Self binding gravel tends to be cheap and locally sourced, rarely travelling more than 30 miles from the source, but some companies have established a national market:

■ Breedon Gravel – (www.breedongoldenamber.co.uk) Golden Amber Gravel has been used to construct the paths in a number of grand houses and golf courses across the country. It is quarried from selected limestone and also contains naturally occurring marl fines, assisting the self-setting properties. Breedon advise that it is suitable for residential use, and by contacting the company directly, they will direct you to your local supplier and installer.

■ Goldpath – (www.stonewarehouse.co.uk) This is almost exactly the same as the Breedon product, and is available for DIY installation through Stone Warehouse for £134 per bulk bag. (It is unclear how much this bulk bag will cover.) It is also available through www.specialistaggregates.com for £148 inc VAT for a 875kg bag, which will cover 22 squared meters.

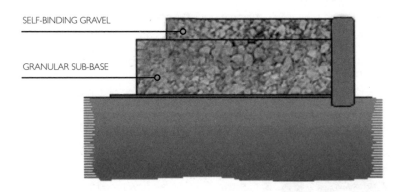

SELF-BINDING GRAVEL

GRANULAR SUB-BASE

7

If loose gravel is preferable to self binding, then websites such as www.stonewarehouse.co.uk and www.specialistaggregates.com supply information regarding a number of gravel or gravel-like products. Stone Warehouse in particular can provide 50 bags of cockle shells, for use particularly on garden paths, weighing in at 500kg, covering 13m2, and costing £150, as well as recycled crushed brick, at the same weight and coverage for £102.

RESIN SURFACING

As with macadam, resin bound paving systems combine loose aggregate with a bonding material, in this case resin, to produce a hard surface.

SureSet UK Ltd produces a range of resin surfaces using a variety of aggregates to create a variety of effects. Typically loose aggregate is sprinkled with resin but ideally the resin and aggregate are mixed to ensure even coverage. This helps the aggregate to bind properly preventing the surface from breaking-up.

The aggregate used for resin surfaces can include everything from recycled ceramics, computers, wires, and crushed CD's to imported marble, or natural, locally sourced gravel and stone. In addition, the resin can be tinted to suit your own, personal design. As such, this resin surfacing can really be used to create a unique, permeable surface. The typical price of the recycled aggregate range is £80 per m^2, supplied and laid on a fully prepared base.

In other respects resin surfacing is similar to tarmac, in the way it is laid, its flexibility in design and its life.

For a list of the approved installers, visit the SureSet website at www.sureset.co.uk. There are DIY kits available also, and these are available primarily through the SureSet Ebay shop.

GRASS PAVERS

Grass paving is essentially a concrete or plastic honeycomb form that carries the weight of people or vehicles and through which grass can grow. It has taken off hugely in the past couple of years and below are illustration of the two principle systems, Netpave and Grasscrete.

■ Netpave 50 – the Netpave system is a grid, consisting of connecting lugs and slots. It is flexible and can therefore be laid over uneven surfaces and gradients. It is in-filled with soil and grass (or for drives and parking areas, gravel) and as the cellular structure is open, it allows development of a strong root system and free drainage. Suitable for permanent car parks, drives and pathways.

■ Netpave 25 – This is a new product and differs from Netpave

7

50 in that it is laid over existing grass rather than having grass planted into it. Again it is extremely flexible and can become almost invisible as grass grows around it. It can also be laid temporarily if need be, unlike Netpave 50, although it has been designed for permanent use.

■ Grasscrete – essentially the same as Netpave (different manufacturer), but is a cellular reinforced concrete system. It is load bearing up to 40 tonnes gross vehicle weight.

Each of these items are easily installed with no pegging required. They are resistant to deformation and rutting and, according to the manufacturers, aesthetically pleasing.

PERMEABLE PAVEMENTS

Essentially these are block paved surfaces for patios and the like, with wide joints filled with fine aggregate. This is then laid on a free draining base. As the water passes through the base course it is filtered and studies from

Grass pavers require little preparatory work, and no more than a non-permeable surface.

Coventry University have indicated that up to 97 per cent of hydrocarbons are filtered out in this process.

Permeable pavements are suitable for all the usual residential applications, including drives, car parking, patios and foot paths. They have the same attributes as the slabs or blocks they are constructed with.

The type of system that you will use will depend on topography and the quality of the soil. An installer should be able to help you determine which is suitable for your home. You will need to ascertain what kind of soil you have and the rainfall levels in your area. This will determine the sub base thickness needed to support the system on top.

This is the usual structure of a block paved area. Directly under the paving units will be a bedding layer, typically sharp sand or 6mm grit. For extra help removing pollutants a geo-

7

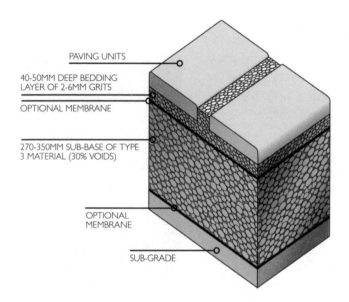

PAVING UNITS

40-50MM DEEP BEDDING
LAYER OF 2-6MM GRITS

OPTIONAL MEMBRANE

270-350MM SUB-BASE OF TYPE
3 MATERIAL (30% VOIDS)

OPTIONAL
MEMBRANE

SUB-GRADE

membrane can be added under the bedding material. It will catch any hydrocarbons as well as any organic material, which can then be allowed to decompose. This is usually only installed in car parking areas. If there is a higher risk of pollutants then another impermeable membrane can be added between the sub base and the sub grade to trap them.

The overall efficiency of the system will diminish over time as the voids have a tendency to become clogged up with salts, mud and silts, but this can be solved with jet washing.

As with all things, especially new things, if you are going to do it, it is best to do it right. The Association of Block Paving Contractors have been set up to promote and maintain the highest standard of practice, develop installation techniques and increase the pool of competent installers. So it seems wise to seek the assistance of an approved installer. A comprehensive list can be found on www.interlay.org.uk.

From the foregoing it can be seen that the real benefit of permeable surface treatments is for the local ecology. Hard surfaces do nothing to help or encourage flora and fauna; they prevent water reaching underground aquifers and reflect heat. They also help to increase the pollution reaching rivers and watercourses. How important that is to the individual builder is a matter for that individual. It is clearly important to the country, if not the world, at large.

THE LAWN

Haven or green desert?

We all take pleasure in a perfectly mown lawn so most of us, when we are designing the garden, will lay most of it to grass, but is it really as 'green' for the environment as we may think?

A good lawn will require around 5 litres of water every square metre, every day throughout the summer, in order to maintain that wonderful green, "Pimms in the midday sun", striped look. This means that even a 10m x 10m lawn requires around 14,000 litres of fresh water in each summer month. What we then have is an environment where most of the animals that make the countryside such a wonderful place cannot actually survive or breed. Apart from the odd beetle, worm and blackbird, a Pimms lawn is basically a desert. The grass is typically a single species and not allowed to flower or seed so it is of limited interest to invertebrates and no interest at all to birds. Almost no organic matter is returned to the soil because the grass clippings have to be removed. We spend time sweeping up autumn leaves so that even earthworms don't get to feed and condition the soil, as they would in their natural state.

As a result the lawn requires the annual application of fertilisers, weed killers and conditioners to maintain that super-green colour that we all seem to be obsessed, to keep the grass growing and to ensure that nothing but grass will grow.

We have to ask ourselves what the lawn is for, and are there alternatives? If we are looking for a play area – soft for the kids, somewhere for the barbeque, sunbathing – then there may be options.

WILD FLOWER MEADOWS

Wild flower meadows are a good play area for kids, reduce maintenance, and add hugely to the biodiversity. Native flower species support native creatures and by using the wild flower system we can justifiably say that we are really doing something positive for the environment. A meadow lawn needs no chemical enhancers, no mowing and the by-product of the wild flower meadow is a pile of hay that can be fed to horses or composted for the vegetable garden.

THE GRAVEL GARDEN

A gravel garden fulfils many of the functions the lawn does, at least for the adult, providing space for the barbeque, for sun bathing or to sit around drinking Pimms. It can take on a Mediterranean feel or follow a cottage garden theme, or maybe a Japanese style. A gravel garden will essentially water itself and will retain water under the gravel for a very long time, allowing most plants to flourish. With care and thought it can be easier to maintain than a

7

lawn, introduce far fewer toxins, fulfil most of the functions and be just as beautiful as a Pimms lawn.

Combine these three garden systems in one space and we tick all the boxes. A garden that is ecologically sound, that meets all the functional needs, that has a minimum water demand and looks beautiful.

COMPOSTING

Composting may or may not fall within the ambit of a book on building homes, but garden and household food waste are resources and therefore the idea falls within the ambit of sustainability.

There are two ways to compost; cool composting and hot composting. Appropriately perhaps, cool composting is the relaxed approach and hot composting requires more effort.

Cool compost is what we usually do with a simple compost bin at the back of the garden. Waste is put in and in a year or two we have usable compost. There may be a little turning of the material but most of the work is done by micro-organisms, worms and insects. It is a well trod path that provides nutrients for the veg plot and reduces waste going to landfill.

Hot composting is basically the same process, but done in an insulated box – typically an old chest freezer (with refrigerant and motor removed). A simple design and construction details can be found at www.cat.org.uk/catpubs.

Hot composting reduces the time taken to produce usable material to around three months but requires a bit more effort in terms of turning the material. The system operates at temperatures of around 50degC to 70degC which will effectively pasteurise the material, killing bacteria, weed seeds and harmful micro-organisms.

What it also does is produce heat. If a few copper pipes are run around the inside of the freezer and water pumped through some of that heat can be extracted and used to heat a greenhouse or cold frame. An elegantly circular process, using plant material to help grow plants.

PATIO HEATERS, POND PUMPS AND GREENHOUSE HEATING

That is, all of those outdoor things that use energy. The arguments around these things rebounds through the newspapers and even the EU Government. The Energy Saving Trust says patio heaters use as much energy in one evening as a gas cooker does in six months. They are acquiring the same social grace as the urban 4x4. Perhaps rightly so but if you want to sit in your garden on a January evening even a really good jumper is not enough. But maybe a chimnea is. A

7

simple wood burning stove will give as much warmth as an LPG patio heater, is CO_2 neutral and more fun to deal with.

All of these things are part of twenty-first century life in the western world, but the application of a little intelligence generally offers a solution to the guilt and angst that increasingly they tend to bring. Pumps with built-in solar PV panels, solar thermal panels (possibly home made) to heat the green house, or hot composting, wood burning stoves instead of LPG patio heaters.

The sustainable builder does not abandon the luxuries of the developed world, she, or he, finds way of supplying them without destroying the planet in the process. As a friendly farmer once said, 'There are better ways of killing a pig than choking it on strawberries.'

NATURAL SWIMMING POOLS

Swimming pools remain a bit of a growth area of UK house building. Increasing personal wealth means that more people can afford to indulge in the not-so-little luxuries. But for the sustainable builder these seem an intractable problem. Swimming pools are biological deserts, need a lot of water, a lot of energy and introduce more-or-less unpleasant chemicals.

Natural swimming pools may be the answer. Natural pools are essentially a swimming pool and pond combined. They use plants, filtration and micro-organisms in reed-bed technology to clean the water and are consequently chemical and energy free.

On the downside, natural pools can take up to twice as much space as a standard pool and are, naturally, outdoors. But they are visually more attractive, use a relatively trivial amount of water and are said to be a much more pleasing swimming experience – probably because there are no chemicals in the water.

The idea started, perhaps unsurprisingly, in the USA in the early 1970s, but was slow to take off there. An Austrian company, Biotop, are probably now the world's largest installer of natural swimming pools. They have been in operation for some 25 years and have 1000s of pools to their name. Their UK distributor is Woodhouse Natural Pools, based in Cambridge (www.naturalswimmingpools.com).

A natural pool will consist of a swimming area and a regeneration zone. The two have a physical barrier between to ensure that the soil and plants in the regeneration zone don't get into the swimming area.

The regeneration zone is the key and is specifically designed to suit the swimming area and the local ecology. Careful, expert, selection of plants is essential, as is the construction of the zone. As a consequence natural pools tend to be a good deal more expensive than a chemical pool, but have virtually zero running costs.

7

Natural pools are usually unheated, for perhaps obvious reasons, but many have been built in hot places in the world where water temperatures naturally get well over 30⁰C. Extending the swimming season with a few solar thermal panels is therefore quite possible. It is also possible to have an indoor/outdoor pool with the swimming area being the indoor bit and the regeneration zone remaining outdoors.

A look at the Woodhouse website will show the variation and beauty of a natural pool. Anyone lucky enough to have been skinny-dipping in a pond or lake will know the silky, sensual feel of chemical free, unsalted water. Sometimes there is a price to pay for sustainability, but the extra investment returns dividends. Natural pools are a case in point. A better swimming experience that enhances the ecology and costs nothing (or very little) to run.

CONCLUSION

The sustainable builder will look at the site whole as a resource, rather than just somewhere to build a house. Considering, designing, the bit of your home that remains outside the house is equally as important as the bit inside – and probably bigger. There are many things that the sustainable builder can do to enhance and improve the outside. Starting with consideration of what that space could be used for will lead further than a simple "it's the garden". There are many potential uses - from play area and hobby to food and energy production – and not everyone will want all of those things. Consideration of what will suit an individual project, now and in the future, is likely to lead to a more attractive, more useful and more fulfilling space. And for the sustainable garden designer all the same issues apply – recycling, water use, energy use, renewable materials – to minimise the impact we have, and to maximise the functional and economic sustainability.

THE WORLD OUTSIDE

7

8 | 100 PER CENT SUSTAINABLE

Do you have the pioneering spirit? You will need to if you want to try and achieve a truly sustainable home. In terms of achieving 100 per cent sustainability the big things – floors, walls, roof – are fairly easy to deal with. Straw bales, sustainable timber, reclaimed roof slates are all relatively easy to source and deal with. The devil lies in the detail. Walls need finishing and even lime plaster is processed and has embodied energy and CO_2. Kitchen fittings can be made from reclaimed timber, but recycled cupboard door hinges are hard to find. Electric cable can contain a high proportion of recycled copper, but the insulation tends to be virgin PVC.

In building a sustainable home we are trying to achieve two things :

■ Reduce the amount of irreplaceable resources used in the building.

■ Reduce the carbon footprint of the building, both embodied carbon and the carbon emitted in running.

To achieve 100 per cent sustainability we would need to reduce both those to zero.

The Government requires that by 2016 (or 2011 in Wales) ALL new homes are 'Carbon Zero'. As has been discussed in the Materials (Chapter 3), an average-size conventionally-built house will embody some 44 tonnes of CO_2 in its materials. A sustainably built house, using modern methods of construction and sustainable materials will maybe halve the embodied CO_2. So the mantra of "Towards Zero Carbon" is a bit misleading to say the least. Even the poor tribes-people of Ethiopia emit 0.1 tonnes of CO_2 per person, and no one is suggesting that Europeans, Americans, Australians, et al, should live like those Ethiopians. Rather that Ethiopians should be helped to achieve the same standards the rest of the world enjoys.

Calculating the carbon footprint of a building remains a nutty problem. What to include in the calculation is still a matter of debate. The question goes, "do we include the energy used to cook the breakfast for the driver of the lorry that delivered the sheep wool insulation?" Or to put it another way, where do you stop?

8

The answer generally is that footprint means what footprint says. Transporting materials has to be a factor and local sourcing is a fundamental tenet of sustainability. But, as has been shown, renewable and reclaimed materials can travel a long way before they take up as much carbon as locally produced virgin material.

Aiming at 100 per cent sustainability is laudable, so long as it is recognised that it is utopia – an unachievable ideal. Reducing CO_2 emissions, even to zero, is a different question. Not only laudable, it is achievable and even desirable.

LOW ENERGY HOMES

Virtually all this book is about reducing the embodied energy in a house and the energy needed to run it. There are a number of examples of houses designed specifically with that in mind, effectively off-the-shelf solutions. Most of these involve off-site manufacture – the modern equivalent of pre-fab (an expression we are not allowed to use in the off-site manufacturer's presence) with all the benefits of modern levels of insulation, air-tightness and consequently thermal performance. But their use of non-sustainable materials, which is often the case, may mitigate against their use of the expression A Sustainable Home. Energy is important – a key issue – but it is not the only issue. It can be argued that a house with low energy demands, perhaps zero CO_2 emissions, but which depletes non-renewable resources in its construction is not a sustainable building method.

None-the-less, low energy houses are a step in the right direction.

BedZED

The BedZED concept was to create a net 'zero fossil energy development' of 82 residential homes; variously flats, apartments and houses, as well as a range of workplaces. The aim was to construct a development that would produce at least as much energy from renewable sources as it consumes. The project also has commercial buildings, an exhibition centre and a children's nursery, in effect a complete working community.

These buildings use concrete and masonry to give thermal mass that store heat during

The BedZED concept was to create a net 'zero fossil energy development'

8

warm conditions and release it at cooler times. They have not adopted the light-tight principles being advocated in some quarters today. In addition, all buildings have a minimum of 300mm insulation. It is interesting to note that the project started in 2001 when 300mm of insulation was considered a lot. At that time the Building Regs called for just 100mm of loft insulation. Today Building Regs call for 270mm minimum loft insulation and Passivhaus and similar standards will use much more.

Houses are arranged in south facing terraces to maximise solar heat gain and each terrace is backed by north facing offices, where minimal solar gain reduces the tendency to overheat.

Emphasis was given to natural, recycled or reclaimed materials and sourced, where possible, within a 35-mile radius of the site. Taken together these reduced the embodied energy and CO_2 in the buildings.

The buildings were designed to be heated principally by solar gain and "casual gains", cooking, appliances, and the like. The design also incorporated passive natural ventilation which taken together significantly reduced the need for space heating.

BedZED receives electrical power from wind turbines and a small-scale combined heat and power plant (CHP) which also provides hot water and supplements the space heating. The CHP plant is fuelled by woodchip and has experienced some problems in operation. One of which was educating the residents in how the houses operated. The immediate effect of this lack of education was that more heat was needed than had been planned for. These problems have been largely ironed out and the plant was fully operational in 2007.

BedZED was a pioneering project that required the co-operation and involvement of the residents to succeed. The first residents moved in during March 2002 and many lessons were learnt and many modifications to the design made as a result of residents' experience..

RuralZED

RuralZED is a spin-off company from the BedZED development, and run by the same man, Bill Dunster. It is said to offer a true zero carbon housing system, focusing on the Code for Sustainable Homes. They offer a range of standard designs which are relatively low-cost and use a very high proportion of traditional and natural materials. The construction method has an advertised design-life of a minimum five generations. Expressed in years that might not sound so long.

As an off-the-shelf solution, RuralZED has a lot to offer. The designs all incorporate a lot of renewable energy, sustainable materials, interesting design features as well as low cost.

8

STEWART MILNE SIGMA HOMES

The Code for Sustainable Homes gives a star rating to new homes; the maximum rating is six stars, which is a building with zero carbon emissions, low water use and a significant proportion of sustainable materials. The house built by Stewart Milne Group – www.stewartmilne.com has achieved five star rating which represents a 100 per cent improvement on Part L Building Regulations, a 30 per cent reduction in water use and zero CO_2 emissions from heating, hot water, ventilation and lighting. It uses timber-frame construction, light and tight, solar thermal panels, PV panels and wind turbines.

It is said to be a commercially viable product for the urban housing developer and to have a host of environment-friendly features, including grey water recycling and rainwater harvesting.

HANSON ECO-HOUSE

This is a masonry built, three-bedroom house, constructed from pre-fabricated brick panels. It gained a four star rating and has high levels of insulation, natural ventilation and PV panels. This means that it is 44 per cent better than Part L Building Regs and uses 12 per cent less water.

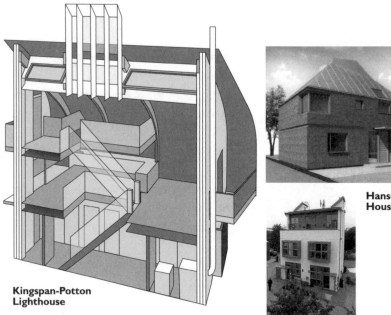

Kingspan-Potton Lighthouse

Of the three best scoring low-energy houses, only the Lighthouse is available to the self-builder.

Hanson Eco House

Stewart Milne Sigma Homes

8

Some way off zero carbon but still acclaimed as a Low-Energy House. Pre-fabricating the brick panels is said to reduce waste by up to 20 per cent but the embodied energy and CO_2 is still high compared to timber-frame.

Whether this is a sustainable method of construction or merely an attempt by an intrinsically non-sustainable building method to gain some green credentials is an interesting question. With the whole of Europe, with the exception of England, majoring on timber frame in one form or another as the preferred building method it is difficult to conceive that brick will feature in the house building industry of 2020.

KINGSPAN-POTTON LIGHTHOUSE

Said to be the most advanced house design ever produced for mainstream construction. It was the first design to achieve a six star rating on the Code for Sustainable Homes which means that it has net zero carbon emissions, uses 33 per cent less water than a conventional house and uses A-rated materials from the Green Guide for Housing Specification.

The building is a $93m^2$ floor area, two and a half storey, two-bedroom house and is constructed using Kingspan Off-Site's TEK Building System. This gives an overall U-value of $0.11W/m^2K$ and airtightness of less than $1.0m^2/hr/m^2$, which reduces heat loss by around two-thirds compared to a conventional house.

One of the more interesting features is a biomass boiler and a waste separation system which enables combustible waste to be used locally in the central heat and power plant. The building also incorporates integrated photovoltaic, solar-thermal array, mechanical ventilation with heat recovery and a roof-mounted wind catcher, which provides passive cooling and ventilation.

POTTON ZENIT

The Lighthouse did not do too well on the sales front and was quickly replaced by the Zenit. Potton have a long history in the self-build market and a deservedly good reputation. What they have done is to take the technological innovation embodied in the Lighthouse and applied it to more, shall we say, functional designs.

The result is a range of self build packages that all have very low energy use, up to zero CO_2 emissions and interesting design features.

OFF-SITE MANUFACTURE

All of the above are essentially off-site manufactured houses, to a

8

greater of lesser extent. We have not included here the range of German and Nordic manufacturers building in the UK. These include names like Hanse Haus, Huf House, Baufritz, Scandia and the like. They all manufacture in basically the same way – single skin timber frame with very high levels of insulation, accurate manufacture and attention to detail, resulting in high quality construction – but there are differences around the periphery. Some use more sustainable materials than others, some focus more on energy conservation and some on energy generation. Hanse Haus are probably making the greatest strides in this direction as they are offering both Passivhaus and Code for Sustainable Homes level 6 houses as standard products.

The big advantage of off-site manufactured houses is that you know what you will get at the outset. There is of course a cost involved in this, but also a high degree of assurance. The same applies to Code 6 or Passivhaus products. If that is what you order, it is what you will get. With conventional building methods there will always be an element of chance (at least until these become the norm for the mass building market), which will involve checking and testing on site at each stage of the construction.

There is a cost involved in using off-site manufacturers, and they are not nor likely to ever be 100 per cent sustainable, but they deliver what they say and that will be what you, the buyer, orders.

GREEN, ECO OR SUSTAINABLE HOMES

A discussion has arisen over the difference between Green Homes, Eco-Homes and Sustainable Homes. The discussion revolves around which of these are meaningful, which are marketing puffs and which should we look for when buying a home.

A Green Home is said to use less energy, water and natural resources; create less waste and be healthier to live in. But that is a bit vague as it does not suggest what it is less than, or by how much.

An Eco-Home is defined as 'A sustainable, healthy and environmentally friendly home, using sustainable building methods, materials, energy, heating and water conservation'. But again, vague. Houses are intrinsically not environmentally friendly. It is just that some are less unfriendly than others. Eco-Homes, or at least those marketed as Eco, tend to have a more radical look and will incorporate some "Eco Features" – a solar panel perhaps, rainwater harvesting, maybe even a green roof (interestingly we don't often see green roofs on houses marketed as being Green). There is still no system of measurement. No way to judge how Eco the house actually is.

A house marketed as Sustainable will often make reference to the Code for Sustainable

THE **SUSTAINABLE** BUILDING BIBLE

8

Homes and have a star rating – one to six stars, with six being zero CO_2 emissions. This at least gives a means of direct comparison. We will know that a 6-star house will have very low energy use and low running costs. We will also know that at least a proportion of the materials used in its construction will be responsibly sourced – the system of measurement used by The Code for materials.

A good definition of sustainability is: 'To meet current needs without impacting on the ability of future generations to meet their needs'. That seems to encompass everything we need to consider but leaves it to the house buyer (or builder) to determine what impact their project will have. That is not always easy and ploughing through the house manufacturer's marketing blurb is not always helpful.

New technologies and new materials are constantly being developed, all aimed at creating greener, more sustainable buildings. They all serve to reduce the overall impact of the building but it has to be accepted that some level of impact will remain.

In short, none of the expressions have any real meaning. It is the reality that lies behind the blurb that matters – how much less energy do they use, what proportion of non-sustainable materials have gone into the house.

CONCLUSIONS ON LOW-ENERGY HOUSING

Reducing energy consumption is important but it is not the whole picture. How the house was built and the materials that went into it will impact on the ability of future generations to build their houses.

The major players in the housing industry, or at least those with something to prove, are all putting forward a product variously labelled as Low-Energy, Zero Carbon, Sustainable, Green or Eco. Whether they actually achieve what they say is a moot point but really not too relevant. The fact that they are investing small fortunes in developing these products and systems indicates two things:

They believe that the market is, or will be, keen to buy their products.

Significantly reducing the energy used in the home and improving a buildings sustainability is achievable.

Whatever else these projects and products have done, they have moved the game on. Some of the ideas coming out of these projects are good and innovatory, some seem plain daft. But it doesn't matter. Kingspan insulation can never be considered a sustainable product, but the fact that the company is prepared to invest millions in developing more sustainable building

8

systems is important and useful. It stimulates and motivates the market by putting otherwise obscure products in the mainstream. It increases awareness of sustainability and reducing energy consumption in those most difficult to reach – the local small builder – and makes life easier for the self-builder or renovator aspiring to sustainability.

THE SOLAR HOUSE

The question is: Can solar power alone provide enough energy to power a house? The answer now is yes. And is has been done – a number of times.

The solar powered house will use solar energy in three forms – passive, thermal and electrical. The idea of the solar powered house starts with design. Using solar energy properly, especially passive solar heat, to ensure the house is functional and that the investment in equipment in minimised, is a design issue.

Solar power for electricity production is not a problem. Photovoltaic systems are well proven technology and it is just a matter of size and not inconsiderable cost.

Solar power for space heating and water heating is a different matter. In addition to a south-facing roof, a south-facing conservatory and glazed roof to collect passive solar heat will be needed; the floors and walls facing the sun need to built with masonry mass to store heat and release it when the sun is not shining. In addition, of course, a substantial array of solar thermal panels to heat water.

The advent of new photovoltaic-thermal technology has made the whole proposition more possible and more attractive (see Chapter 4-Renewable Energy). Operating at a heat to electricity production ratio of 3:1 if a big enough array to meet the electricity demand is installed, it is likely to produce an excess of heat.

For example: If we assume that our 200m² house needs 5,000kWh of electricity per year, the PV-T system will also produce 15,000kWh of heat in the year. If the house only has meets current Building Regs standards it will only need 11,000kWh for space heating and perhaps 3,500kWh for hot water – a total of 14,500kWh. A 6kWp PV-T system can therefore meet the whole of the heating, hot water and electricity demands, with perhaps a bit over. Cost may be an issue; at £30,000 to £35,000 this is not a cheap option.

Heat recovery ventilation will also be needed to capture casual heat gains (from cooking, lighting, showers, etc.) as will high performance double-glazing. Construction costs should then be similar to a traditional house of the same size with money going to design and insulation rather than central heating and renewable energy equipment.

Even then, a top-up to solar energy with an immersion heater in the hot water tank and

8

maybe a log burning stove is likely to be necessary. On clear frosty days there's enough sun to generate the heat needed, but on cloudy winter's days probably not.

The Feed-in Tariff and Renewable Heat Incentive also begin to play a part. The 'profit' from these annual payments can be used to off-set the cost of buying more energy.

For example, if we reduce the size of our PVT array to 4kWp it will generate 3,200kWh of electricity and 9,600kWh of heat. If this qualifies for both FiT and RHI payments (at the rates published in 2010) it will produce an income of £2,870 per year. We have a shortfall in energy of 6,700kWh. If that was purchased from the grid it would cost (at 2010 prices) less than £1,000. And the capital cost of the equipment has reduced as well.

The conclusion; solar heating works, and it has been done, notably in Cornwall. But it probably does not work quite as well in Orkney. The UK can provide plenty of free energy – in Cornwall it may be solar and in Orkney probably wind – and the key is designing a house to take advantage of what is available. Done properly it will work but the investment will be in design and equipment rather than running costs.

SUSTAINABLE CONSTRUCTION

The number of people actually attempting to build with cheap, natural materials like mud, hemp and straw is very small. One of the main stumbling blocks tends to be raising finance and by the end of 2006 only two mortgages had been given by the Ecological Building Society for straw-bale homes. Since then the demand for this sort of construction has grown and more building societies, like Principality and Norwich & Peterborough have entered the market. It is becoming easier to raise finance but still cannot be considered easy.

There are people alive today who were born and raised in cob houses. It must also be considered that although the raw material is cheap, the cost of the building will not be much less than a conventional build, if at all. These materials and methods only apply to the walls and are off-setting the cost of timber-frame or masonry. The costs involved in the rest of the property remain the same and the time taken to build a straw-bale or cob wall will probably absorb all the cost saving in materials, unless there is lots of free labour to hand.

Although many people start out thinking that it is a cheap building method, it is not principally about cost saving. It is about sustainability, a tiny embodied carbon footprint and about lifestyle. It is labour intensive, it means learning new, rare skills, it requires determination to get it past the regulators, it needs careful thought and even more careful planning. But the sense of satisfaction from completing a home of this sort can only be wondered at. It is

8

something you do because you want to and when you're finished it is guaranteed to make you smile.

COB HOUSES

Cob is an old word for a mud wall. Devon and South West England probably have more cob than anywhere else in Britain, with cob being Devon and Cornwall's traditional construction material from the fourteenth century. There are still houses standing in the West Country built over 400 years ago. In 1998 Bob Bennett, a specialist in single skin wall construction, together with a small team of enthusiasts, built a single storey cob house in one day, in a clearing in the New Forest. The object was to prove a piece of folklore that in mediaeval times, if a peasant without rights could build a house on common land between sunrise and sunset, he could claim the building for his own.

Cob is a mixture of straw (around three per cent by dry weight), and sometimes dung, added to a clay sub-soil. In some parts of the country, notably Hampshire, chalk is also added. The straw and dung (although some sources maintain that the dung element is a myth) are added to reduce cracking problems in the clay during drying. Traditionally cattle would be used to tread the mixture, so the addition of dung would seem to be inevitable. Today a JCB or similar is used to mix the straw and clay, and dung is an optional extra. As about 70 per cent of the earth's land mass is clay, this seems like quite a good material in terms of sustainability.

The cob is mixed with water to a 'just workable' consistency and the walls built up in layers, with each layer being rammed and given time to dry before the next one is added. Shuttering can be used to aid stability during the construction and the wall finished with a "bag rub" – literally rubbing with a hesian sack to give a smooth, textured finish. This construction method brings one of the great advantages of cob. It can take on a much wider variety of lateral shapes. Sweeping curves and round corners are no more difficult than straight lines and can lead to interesting design ideas.

A good-quality cob can survive quite well without rendering, but normally it is coated with a lime render, followed by a lime wash.

WWW.COBCOTTAGE.COM

A typical cob house with thatch roof. A modern version would be almost indistinguishable to this old example.

JEREMY PHILLIPS

Cob incorporates site soil and locally sourced clay, with straw acting as the binding ingredient.

These coatings have the important property of being porous, or 'breathable', so that any moisture that gets into the cob, via penetrating rain or rising damp, can evaporate out through the render. Moisture is the death of cob (for obvious reasons) and good cob walls are said to have "a good hat and a good set of boots". The good hat is the roof covering which is traditionally thatch but does not have to be, and usually has widely overhanging eaves to ensure there is no rain water penetration to the top of the wall. The good boots are a stone or masonry foundation plinth. The plinth will usually be up to 600mm above ground level, to minimise splashing from rainwater hitting the ground, and will have to incorporate a DPC to comply with current building regulations (although strictly it is not necessary as cob walls work by allowing any moisture penetration to drain away). Often draining foundations are used, which are a cavity stone or block wall with a loose stone infill to allow any moisture in the cob to drain completely away.

Built properly cob walls are extremely durable. Most modern coatings, such as cement render, gypsum plaster and vinyl paints, do not allow the cob to dry out after a spell of wet weather, so that it gradually accumulates moisture until it eventually starts to crumble. Ensuring that any coating, internal and external, applied to the cob is moisture permeable is essential to the success of the wall.

So far as Planning Permission is concerned, cob wall buildings would be treated in exactly the same way as those with walls of masonry or timber-framed construction. The issues revolve around the appropriateness of the building in that location, design, finishes and the like, not with construction materials and methods. Compliance with the Building Regulations can be a different matter as it is likely that the Building Control officer will not have a great deal of knowledge on cob walls. It will probably be necessary to supply a lot more information than would otherwise be the case. The Plymouth University School of Earthen Architecture can help with soil analysis, thermal performance and the like.

Thermal performance can be a problem but compliance with Building Regulation Approved Documents is not necessarily mandatory if another method can be shown to be as effective in achieving the desired end. Building Regs to be implemented in October 2010 switch the emphasis from achieving specific U-values to hitting CO_2 targets. Cob is well known for being a very comfortable material in which to live; in part this is due to its excellent thermal properties, being a combination of high thermal resistance and thermal storage and good humidity regulation.

However, from a building regulation point of view thermal resistance is still an issue. An 850mm thick cob wall (which is much thicker than a traditional cob wall) will give a thermal resistance of 0.45w/m/k, higher than the maximum of 0.35 allowed. A study carried out by Equipe Matériaux et Thermique des Bâtiments, INSA de Rennes, France in 2004 concluded that the thermal behaviour of a 500mm thick cob wall is about the same as that of concrete block cavity wall with 75mm of insulation. What this means is that while a 500mm wall would fail miserably on the U-value test, the house as a whole can pass the new Building Regs CO2 targets test.

Many new cob structures have been built over the past few years, all with Building Regulations approval. Kevin McCabe's houses at Keppel Gate and the Cob Tun House, which won an RIBA award in 2005, are a couple of examples. The technical and thermal performance of the particular mix of cob needs to be evaluated, with regard to its density, shrinkage rate, and compressive strength. These in turn will dictate the thickness of foundations. Again the Plymouth University Centre for Earthen Architecture can help with this (for a reasonable fee).

Another issue to bear in mind is that cob walls offer very high thermal mass; they are good at storing heat, both internal and from the sun. As a result they do not heat quickly and cob

8

houses do not perform well with instantaneous heating systems – particularly heated air. They take time to reach a comfortable temperature but will maintain a relatively constant temperature, irrespective of the vagaries of the weather.

Fortunately the traditional skills, almost lost in the second half of the twentieth century, have been saved so that now there are professional suppliers and builders who are able to build structurally stable and aesthetically pleasing cob structures.

The Weald & Downland Open Air Museum run courses on cob construction, or get more information from :

■ www.buildsomethingbeautiful.com

■ www.jjsharpe.co.uk

■ www.earthedworld.co.uk

■ www.abeysmallcombe.com

■ www.tech.plym.ac.uk/soa/arch/earth.htm

■ www.cat.org.uk

STRAW-BALE HOUSES

In many respects straw-bale construction is very similar to cob. Both suffer if moisture penetrates, both require a 'good hat and a good pair of boots', both offer good thermal and sound insulation, and both require particular skills to build well.

Unlike cob, straw-bale construction is relatively new. It was first developed in the USA in the nineteenth century (when baling machines became more common) by pioneer farmers short of building materials. Straw, as a waste product from wheat production, was used as it was readily available, if not all that was available, in the prairie states. Initially buildings were intended to be temporary, until more substantial materials came to hand, but the straw house proved so comfortable and durable that the farmers decided to continue with them. The technology has not advanced much since those early days and in truth it is difficult to see how it could advance.

As with cob, water is a key factor in the straw-bale construction process. Cob starts wet and is allowed to dry, straw bales start dry and have to stay that way. If the moisture content gets over 20 per cent the straw will rot, with predictable consequences. On that note, if a straw-bale building fails structurally it tends to be fairy undramatic. It does not suddenly tumble in a cloud of rubble and dust, but rather it gently subsides as the straw gradually gives way to unsupportable compression.

The three big scares with straw-bale are:

■ Fire – straw is flammable and will burn. It is actually no greater a

8

fire risk than timber-frame construction with timber cladding. If the straw is lime rendered it has the same fire risk as masonry and passes all Building Regulations tests.

■ Durability – Straw is an insubstantial material and cannot last. Straw-bale houses built 100 years ago are still standing. Until the 1990s the design life for UK houses was 60 years. As with all things, it is the care given to the construction detail that determines the durability of the building.

■ Vermin infestation – Straw will be a welcome home to rats and mice. Rats and mice do not particularly like straw (although they do like hay) as it is a poor food source and poor nest material. In addition they would have to chew through lime render to get at it. There is no more risk of vermin infestation than with any other construction method.

Using straw bales allows a greater flexibility in design. As with cob, curved walls are easy and interesting.

Straw is a relatively light weight material and consequently foundations can be lighter. But the need to prevent rising damp reaching the straw tends to counteract this. As with cob, a plinth foundation wall of 300mm to 500mm above ground level is used to prevent rainwater splash. Straw does not "wick", that is draw up moisture. Rising damp will not be drawn into the wall and rain will only penetrate as far as the wind drives it. Therefore water penetration to the bottom and sides of the wall is less critical than penetration at the top.

Straw bales can either be used to form the structure of the building, i.e. to be load-bearing, or as infill to an oversize timber-frame. This last method is the one most approved by building societies and the only one likely to release a mortgage.

LOAD-BEARING OR NEBRASKA METHOD

This is the original method pioneered by the Nebraskan farmers, from whom it derives its name. In this method there is no structural framework and the bales themselves take the weight of the roof. They are placed together as brick or concrete blocks would be in a masonry wall and pinned to the foundations and to each other with wooden stakes – hazel is most commonly used in the UK. They have a wooden roof plate on the top course, again fastened to the bales with stakes

8

and tied down to the foundations. The roof is then constructed on top of the roof plate. Typically this is a cut timber roof, but there is no impediment to using trusses. The roof covering is also a matter of choice, but it is often turf or thatch, which is probably more to do with enhancing eco-credentials than because they are intrinsically better materials. Timber shingles or reclaimed slates would work just as well. Whatever the roof covering, an extra eaves overhang is needed, up to 600mm, to ensure there is no rainwater penetration to the top of the wall.

Windows and doors are placed inside structural timber box frames, which are pinned into the bales with hazel stakes as the walls go up. To maintain stability and avoid bale-wobble, windows and door openings cannot take up more than 50 per cent of the wall's surface area and a wall cannot be more than 6m long unbraced.

It is now common practice to bind the bales with wire straps as the walls go up to prevent "bale-wobble" and help compress the bales until the roof is on. The weight of the roof tends to compress the bales and adds structural stability.

The advantage that this method has over other methods is that it is possible to learn how to build a bale wall fairly quickly and to undertake the construction as a DIY project. Which is not only fun and satisfying but also saves money. Our 'standard' house will need 400 to 500 bales at a cost of perhaps £3 to £3.50 per bale (delivered). Added to this will be the cost of coppiced hazel stakes and the other timber for door and window openings and wall plates – perhaps £1,000. A similar brick and block cavity wall will cost around £10,000 to build – and will not produce much fun.

LIGHTWEIGHT TIMBER-FRAME

This design idea was developed by Barbara Jones of Amazon Nails – the definitive source of information on straw-bale building in the UK – to retain the benefits of the load-bearing style and enable the roof to be constructed before the straw walls are built. The importance of protection from the weather throughout the construction process cannot be over-emphasised. Even slightly damp bales will rot. It is not uncommon to erect a scaffolding "tent" over the whole site to make sure it is fully protected from the elements.

This method uses a light-weight timber framework that needs temporary bracing and acrow props to give it stability until the straw is in place. The straw is an essential part of the structural integrity of the building, and still the main load-bearing element. Timber posts are located at corners and either side of window and door openings, and are designed such that the wall-plate at first floor and/or roof level can be slotted down into them once the straw is in place, thus allowing for compression on the bales. Compression of the bales is essential for the stability of the wall. Walls are constructed in such a way that the wall-plate and roof are kept 100mm above the finished straw wall height whilst the wall is being built, allowing for compressive settlement of the straw wall once the bracing and props are removed. A wall seven bales high will compress up to 50mm.

POST & BEAM

Essentially the same as any other post & beam construction. A structurally stable timber frame is constructed, up to and including roof covering, and straw-bales used as infill to the walls. In this case the straw takes no load bearing and is subject to less compression. As a result the bales are less stable and need to be well pinned in to the frame.

This method is the one preferred by architects and building societies. Being essentially traditional post & beam it is well understood and does not use what might be considered experimental construction methods.

Compared to either of the other methods it uses a lot of good quality timber and requires a high level of carpentry skill. It is not really for the DIY builder. The timber used in the frame does not need to be top quality oak or similar, as would usually be used in post & beam, as the frame is not exposed but it still needs to be good quality softwood.

Although more complex and expensive than the other methods it brings all the flexibility advantages of post & beam being more adaptable to extension or modification. The costs of taking down and rebuilding a straw wall is trivial.

THERMAL PERFORMANCE

All straw-bale buildings share the same high levels of thermal resistance. Building Regs require a U-value for external walls of 0.35. A typical bale of straw has a U-value of 0.13 – significantly better thermal performance than regulations require and as good as the German Passiv Haus standard with its high-tech, highly insulated walls.

More Information

The best source of information is Amazon Nails at www.strawbalefutures.org.uk who publish a very useful guide to building straw-bale houses and run regular courses on all the construction methods.

HEMP WALLS OR HEMCRETE

Using hemp as a building material is a fairly new idea. Hemp shiv (the waste product left when

8

the more valuable hemp fibre is extracted from the plant) is mixed with a lime binder to produce a filling and insulation for timber-frame walls. This mix is generally known as hemcrete. A plywood shutter is fixed around the timber-frame wall and the hemcrete poured and rammed in place.

There is some discussion over whether hemcrete is a structural material or not. It is generally used as a single-wall construction of 300mm thick at which thickness it is not strong enough to be structural and needs a timber-frame for stability. Used in this way it removes the need for a second skin to the wall and the structural improvement it provides means that a lighter timber frame can be used – 100mm rather than 200mm, which would be usual for a single skin timber-frame.

When the shutter is removed the surface of the hemcrete is ready to accept a lime render, internally and externally, and finished with limewash. As with other natural materials, hemcrete is a breathing material and needs breathable finishes to allow moisture to dissipate. Another effect of this is to move moisture away from the timber frame, protecting it from decaying influences and increasing its longevity.

Most importantly hemcrete provides excellent thermal performance. The actual thermal resistance will vary with the mix, proportions of hemp to lime, but approximate U-values are :

■ 300 mm wall 0.29 W/m^{2}K

■ 400 mm wall 0.22 W/m^{2}K

■ 500 mm wall 0.18 W/m^{2}K

Remembering that the Building Regs Part L call for a maximum U-value of 0.35, even 300mm is a 30 per cent improvement and 500mm is close to Passivhaus standard.

A result of combining lime and hemp is to allow it to act as a carbon sink. As the hemp grows it absorbs CO_2, which would normally be released as the plant decays. Mixing with lime prevents, or at least delays, the decay and data from Lime Technology Ltd suggest that 50 Kg of CO_2 can be locked up per $1m_2$ of hemcrete walling (at 300mm thick), which in addition to embodied energy savings is a useful one-off carbon saving

This one-off skewing of the carbon cycle is a useful bonus, using materials that lock-in carbon in its unoxidised state, and preserving it there, warm and dry, for the foreseeable future. This may only be a postponement of its inevitable rotting or burning, but it is postponed for at least the life of the building. Hemcrete, like most natural materials, is eminently recyclable. The hemcrete can be broken up, mixed with more lime binder and reused. So the delay in releasing the locked-in carbon could go on for quite a long time.

8

The argument applies equally to all plant materials and can be extended to using as much timber as possible for construction. It is also the best, possibly only sound, argument for paper recycling.

More information
■ Lhoist UK Ltd www.lhoist.com
■ The Hemp Lime Construction Products www.hemplime.org.uk
■ Ralph Carpenter, Modece Architects, Bury St Edmunds.

Further Options
The three methods discussed are, perhaps, the most popular options. Cob has a long tradition stretching back 500 years and is being actively revived. Straw is a comparative newcomer being only around 100 years old. It has a good deal of enthusiastic support as it is a material that is readily available, easy to work with and that locks-in CO_2. Hemcrete is a very new idea (using old materials), and brings together many of the benefits of the other two. But there are more options :

■ Rammed earth – as the name implies, earth is rammed into a shutter to form the wall. Very similar to cob but tends to be used in chalky soils and is rammed almost dry.

■ Cob blocks - again as the name implies, cob (clay and straw mix) in block form. These have been produced for many years principally as a repair material for pre-existing cob buildings. New build with cob block is gaining popularity as it provides all the advantages of cob, but without the labour-intensive construction process (but with proportionately higher cost).

■ Unfired Clay blocks – there is a good deal of research into unfired clay blocks, by people like Hanson, Ibstock and Plymouth University, and as such it seems to have the backing to make it as a 'standard' building method. It is similar in many ways to the clay-lump or adobe, the universal mud brick. Adobe is found mostly in East Anglia where it has been used since the end of the 18th century. Construction is similar to brickwork with regular bonded courses, but the dried blocks are much larger and are usually laid in a mortar of clay, rendered over with more clay or, more usually, lime.

■ Wattle & daub – a method that everybody learnt about at school. Most usually wattle & daub is used as infill to a post & beam structure. A woven panel of oak or hazel (the wattle) is fixed in place and "daubed" with a mixture of clay or earth with straw and dung. Does not really have anything going for it as it is non-structural, a poor insulator, labour intensive and uses a lot of dung

8

EARTHSHIP

An Earthship is essentially a combination of rammed-earth and old tyres. Tyres are stacked in a brick-bond manner and earth or clay rammed in. It therefore offers the advantages of a rammed earth structure with the stability during building of a bonded wall. Earthships have evolved over the last thirty years from the pioneering work of Michael Reynolds, who now runs Earthship Biotecture in Taos, New Mexico, selling the idea and some designs

Houses are designed to use thermal mass and have lots of south-facing glazing, passive ventilation and renewable energy for heating and power and rainwater harvesting.

Internal, non-load-bearing walls are often made of recycled cans or bottles joined by mortar and lime plaster finished. This construction allows for a thinner wall than using tyres would.

The first Earthship in England was a community centre built in Brighton in 2001. There is no question that the idea works – rammed earth technology has worked for hundreds of years. Earthships seem to just add tyres to a well recognised building system.

That is not say it is a bad thing, or that the work of Biotecture is pointless. Quite the reverse. Putting a new spin on an old idea is often very beneficial and what Earthships bring to the party are two things: the notion that this very old technology has a place in the twenty-first century and that adding renewable energy and rainwater harvesting in a well orchestrated design brings that higher level of sustainability.

CONTAINER HOUSES

That's right, houses made from shipping containers. Even though they are cheap, strong and readily available, you have to wonder why.

It is true that they are immensely strong (they are built to withstand ocean crossings, after all) and that they are made from largely recycled steel. It is also true that they have been used to replace many homes lost in the Florida hurricanes. But they are still a long, narrow, low steel box. At best they provide a shell that needs all of those other things that go to make up a house – doors, windows, stairs, insulation, walls, floors, ceilings, electrics, plumbing, etc. etc.

They are touted as a Green Alternative, one American supplier even suggest they are the most environmentally sound housing option, but they are not. In terms of sustainable house building what they actually replace is the timber in a timber-frame house. Everything else remains the same.

Conclusion

With our increased awareness of the effect we have on the planet

8

it is perhaps not surprising that there is a burgeoning movement to construct our homes from materials that are from the earth; using methods that are simple, non-invasive and self-reliant. They are all ancient methods, in some cases modified by modern understanding and technology, in some cases exactly as they have always been.

The fact that they work in providing comfortable, affordable housing has been proven over centuries. The fact that they present problems in meeting regulations says more about the blinkered thinking of the regulators than it does about the materials and methods.

The 2010 Building Regulations switch the emphasis from a simple elemental U-value compliance (walls must be no more than $0.35W/m^2$, roof $0.16W/m^2$, etc.) to an overall reduction on potential CO_2 emissions. That is, a reduction on a notional house of the same size built to 2006 standard. Which is good news for anyone wishing to use these old, traditional building methods.

CO_2 emissions are calculated on thermal resistance and fossil fuel consumption. A cob or straw bale house, for instance, will have good thermal performance, even though the elemental U-values will not be great. So even if the house is heated by an oil-fired boiler, it still has a good chance of passing the SAP calculation test.

Are traditional, sustainable construction methods still just a dream? It still depends on how determined you are.

9 HEAT AND POWER FOR FREE

I n Hinduism nirvana can be defined as an ideal condition of rest, harmony, stability and joy. A state similar to that enjoyed by people with free energy. Having free energy, at least enough to run the house, is fast becoming the nirvana, the ultimate goal, and it is surrounded by the same mysticism. The reality is that, unlike that harmonious state of mind, you only need two things to get free energy:

■ To be in the right location
■ Have enough money to fund it.

Free energy involves some decision-making, and sometimes hard choices. But, if we project forward even 10 years it may be that what seems like a hard choice now will, in hindsight, seem a no-brainer.

Of course obtaining free energy will have a cost. It will require a significant investment in renewable energy technology, and in reducing energy consumption, but it may turn out to be the cheap long-term option. It has to be accepted that there are few short-term benefits to renewable energy. Even with Feed-in Tariff payments it is still five to 10 years before we get full payback. It is an investment for the long-term benefit – financial and environmental.

If you are reading this book then the probability is that you own or are buying your own home. Ask yourself why you are doing that? Why not rent and save all the responsibility of ownership, the expense involved in the act of buying and the on-going cost of maintaining your house? The answer probably is for the security it brings, for the investment, and because in the long term it is far cheaper than renting. Rent is lost money. It goes to the landlord to pay his mortgage. He gets the long-term benefit of the investment, the profit, because he had the financial means.

The same argument can be applied to energy. Buying energy – electricity from the grid, oil or gas for the boiler – is cheaper in the short-term because it involves little or no capital investment. In the long-term the profit goes to the energy company. Conversely investing in renewable energy

HEAT AND POWER FOR FREE

equipment has a significant capital cost but adds value to the property, brings security from rising energy prices and produces energy at a lower unit price. So much so that it is now (under the new Feed-In Tariffs – see Chapter 5 – Renewable Energy) possible to make a profit.

The problems to be overcome in achieving our nirvana are different for the self-builder and the renovator, but both have to deal with the same initial issues.

HOW MUCH ENERGY IS NEEDED?
Before setting out on the quest for free energy there are three questions to be answered:
■ How much energy is needed – that is, how much does the house consume, how much electrical energy and how much heat energy.
■ How much renewable energy equipment can be afforded?
■ How much energy do you want to produce? Meeting the needs of the house, a proportion of those needs or exceeding those needs with a view to producing an income stream? Obviously this relates to available budget, and to the resources available on the site – is there wind or water, for instance?

CALCULATING ELECTRICITY CONSUMPTION
Put simply you don't calculate, you read the meter. It is possible to establish the demand of each piece of electrical equipment in the house, and to take a guess at how long it is used for each day or week, and thereby get an estimate of the total annual consumption, but it is far easier, and far, far more accurate to look at the bills and read the meter.

Even if you are moving to a spanking new house your consumption is likely to remain pretty much the same (unless you are changing from gas to electric cooking and heating) as consumption tends to relate to the people in the house rather than the house itself. If you are changing to electric cooking and heating it should be fairly easy to obtain estimates of annual consumption for those new pieces of equipment and add that to the figure.

Find the oldest electricity bill with an actual reading on it – not an estimated reading. Read the meter today, subtract one from the other and you have the actual consumption for the period from the date of that bill. Hopefully that old bill is more than a year old and you can then calculate the actual annual energy consumption.

The UK national annual average consumption is 5,000kWh per year per household. Which, like all averages, is a bit misleading as it takes in houses large and small, with single and multi-occupancy. But it is surprising the number of times a figure between 5,000 and 7,000 comes up as the actual consumption and therefore we will take 6,000kWh p.a. as our working figure.

9

CALCULATING HEAT ENERGY

The energy needed for space heating in a new-build is a relatively simple calculation of energy consumed per square metre floor area, multiplied by the floor area.

A house built to 2006 Building Regs, Part L1A should consume not more than 55kWh/m²/year, but this assumes good quality control systems and that the drawings and specification have been strictly adhered to. That is the way the figures work out when the elemental U-values are applied to calculate the heat loss from the house. It takes no account of casual heat gains (from lighting, boiling the kettle, making toast, generally living in the house) or from solar gains. The actual demand is therefore likely to vary from 55kWh/m² but a cautious approach would lead us to accept that figure.

There is an issue here to deal with the difference between design U-value and actual U-value. Take a typical brick-and-block wall as an example. A design U-value of 0.35W/m² (complying with current Building Regs) will require an outer skin of brick, a 50mm cavity, 70mm of PUR insulation, and an inner skin of insulating blocks. Calculating that U-value across that wall assumes that there are no gaps between insulation boards and takes no account of the mortar between the blocks, nor of the cold bridges created by the cavity ties. The calculation assumes an homogenous, perfectly constructed wall, which is seldom, very seldom, the actuality. A survey carried out for NASA in the early 1990s found that gaps in insulation amounting to five per cent of the total area of insulation accounted for 50 per cent of the heat lost.

The real U-value for a wall constructed in that way to normal quality standards is likely to be nearer 0.5W/m² than 0.35. The same problems will exist for all elements – the roof, the windows, the floor. Then the affect of wall and roof penetrations for pipes and cables need to be factored in to arrive at an accurate overall heat loss figure.

Some of the better U-value calculators take some of these issues into account and arrive at more accurate figures but it is difficult to know what the software is actually doing. In addition, the software can take no account of build quality on site. A sloppy bricklayer leaving thick joints and gaps in the mortar will have a serious impact on the actual U-value.

Historically this has not been a noticeable problem. Gas and oil-fired boilers are oversized as a matter of routine and can comfortably modulated their output to suit. A house with a probable peak load of 15kW will have a 25kW boiler that can modulate from 5kW to 25kW. The house stayed warm and energy was cheap so it did not matter that the design consumption was exceeded.

For the sustainable builder trying to improve thermal

9

performance build quality is a critical factor – striving to get that homogenous brick and block wall. It is one of the reasons that off-site manufactured houses do so well in this respect. Build quality is largely controlled in the factory and the repetitive nature of the process allows for improvements in design to have a real effect.

The answer is that there is no easy answer. Building a thermally efficient house requires attention to detail. Attention at the design and calculation stages and attention on site – far more attention than is the norm on a UK building site.

The typical route at the design stage is to calculate the heating energy consumption that results from the design. What the sustainable builder will want to do is set the energy consumption figure as a design criterion and design the construction of the house to suit. So the figure may be 55kWh/m² if we build to Building Regs standard, but may be down to 15kWh/m² if we go to Passivhaus standard.

Taking our 200m² house as the example, and sticking with the notional 55kWh/m² we then calculate heat loss at $200 \times 55 = 11,000$kWh/year.

We also need hot water for sanitary purposes – washing dishes, washing ourselves, etc. There is a law of physics which tells us that it takes 1.16 Watts of energy to raise 1 litre of water through 1degC.

Average hot water consumption is 50 litres per person per day. If we assume four people living in the house we need 200 litres. Incoming cold water is generally about 7degC and we will need to raise it to 65degC to kill legionella, so a 58degC temperature difference. Therefore the calculation is:

$1.16 \times 200 \times 58 = 13456$ Watts or 13.46kW

That energy is needed each and every day, as we need hot water each and every day. There will be variations for holidays, guests visiting and the like but the figures tend to work out across the year. We can also argue that the temperature of the incoming water can vary and that we only need 65degC once each week, but the generality remains true, and accurate enough for these purposes. So annual consumption is $13.46 \times 365 = 4,911$kWh/year.

The total energy demand for our example house is therefore:

Total demand 6,000 + 11,000 + 4,911 = 21,911kWh.

At this stage we make no distinction as to the fuel or resource to supply that energy. We

9

merely wish to get a handle on the size of the problem. We are setting the benchmark.

The other obvious benchmark is the CO_2 emissions from this house if all that energy comes from conventional sources. Let's assume that the electricity comes from the grid and the heat from a condensing gas boiler.

Each 1kWh of electricity from the grid produce 0.43kg CO_2

Each 1kWh of natural gas consumed in the house produces 0.19kg CO_2

You may wonder why there is such a significant difference when most power stations producing the electricity are running on natural gas. The answer is that the electricity coming out of the plug socket in the house is about 27 per cent of the energy that went into the power station. The rest, 73 per cent, being lost as heat and grid inefficiencies.

We need to factor in the efficiency of the gas boiler. A good condensing boiler will operate at around 85 per cent efficiency (for 10 to 12 years from new if it is regularly maintained). That means that to generate 11,000KWh of space heating and 4,911kWh of hot water will take $(11,000 + 4,911) \times 1.18 = 18,774$kWh of natural gas.

CO_2 emissions are therefore :

6,000kWh of electricity at 0.43kg = 2.58 tonnes CO_2

18,774kWh of gas at 0.19kg = 3.57 tonnes CO2

Total emissions = 6.15 tonnes CO_2 per year.

ENERGY CONSERVATION – POWER

This is the area that is focused on most clearly and most often by the Government and their various agencies. The reality is that it is the area in which we can make the least impact. There are three main reasons for this:

1. We start from a comparatively low threshold. Average consumption is about 5,000kWh per year. Most houses are not average (otherwise the average would be different) so let's say that the actual consumption is 7,000kWh. That is still less than half the energy needed for heating (space heating and hot water) in the conventional house.

2. Doing all the easy things has a small impact. Switching to all low energy lamps will save about 300kWh per year and switching stuff off rather than leaving it on standby another 250kWh (for the average house). Even changing appliances to A-rated efficiency is only nibbling at the edges. Taken together these measure might reduce overall consumption by 15 per cent to 20

9

per cent - not insignificant in money or CO_2 terms, but not huge. The reason we are urged to do it, and the reason we need to do it, is because of the disproportionate effect on CO_2 emissions that grid electricity has.

3. Consumerism. The annual average electricity consumption has risen by a fairly steady four per cent per year, every year since 1950. The reason being the stuff that last year we did not need but that now our lives would be empty without – MP3 players, mobile phones, fridges the size of a small bungalow, TV's in every room, hot tubs, games consoles, the list goes on. So even if we go to the max in terms of reducing consumption the probability is that we will be back where we were in four to five years.

But it is not electricity consumption per se that is the problem, but the CO_2 emissions that using grid electricity causes (plus, of course, the embodied CO_2 in the stuff we buy). It is free electricity that we are striving for and that will, of its nature, have zero CO_2 emissions. The answer is not to deny ourselves the benefits and pleasures of living in the western world in the twenty-first century but to invest in the technology that allows us to enjoy those benefits responsibly.

It is also worth noting that low energy lamps (particularly Compact Fluorescent Lamps) might not be as good as the advertising suggest. Which will comes as a big surprise to us all. An 11W CFL is said to be equivalent to a 60W tungsten and an 23W CFL to a 100W tungsten, a ratio of about 4 or 5 to 1. New guidelines being proposed by the EU, and based on research by various agencies, including the Building Research Establishment suggest that a ratio of 3:1 is more accurate. Still a reasonable saving in consumption but a more powerful lamp will overcome the problems of CFL's being considered a dim idea (is that a pun?). Look for the Energy Star logo, currently about the best available.

ENERGY CONSERVATION – HEAT

Heat divides into space heating and hot water. Hot water is like electricity in that there is little we can do to reduce consumption. Living standards have change over time and we need more hot water. We can fit flow regulators and aerated taps, and those are good things to do, but like electricity a reduction of 15 per cent to 20 per cent in annual consumption would be a good result.

Space heating is a different matter. A sustainable builder or renovator may well be aiming at a better level of insulation than suggested by Building Regs Part L1A and therefore a lower energy consumption figure. If the ethos of setting the energy consumption as a design parameter, as

9

discussed in Chapter 1 – Design Right, is followed then the figure of 55kWh/m² can change to anything you like. A Passivhaus, for instance, would use a figure of 15kWh/m² and at that level the casual and solar heat gains become far more significant as they make a much greater proportional contribution to space heating. At Part L1A standard casual and solar heat gains will amount to only around 10 per cent to 15 per cent of the total space heating load – it will vary with glazing, orientation, etc. At Passivhaus standard those heat gains could get to 100 per cent of the total space heating demand – that is why it is called Passivhaus.

We might suggest that 30kWh/m² is a good target design parameter and that therefore the space heating demand is (200m² × 30kWh =) 6,000kWh. Let's assume that casual and solar gains amount to 1,500kWh meaning that we need to generate 4,500kWh of heat per year. At this level, and taking into account the issues discussed above around actual heat loss compared to design heat loss, it would be prudent to ignore these heat gains and assume a design heat load of 6,000kWh. Having said that, it depends on the glazing. Large areas of south-facing glazing can produce a much higher solar gain, potentially to the point where cooling is needed. That would need calculating accurately and factoring in.

It needs to be considered that reducing the heat demand to this extent has a cost, in extra design work, extra insulation and improvements in air-tightness. The actual cost will vary with the design of the house, the location and the construction method (improving air-tightness is much easier with SIPS, for instance, than with brick-and-block construction). If we assume an overall build cost of £1,200 per m² the extra cost of improving the thermal efficiency is likely to be less than 2.5 per cent, so less than £6,000

NEW CALCULATIONS

If we assume that the project achieves a 15 per cent reduction in electricity consumption and a 15 per cent reduction in hot water use, and that the proposed levels of insulation and air tightness are adopted then the total energy consumption for our example house is:

To reset the benchmark for CO_2 emission, hot water and space heating are still from a gas boiler at 85 per cent efficiency, (6,000 + 4,174) × 1.18 = 12,005kWh natural gas.

Electricity	6,000 less 15 per cent	= 5,100
Hot water	4,911 less 15 per cent	= 4,174
Space heating		= 6,000
Total consumption		= 15,274kWh per year

This represents a saving of almost 7,000kWh each year.

9

CO^2 emissions are then :

5,100kWh of electricity at 0.43kg	= 2.19 tonnes CO_2
12,005kWh of gas at 0.19kg	= 2.28 tonnes CO_2
Total emissions	= 4.47 tonnes CO_2 per year.

This represents a saving of over 2 tonnes CO_2 each year.

So an investment of perhaps £6,000 brings significant reductions in energy consumption, running costs and emissions, but the next steps will vary with the project.

THE SELF BUILDER

In the search for free energy finding a location with good wind power potential or even a stream good enough to support a hydro scheme makes eminent sense. The potential then exists to not only have enough free energy to run the house but perhaps to produce an income stream.

The challenge is to produce a total of 15,274kWh of energy, but it may be that the figure can be reduced still further with a little thought. The bulk of the energy goes in heating and hot water. A solar thermal system will produce around 60 per cent of the hot water demand, reducing the requirement to 1,670kWh. If we install a ground source heat pump with an annual average COP of 4 then the space heating load drops by a factor of four to 1,500kWh.

A house with an energy consumption requirement of 30kWh/m²/yr will need to be fairly air-tight. The Building Regs requirement is not more than 10m³/m²/hr. To achieve 30kWh/m² will mean achieving an air-tightness of around 5m³/m², at which level mechanical ventilation will be needed. That will add maybe 200kWh to the electrical energy consumption. If the house has a good area (up to 20m²) of glazing on the south-facing elevation adding heat recovery to the ventilation could save as much as 1,000kWh per year. That figure needs to come off the gross space heating load, before the COP factor is applied. That then brings the energy demands to:

Electricity	5,300kWh
Hot water	1,670kWh
Space heating	1,500kWh (but this is now electricity to run the heat pump)
Total	**8470kWh**

If the project is in the right location with access to good wind power or a reasonable stream,

9

then the problem is very small. An all electric house is the obvious choice and a 5kW wind turbine (given an average wind speed of more than 5m/s) will do the job nicely. As will a 1.5kW hydro turbine. Both would produce in excess of 9,000kWh each year. Chapter 5 – Renewable Energy gives more details of costs, but broadly a 5kW wind turbine will be around £25,000 installed and connected to the grid. The price of a hydro turbine will vary with the site.

A smaller, 2.5kW, wind turbine will produce about 4,000kWh per year. Which is obviously not enough but, under the new feed-in tariff scheme, such a machine would pay 26.7p per kWh generated, so £1,068. That sum would buy around 6,000kWh from the grid (at 2010 prices), more than enough to make up the shortfall. (The same applies to a 5kW wind turbine, so the larger machine would produce a small income as well as free energy).

As an alternative to buying electricity from the grid with our £1,068 we may choose to install a biomass stove with back boiler to make up the heating shortfall instead. Some electricity will still need to be bought from the grid as the turbine, big or small, will not meet peak demands in the house, but that should amount to no more than 2,000kWh at about £300. Assume the biomass stove/boiler replaces the heat pump and therefore needs to produce 7,670kWh of heating and hot water. Running on wood pellet the machine would consume around 1.6 tonnes of fuel each year. That would not qualify for bulk discount so price would be around £230 per tonne or £368 per year.

To summarise:

A 5kW wind turbine (or similar hydro turbine) with solar panel and a heat pump will meet all the power, heating and hot water demands of the house and produce an income of up to £2,000 per year. Costs will be £20,000 to £25,000 for the wind turbine, £4,500 for the solar panels and £6,000 for the heat pump. There may be ancillary costs relating to installation and grid connection but these will vary with the site.

A 2.5kW wind turbine, solar panels and biomass stove/boiler, will meet the heating and hot water demand, but come up short on electricity production. But the revenue received for generating the electricity will pay for extra electricity and the wood pellets AND leave a surplus of around £250. Costs will be £12,000 to £15,000 for the wind turbine, £4,500 for the solar panels and £4,000 for the stove boiler (although stove boiler prices can vary hugely).

Obviously the 5kW turbine option is more expensive (by a margin) but produces more income and is cleaner and more convenient than the biomass stove/boiler option. But both work. Both will do the job of providing 'free' energy for 20 years plus with different levels of

9

investment. But both are predicated on the availability of wind as an energy resource.

If a stream is available it is likely to be a better resource, although the installation cost can only be established with an on-site survey (which is why it is largely ignored here). The rule is; if the head is more than 5m head think about getting a proper survey done. If there is more than 10m head don't think about it, just do it. As a reminder head is the vertical distance the stream falls as it crosses the property and is unrelated to the horizontal distance the stream travels. For more details on hydro schemes turn to Chapter 5 Renewable Energy.

If neither wind nor hydro is available the only other option is solar power, which is dealt with in The Solar House, below.

There is one other option; to improve the thermal efficiency of the house still further, but a little caution is needed. If the all electric option is being considered, and by implication a heat pump installed, that will reduce the space heating energy demand quite significantly. Increased thermal performance does nothing to reduce the hot water and power demands so the proportional impact of the space heating load is quite small. If the levels of insulation discussed are adopted and a heat pump with a COP of 4 installed the space heating energy demand is 1,500kWh, compared to almost 10,000kWh for hot water and power. Increasing thermal performance may have only a marginal effect on the actual energy demands and if the energy comes from a renewable source the extra investment (which will not be insignificant) in design, extra insulation, air-tightness and the consequent improvements to build quality control may be misplaced.

What is attempted here is to provide an illustration of the thought process involved in arriving at a design that enables free heat and power. Whether the option is right for any given location cannot be determined here and what level of generation is right will be a matter for the self-builder.

REQUIRED INVESTMENT

The cost of the two options discussed in detail above, over and above the build cost for a Building Regs compliant house, will be in the order of:

All electric option

Improve thermal performance	£6,000
Solar thermal panels	£4,500
Wind turbine	£25,000
Ground source heat pump	£6,000

9

Heat recovery ventilation	£3,500
Total	**£45,000**

Turbine & Biomass option

Improve thermal performance	£6,000
Solar thermal panels	£4,500
Wind turbine	£15,000
Biomass stove/boiler	£4,000
Heat recovery ventilation	3,500
Total	**£33,000**

It must be noted that these figures are little more than guesstimates as the real cost would need to be established for each individual project. But they serve to give an order of scale.

REALLOCATING FUNDS

The immediate reaction to those sort of figures might be that it is a high price to pay, too steep, a bit salty, can't afford it. But it needs to be seen in the context of an overall build cost. Average build costs for the self builder tend to be in excess of £1,200 per m^2 so our 200m^2 house will cost £240,000. The extra for 'free' energy is then just 14 per cent or 19 per cent which is possibly less than some self builders will spend on the kitchen.

But consider, does the sustainable self builder really need 200m^2? And 200m^2 is actually on the small side for the self builder.

Returning to our mantra, our definition of sustainability – meeting our needs without impacting on the ability of future generations to meet their needs – it starts with meeting our needs. Not exceeding them, not building a house as a status symbol, not building what is not needed. Size is important. Each square metre of a conventional house will embody 0.4 tonnes of CO$_2$. So building a house that meets our needs and designing in the flexibility to meet changes to those needs may be the way to go.

It also needs to be considered that the self-build will, almost by default, be cheaper than a comparable house built by a developer as the self-build extracts the developer profit element (and replaces it with sweat, frustration and anxiety). That profit element is often around 20 per cent of the build cost so it might be considered that there is a bit of elbow room in the budget.

Taking the average build cost of £1,200 per m^2, and assuming that £240,000 is an immoveable budget, paying for the free energy

9

option could be done by reducing the size of the build by just 37.5m^2 for the most expensive option. A house of 162m^2 is not so much smaller than a 200m^2 house – almost unnoticeable to the outside world – and it will have 15 tonnes less embodied CO_2, and free energy (with the consequent increase in value that that will bring) at the same build cost.

THE RENOVATION

A renovation project is more difficult to deal with as the term can cover everything from an urban Victorian terrace to a rural barn conversion. And everything from a redecoration to a complete rebuild. But the rules are largely the same, it is their application that varies.

Insulation is still king and improving thermal performance is the primary requirement. The problem is establishing the existing thermal performance so as to judge the level of improvement needed. This is where investing in a U-value calculator will be useful. There are a few available on the internet, Build Desk being a good one and free to download – although a bit complex to use. The various bits of software will achieve various levels of accuracy but whatever they achieve is better than a finger-in-the-air guess. They at least provide a baseline from which to work.

The rules for power and hot water energy consumption remain the same as they apply to the people rather than the house. The calculations around heat loss and the amount of energy needed for space heating remain necessary and will be largely the same as for a new build, once the baseline figures are established. These then lead to the same decision-making process, first of which is the preferred level of space heating demand.

It is equally possible for the renovator to elect to achieve a given level of space heating energy consumption as it is for the self builder. And equally possible to implement all those other energy saving measures. But it may be more difficult, impossible even, to achieve the higher levels of efficiency available to the self builder. A pragmatic approach needs to be taken, and budget may play a part in this. The urban renovator is likely to have less access to renewable energy that the rural barn converter so investing more in improving insulation, reducing hot water consumption and limiting power consumption will make more sense.

For people still looking for their urban renovation project, finding one with a south-facing roof elevation make sense, to allow the installation of solar panels – thermal and/or PV.

AN ENERGY AUDIT OF THE BUILDING

The scale of the renovation will determine, to some extent, the potential to achieve a 'free energy' property. The place to start is with a full audit of the property.

■ What features of the property are useful to retain? Thick stone walls, south-facing glazing.

■ Which features aren't, and should be changed? Thin brick walls, single-glazed windows.

■ Does the property have a renewable resources, i.e. wind, water or solar power?

■ Is there a south-facing roof? How big is it and does it need roof lights?

■ Is more glazing needed to increase natural lighting?

■ Can passive ventilation be designed in?

■ Where are the draughts coming from and can they be blocked?

■ Is there good access to the roof to install insulation?

■ Is there access beneath the ground floor to install insulation?

The list will vary with the project and likely to extend as the renovator gets into the swing of it. All the relevant issues are discussed in various places in this book and it is a matter of approaching the audit with an open mind and an eye on completeness.

AN ENERGY-BASED RENOVATION PLAN

As with a new build, putting energy at the centre of the design is the best way to ensure that the energy needs are met. It has to be accepted that the urban terrace house is unlikely to be able to achieve 100 per cent free energy. The location, the proximity of neighbours, the fabric of the house all impose too many constraints to make it practically possible. At the other end of the scale the rural barn conversion can be as easy as a new build.

Putting energy at the centre of the plan allows full consideration of the opportunities and constraints.

Solar thermal is likely to feature in any renovation project. To put it another way, if solar thermal is not possible on this project, then you are probably renovating the wrong house.

Solar PV, on the other hand, requires a much greater area of south-facing roof to make a useful contribution, needs to be much closer to due south (solar thermal can be up to 40deg east or west of south and still be effective), and is far more expensive. The same issues apply to PVT and the suitability of these systems will vary with the project and the budget.

Wind power is unlikely to be available in an urban location but may well feature in a rural project. Similarly biomass, in the form of logs, is more likely to be available, perhaps even free, in a rural location. Many towns and cities still have smokeless fuel legislation, and while many biomass boilers have no smoke emissions, they tend to be limited to wood pellet as the fuel.

The key is to understand what the property has to offer; what is essential, what is achievable and what cannot be done, in terms of

9

energy conservation and energy production.

In terms of pure sustainability it has to be recognised that the renovator starts a step or two ahead of the new-builder. A renovation is effectively recycling all the material, and retaining the embodied CO_2, in the house. That advantage can be off-set by the greater design flexibility that the self builder has and the renovator therefore has to be more creative and, if the goal is free energy, more determined.

A good source of information on what is achievable and the problems that may need to be overcome can be found at the BRE renovation website: www.rethinkinghousingrefurbishment. co.uk

THE SOLAR HOUSE

The concept is for a house powered entirely by solar energy. The gross amount of solar energy available is largely the same across the UK., about 1.11kWh per square metre. There is some difference south to north but not enough to make a material difference, until you get to the extreme north. The problem is more to do with space. Having enough of it to install a large enough solar array.

There are fundamentally two ways of approaching the Solar House concept and both suffer with the same underlying problem; energy is produced when the property does not need much of it, and not produced when the property needs lots of it. There are a couple of solutions, as discussed in Chapter 5, using boreholes or Phase Change Material. But both add to the cost and neither are easy. The approaches are:

The piecemeal approach

This would involve passive solar energy (which is largely a matter of design rather than equipment), solar thermal energy and solar PV energy. A bit like old hi-fi systems where you get lots of different bits of kit and bring them all together with spaghetti-like wiring. This approach suffers in the same way in that the equipment will be from different manufacturers, and probably different suppliers, and will need to be brought together with pipes, hot water tanks and control systems, in a design specific to the property.

Producing sufficient heat energy will be the biggest problem with this approach, and consequently minimising heat demand, for both space heating and hot water, the key design issues.

The PVT approach

Effectively a unified system producing both heat and electricity, overcoming the problems

9

relating to specific plumbing and control systems. PVT produces lots of heat therefore less thermal improvement needed. The concept of PVT is to provide year-round energy so using seasonal heat storage is better understood.

The advantage the piecemeal approach has is availability. The PVT option is only available from a single supplier in the UK, and is imported from Germany. A number of other manufacturers are trying to develop the technology, notably Phillips and Sharp, but so far have nothing on the market and no forecast as to when products may be available. That presents the obvious pragmatic problem that if the sole UK supplier goes under then the unhappy owner has an unsupported system.

Whether the system is to be mounted on the roof or ground mounted, both approaches need a south-facing aspect. More than 5deg east or west of south and the efficiency begins to drop off – over 20deg and it gets worrying. As it does if the inclination falls outside parameters – the array will need to be between 30deg and 40deg from the horizontal to work well. Neither option is cheap and both will probably need a wood burning stove to top-up space heating in deepest winter,

The piecemeal approach will need high levels of thermal efficiency, ideally up to Passivhaus standard. The solar thermal system will typically be used primarily to produce hot water rather than for space heating. The house will rely on Passivhaus technology to retain heat and on passive solar heat, topped up with a small heat pump. The heat pump, and everything else in the house, will be powered by the PV array (the more heat required, the bigger the heat pump, the more solar PV panels needed, the greater the cost). There will be a need for a heat storage system but generally this will be short-term rather than seasonal – so a big hot water accumulator or thermal store. ('Big' will be defined by the house and the number of people in it, but generally in excess of 350 litres). Design and calculation are critical to success with this approach. The house will be reliant on the PV array and it will require a significant investment. Designing and building to minimise energy demand will be essential, as will calculating exactly the energy demands of the house.

The PVT approach assumes year-round heating, so the principal difference is the need for seasonal heat storage. The need for thermal efficiency is not so great, but still exists, as the PVT system will produce a lot of heat, especially in summer. Storing that heat requires different technology and adds significantly to the cost. Generally the system will be sized to meet the electrical demand and the heat taken as a bonus. This means that there can be a disparity between heat demand and available heat energy. In this case too much heat energy, which is entirely possible, can be a bigger problem than too little.

Anafsolar, an Italian company, have developed a PVT system than incorporated a heat pump to overcome this problem. The product is due in the UK market in mid 2011.

To put this in context, a PVT system producing 5,000kWh of electricity each year will also produce at least 15,000kWh of heat energy. The house we are considering has a demand for around 11,000kWh of heat energy to meet both hot water and space heating demands. An excess of 4,000kWh. The seasonal storage system, especially PCM, has a finite capacity, although boreholes offer greater scope in this respect. PCM certainly will fill-up, not be able to accept any more heat. The need will exist to maximise electricity production while the sun shines, to ensure the annual demand is met. But the system will also go on producing heat, whether it is wanted or not.

Heat can be dumped – to a pond or swimming pool or into the earth – but to avoid this waste needs careful consideration of heat consumption, and careful design of the house and the system.

It is likely that the best designed system will still fail to meet the peak space heating demand, for those really cold days in the depths of winter. A small, log-burning stove will suffice to meet the shortfall. While this means that the project is no longer a 'solar house', it still works.

PROBABLE ECONOMICS

Remaining with the energy demand figures set out for the new build project discussed above and implementing the suggested measures to reduce energy demands, the requirement is:

Electricity	6,000 – 15 per cent	= 5,100
Hot water	4,911 – 15 per cent	= 4,174
Space heating		= 6,000
Total consumption		**= 15,274kWh per year**

Option 1 – the piecemeal approach could work out as:

Extra house design costs	£5,000
Improve thermal performance	£6,000
Passive solar – design	£2,000
Heat recovery ventilation	£3,500
Air source heat pump – 3kW	£1,500
Solar thermal	£4,500

9

Solar PV – 7.5kWp array	£34,000
Heat storage	£1,200
Extra for pipes, controls, etc.	£1,500
Log burning stove	£ 500
Total	**£59,700**

It can be argued that some of these elements, notably heat recovery ventilation, log burning stove, improved thermal performance, could be included in the general build cost as they would be done anyway. And again, none of these figures are accurate for a given project but indicative of scale only.

In this case we assume that the thermal performance is close to Passivhaus standard and that the heat pump is linked to the heat recovery system. This means that an under floor heating system is not needed. The system will produce 6,000kWh electricity each year, enough to power the house and run the heat pump, if the energy is used very carefully.

We also assume that 50 per cent of the electrical energy produced is used on site and 50 per cent exported to the grid (as the PV array is not able to meet peak demand and electricity is produced at times when it is not needed in the house). Returns are then:

Generation tariff – 6,000kWh @ 36.1p	= £ 2,166 p.a.
Export tariff – 3,000kWh @ 3p	= £ 90 p.a.
Import cost – 3,000kWh @ 12.5p	= -£ 375 p.a.
Net Return	**= £1,881 p.a.**

The investment of close to £60,000 produces a super thermally efficient house that produces enough energy to run itself for up to 40 years, with zero CO_2 emissions and an annual income of £1,881 per year.

Consider that without that investment the same house is likely to cost around £1,700 per year to run, at today's prices. Therefore a difference of £3,260 per year.

Predicting how energy prices will rise over the next few years is a difficult business. Rise they will and the perceived wisdom is that it will be anything between 10 per cent to 20 per cent year-on-year. Even at the lower figure it means that real terms payback will be less than 15 years. At the higher figure payback will be under 10 years.

Option 2 – PVT approach

9

Improve thermal performance	£6,000
Heat recovery ventilation	£3,500
Air source heat pump – 3kW	£1,500
Solar PVT – 6kWp array	£30,000
Design costs	£2,000
Seasonal heat storage	£10,000
Log burning stove	£ 500
Total	**£53,500**

Again, none of these figures are accurate for a given project but indicative of scale only. The system will produce 5,000kWh electricity and potentially 15,000kWh of heat energy each year, meeting all the demands of the house but again the electricity needs to be used carefully. And that may not be a realistic option. Adding more simple PV may be needed, moving back towards a piecemeal approach but overcoming the electricity shortfall without producing excess heat. Improvements to thermal performance are reduced but an underfloor heating system may be an alternative to the air source heat pump. This will be a matter for the design of the house.

We also assume that 50 per cent of the electrical energy produced is used on site and 50 per cent exported to the grid. Returns are then:

Generation tariff – 5,000kWh @ 36.1p	= £1,805 p.a.
Export tariff – 2,500kWh @ 3p	= £75 p.a.
Import cost – 2,500kWh @ 12.5p	=£312.50 p.a.
Net Return	**= £1,567.50 p.a.**

Without the investment of £53,000 the same house is likely to cost around £1,700 per year to run, therefore a difference of £3,200 per year.

This option gives a real terms payback of nine years, being the compounded increase in running cost for a conventional house plus the income from the feed-in tariff. That figure does not include the Renewable Heat Incentive scheme payment, which is likely to be an increase in income equivalent to £300 per year.

CONCLUSION
Three things come out of this:

THE **SUSTAINABLE** BUILDING BIBLE

9

1. Heat and Power for "free", including the Solar House are possible, in fact they have been done. A building system has been developed in Denmark called Activhaus – which is just that.
2. It is not cheap.
3. It is not easy.

It is probable that within 15 years all new houses will make a trivially small call on the national grid for any form of energy. Building Regs and feed-in tariffs are aimed specifically at encouraging micro generation, and the use of renewable energy is becoming increasingly essential. As well as being an ecological and moral issue it is also a political and commercial one. House use 27 per cent of the nation's energy and are responsible for 24 per cent of the nation's CO_2 emissions. Dealing with these issues has more political impact (is more visible, more tangible) than dealing with cars and factory's. The house building industry is not hindered (or supported – depending on your point of view) by the strong political lobbies of the oil and motor industries. We are a softer target. And we are willing to fund, at least in part, the necessary changes ourselves.

The ultimate aim of renewable energy is not a largely pointless wind turbine bolted to the chimney, it is the 'free' energy house – the Activhaus – that makes a net contribution to the nation's energy demands. We are probably some way off renewable energy technology being the norm but in the 1960s central heating was a rarity, in the 1980s double glazing was the new idea. Now it is time for renewable energy and it will still be the early users that push, and fund, the development of better, more useful, more affordable machines. While we wait for that better technology we will still have a comfortable, attractive, valuable house that cost little or nothing to run.

HEAT AND POWER FOR FREE

9

APPENDICES

APPENDIX 1: WHAT IS THE LEGISLATION?

For the time being at least building a low energy home is, for the self-builder, a matter of choice. The 2010 Building Regulations have ramped up the requirements again but beyond that there is no legislation around building sustainably, and Building Regs have little on no impact on materials or design.

Planning Policy Statement 22 (in England) and Technical Advice Note, July 2009 8 (in Wales), requires or suggests that developments of 10 or more domestic properties produce at least 10% of their energy needs on site. Some local authorities, most notably Merton, have decided to increase this minimum requirement to as much as 25 per cent and this minimum requirement has been embodied in the 2010 Building Regulations (see section 3 – Building Regulations, below). Ruth Kelly stated, on behalf of the last Government, that all new homes built after 2016 (2011 in Wales) have zero carbon emissions and groups have formed all over England and Wales to discuss how this can be achieved. So far the answers are far from clear. The plan is to rack-up the minimum requirements under Building Regulations Part L1A on a 3 year cycle until zero carbon emissions are reached in 2016. By that time Wales will be independent of English Building Regulations (as Scotland already is) and will have set their own standards.

In addition a number of local authorities are now requiring that some new planning applications meet Code for Sustainable Homes level 4 as a minimum. Powys in Wales requires this for developments of three or more houses. Other authorities implement this is different ways.

It seems unlikely that this movement towards sustainability and energy efficiency will be reversed so the expectation has to be that achieving low energy housing for all house builders, and those carrying out major renovations and extensions, will become the norm. They will be come compulsory by 2016 in any event.

The Building Research Establishment (BRE) produces a booklet called The Green Guide to Housing Specification that lists and grades materials used in house construction. BRE is also responsible for drafting the Building Regulations on behalf of the Government and for producing the Ecohomes standard and The Code for Sustainable Homes. Currently there is no legislation around using sustainable materials in private house construction, merely encouragement in the form of these two standards. However, housing associations and any housing receiving local or central government funding have to achieve at least Level 4 under Code for Sustainable Homes.

As has been shown there is at least 44 tonnes of CO_2 embodied in the materials of the average house. Under 2006 Part L standards this amounts to nine years of CO_2 emissions. Under 2010 Part L standard nearer 12 years. It does not take a great leap of imagination to conclude that we can look forward to legislation around the sourcing and energy content of the materials we use.

For those wishing to investigate further the environmental impact of materials, Bath University publish an Inventory of Carbon & Energy, known as the ICE Database, V1.6a. It is available free to download or is published in hardcopy on a not-for-profit basis. The database lists all commonly used building materials (and a fair few less commonly used ones) and is available at www.bath.ac.uk/mech-eng/sert/embodied/

APPENDIX 2: EXAMPLE SAP CALCULATIONS

The Standard Assessment Procedure (SAP) was devised by the Government as a means of assessing the energy performance of a building. The SAP calculation gives a rating of one to 100 where one is the worst and 100 will indicate no heating/hot water cost. It is determined by comparing the Target Emissions Rate (TER) and the Dwelling Emission Rate (DER). The TER is calculated based on a notional building of exactly the same size and shape as the actual dwelling that conforms to the minimum energy performance requirements of the 2002 Part L1a, less 20 per cent. The DER is the emission rate for the property as designed. So the new dwellings must be 20 per cent more efficient than the previous minimum standards of 2002 Part L1A. The 2010 Building Regs ramp that up by a further 25 per cent on the 2006 Standard. It is possible to achieve a higher score than 100 with the use of micro generation where a property generates more energy than it uses and is a net exporter to the national grid.

THE STANDARD ASSESSMENT PROCEDURE

APPROXIMATE ENERGY RATING

Very energy efficient house   100

New house to 1996 regs   80

Average of UK housing stock   40

Typical 1960s-built house   30

Very energy inefficient house   1

In simple terms SAP calculations allow comparison of the energy running costs of dwellings anywhere in the United Kingdom, in a similar manner to the comparison of fuel economy in cars expressed in miles per gallon. A SAP calculation is normally a desk exercise. The client submits drawings, plans and specifications of the development to the assessor who then runs it through specialist software to get the result. This will come in two forms; a standard form and an Energy Performance Certificate, similar to those on fridges, washing machines and the like. The difference that

2010 Building Regs brings is timing. From October 2010 it is now necessary for the SAP calculation to be carried out and submitted with the Building Regs approval application, i.e. prior to work starting. The notion is that the building inspector will ensure that the house is built in accordance with the drawings and specification and that the SAP prediction is met.

SAP Calculations generally involve four stages:

1. Design: draft stage

From the plans and drawings the assessor prepares various bits of information; dimensions of walls, floors, windows doors etc. From the specification the assessor can calculate the thermal performance of each element - heat loss through floors, walls, roof, etc.

The assessor uses the specialist (and Government approved) software to complete SAP calculation, entering data on:
- The type of dwelling
- Floors
- Walls
- Roofs
- Openings (windows, doors, rooflights)
- Ventilation
- Main and secondary space heating
- Hot water generation
- Use of renewable technologies such as photovoltaics and solar water heating
- Lighting

There are in excess of one hundred data items involved in the calculation. The software determines whether the proposed dwelling will pass the Building Regulations Part L1A – and therefore be allowed to be built. The assessor is able to use the software to model different variations of the dwelling design.

The assessor then reports back to the client so that he can check that the information used in the assessment is correct. It also provides the opportunity to change the design and get a better rating.

2. Design: final stage

The client and the assessor agree a finalised version of the design, sometimes following several amendments to the initial design, and the calculation is repeated. The assessor will then provide the documentation needed for building control.

3. As built: draft stage

For new dwellings an air pressure test will normally be required, if the specification calls for a permeability of $10m^3/m^2/hr$ or less but as with all elemental values the design will need better permeability to get a good SAP result. The client reports back the results of the air pressure test to the assessor, together with confirmation from building control as to any variations from the previously agreed specification. The assessor then completes the As Built assessment – which if all went well with the build will still be a Pass.

4. As built: final stage

The assessor finalises the SAP calculation and creates the **On Construction Energy Performance Certificate (OCEPC)** – that provides a rating of energy performance based upon the dwelling as built. The OCEPC must, by law, be displayed in a new dwelling put up for sale on the open market.

A Carbon Index (CI) calculation is a relatively new method of rating a property's energy efficiency and thereby compliance with Part L1A. It measures the amount of carbon dioxide emitted by a property's heating systems. The CI is based on the CO_2 emission figure, but adjusted for floor area so that it is essentially independent of dwelling size for a given built form. It is expressed on a scale of 0.0 to 10.0, the higher the number the better the performance. A carbon index of 8.0 is roughly equivalent to a SAP of 100. The achievement of a specified level of the CI is proposed as one way of demonstrating compliance with the next revision of Building Regulations Part L1A.

The key issue in the SAP calculation is the DER, calculated from the design specification of the house in question (at the design stage, so it is not the actual emission rate) and both figures are given in kg of CO_2 per sq m of usable floor area. To demonstrate compliance the DER must be less than the TER and this constitutes a pass or fail of regulations 17A and 17B, and thereby a pass or fail of Part L1 as a whole.

The DER is effected by the following factors :-
■ Air permeability
■ Heating & ventilation systems
■ Insulation
■ Element U-values
■ Renewable energy

■ Glazing

It is possible to trade one off against another to achieve the desired DER figure, and there is a good software tool to help with this is at www.playtheregs.com It is very easy to use, and free, but it is not definitive and only provides an idea of what can be done. Ultimately a SAP calculation provided by an approved SAP assessor showing an appropriate DER figure is needed to comply with the regulation.

A full copy of the SAP specification, setting out exactly what is assessed and how, is available at www.bre.co.uk/sap2005 The document is 74 pages long, very difficult reading and goes to show that this is perhaps a misleading, not to say misconceived, way of assessing the energy performance of a house. It should also be noted that this assessment method only applies to houses of less than 450m², larger houses are assessed using standards set for commercial buildings, which are becoming even more stringent.

In summary, SAP 2005 is a compliance requirement that serves little useful function for the sustainable builder. The problem with it is that there is a danger that a PASS is considered good enough. For the sustainable builder a PASS is little more than a starting point.

The potential impact of the Energy Performance Certificate also needs considering. The example above shows a rating of C to D for energy consumption and D for environmental impact. This reflects a house achieving, broadly, compliance with 2010 Building Regs. Which, as of date of publication, is all that needs to be achieved to comply. It is often the case that the sustainable house will potentially achieve a far better rating but that the architect or builder will deliberately omit details from the drawings or specification to avoid the necessity of having those details inspected and approved by building control. The outcome is a house that actually performs quite well but has a D-Rating on the EPC.

This is all well and fine and plays the Regs quite well, at first glance. But consider, from 2016 ALL new houses will have a SAP rating of 100 and an A-Rating on their EPC. Ask yourself, how much discount would you need to persuade you to buy a similar house with a C or D-Rating? In this case playing the Regs may not be the smartest move. By 2020 there are likely to be up to 1 million homes in the UK with A-Rating.

APPENDIX 3: BUILDING REGULATIONS 2010

A complete version of the Building Regulations is downloadable from http://www.
ukbuildingstandards.org.uk/ It is published as a series of Approved Documents
which provide explanation and guidance around the meeting the regulations and
breaks the full regulations down into the following parts:

- Preparing for flood
- Basements for dwellings
- Broadband
- Part A – Structural safety
- Part B – Fire safety
- Part C – Resistance to moisture and weather
- Part D – Toxic substances
- Part E – Resistance to sound
- Part F – Ventilation
- Part G – Hygiene
- Part H – Drainage and waste disposal
- Part J – Heat producing appliances
- Part K – Prevention from falling
- Part L – Conservation of fuel and power
- Part M – Access to and use of buildings
- Part N – Glazing safety
- Part P – Electrical safety

The sections relevant to energy and sustainability for the house builder (and those carrying out major renovations) are Part C, Part F and Part LIA.

The current version came into force in October 2010 and is a revision of the Building Regulations 2006. The new Part L requires a step up of around 25 per cent in the energy efficiency of new builds on the previous Part L and it now also applies to major extensions and renovations as well as new build. A major extension is generally considered to be more than 50 per cent of the pre-existing floor area and a major renovation to be one that requires works to the fabric of the building envelope (walls, floor and roof) but not just decorative work.

A

Amongst many other things it increases insulation levels, requires improved air-tightness and increases the proportion of energy efficient light fittings.

PRÉCIS OF PART C

Part C deals with the Resistance to Moisture and Weather. So far as the sustainable builder is concerned it has a couple of effects.

The regulations require that the fabric of the building resists the penetration of water (rain or other precipitation – not flood water) through the roof, the top of an external wall, the bottom of an external wall and from the external surface of an external wall to the internal surface. At first glance no one would argue with any of this, we need to keep the rain out. But for a straw-bale, cob, post & beam or any single skin wall construction, including the renovation of a stone barn, it presents problems.

Water penetration through the roof and at the top of the wall is, in all cases, to be strongly resisted. Penetration from the bottom of the external wall, and from the external surface to the internal surface is another matter.

Take the case of converting a stone barn (that may have stood doing its job, being wind and water tight for 200 years or more). The walls will be single-skin stone, maybe 450mm to 800mm thick. The stone is likely to be laid in a lime mortar and the design of the wall is to allow rain-water to penetrate and to drain out of the bottom of the wall into the ground. It was recognised 200 years ago that lime and to a greater or lesser extent, stone, are porous and that it is impossible to prevent rain-water penetrating. The design did not have a damp-proof course at the bottom of the wall (although this technology existed 200 years ago and was used) as this would prevent the moisture draining out. The regulation insists that an injected damp-proof course be incorporated, irrespective of the fact that this will hold water in the wall, some of which at least will exit via the internal surface.

This rationale holds true for any single-skin construction being more of a problem for some construction methods – straw-bale, cob, post & beam – than others – single-skin timber-frame, single-skin block. The irony is that the majority of building control officers seem to recognise that it is an anomaly but feel bound to enforce the regulation.

A strict interpretation of the regulation will also not allow lime render as a weather-proofing coating as lime is, by its nature, permeable, which is why it is being used.

PRÉCIS OF PART F

Regulation F1 states that 'There shall be adequate means of ventilation provided for the people in the building'. There then follows a 53-page document setting out what 'adequate' means, and how to achieve it.

The regulation, like all the regulations, deals with all types of buildings from houses to factories and the ventilation requirements vary hugely with the type of building and what is going on in there. Factories can produce all sorts of pollutants, offices more than enough body-odour, restaurant kitchens excessive heat or moisture. The regulations have to deal with all these potential extreme conditions.

The house builder has to deal with just three issues:

■ Extraction from kitchen, bathrooms and utility rooms
■ Fresh air infiltration to habitable rooms
■ Meeting the air permeability standard set out in Part LIA

There are two basic methods of achieving this:

■ **Infiltration** – which is perhaps the normal method, using extractor fans and trickle vents. The regulations allow for windows to be opened to provide what is called 'purge ventilation'. That is the removal of extraordinary pollutants from, say, decorating or burning the dinner. Extractor fans have to be fitted to the kitchen, bathrooms and utility room and minimum standards are set.

Typically intermittent extractors are used (those that are only switched on when necessary) and in the kitchen need to have a minimum capacity of 60 litres per second (l/s) or 30 l/s if it is a cooker hood. Bathrooms need a minimum of 15l/s, as does a utility room. A WC (not in a bathroom) only needs 6l/s. The purpose of all these is to remove moisture and odour.

In addition, habitable rooms must allow outside air in, to refresh the internal air and to replace that air extracted. In the case of bathrooms, kitchens and utility rooms a 10mm gap on the bottom of the door is sufficient, for other habitable rooms a trickle vent is fitted, usually over the window. The regulations set a minimum height of 1.7m above floor level for the avoidance of draughts. Calculating the size of trickle vents is a complex process. It is based on the permeability of the building at 50 Pascal's and the infiltration needs to be at least 1/20th of the air leakage rate. (Air leakage is measured under positive pressure and infiltration is at normal atmospheric pressure – which explains the difference.) In addition the size of the room being ventilated is taken into consideration. The answer is to consult with the window supplier and / or architect who should be familiar with ventilation rates, trickle vents and the regulations, but the low energy house with better levels of air tightness will not have trickle vents in any case. See Controllable Ventilation below.

■ **Controllable ventilation** – Or mechanical ventilation systems, with or without heat recovery. If the regulations in Part L are stepped up as planned from the existing 10m³/hr to 3m³ per hour, mechanical ventilation will become essential. At below 5m³/hr there is insufficient air leaking into the house to dilute or remove the exhalation CO_2 and provide a comfortable atmosphere.

The minimum requirement is a ventilation rate of 0.3l/s per m² of internal floor area, which applies whatever type of ventilation system is installed.

The purpose of this regulation is to place emphasis on the need to control the ventilation. It follows from the air permeability regulations that if the rate at which air leaves the building is to be limited to provide greater thermal efficiency then the rate at which air enters the building must also be controlled. Mechanical ventilation systems not only control the amount of air entering the building, they can also control the moisture content, pollutants, pollen, and even the temperature. All of which are of course essential if the interior of the building is sealed off from the outside world.

Designing these systems is another complex business and will vary with the design of the house and the type of system being installed. The Approved Document provides guidance, but it is a matter best left to the experts. There are plenty of Mechanical Ventilation and Heat Recovery systems suppliers able to assist. It should be kept in mind that these systems seldom work well in retrofit situations. They need to be designed to the building and installed in the fabric of the building. Which is possible in a new build or a major renovation, but seldom otherwise.

All such system should be 'Appendix Q compliant'. This means that they have been tested to minimum standards and the rates at which the remove and inject air is accepted as fact. The figures for these system can then be safely included in the SAP calculation.

PASSIVE STACK VENTILATION

This is a whole house ventilation system that relies on pressure differential, internal to external, to draw air from the building. It does not use fans but ducting is installed to each room in the house (normally mounted on the ceiling) and connected to a roof stack. There is a basic requirement to have a long stack over a warm, wet room which allows convection currents to gain momentum and overcome external air pressure. Wind passing over the stack draws air from the ducts and thereby from the rooms (exactly the same principle as a chimney over a fire).

The BRE Innovation Park at Watford has an office building ventilated with a PSV with the

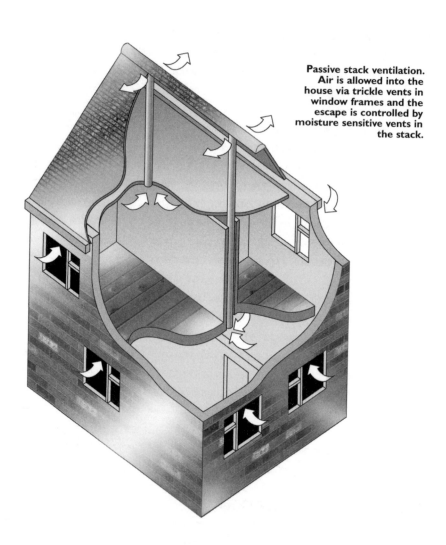

Passive stack ventilation. Air is allowed into the house via trickle vents in window frames and the escape is controlled by moisture sensitive vents in the stack.

stack built on the outside of the building. The external surface of the stack is made of glass bricks which allows the sun to warm the air in the stack and create stronger convection currents.

The system is becoming very popular with sustainable builders and is used extensively on the BedZed development, for instance.

Designed properly they provide effective ventilation with no energy input. Again design is the key issue and it will vary with each building. As with mechanical ventilation, it is difficult to install effectively in a renovation or refurbishment.

PRÉCIS OF PART L1A

Target CO_2 emission rate (TER)

The TER is the minimum energy performance requirement for new dwellings approved by the Secretary of State in accordance with Regulation 17B. It is expressed in units of kilograms per square metre of floor area per year ($kg/m^2/yr$) emitted as a result of the provision of heating, hot water, ventilation and internal fixed lighting for a "standardised" household.

The calculation of the TER is a part of the SAP calculation and can only be done by software approved by BRE.

Calculating the CO_2 emissions from the actual dwelling

This is the Dwelling Emission Rate (DER) and again forms part of the SAP calculation and can only be done with approved software. Although they use the term 'actual dwelling', they mean the dwelling at the design and specification stage. All the data used is the calculation is taken from the drawings and specification, including the anticipated air permeability. There is a reliance on the builder and the building control officer to check that the building is built as specified, with the exception of air permeability when a test certificate must be produced.

Secondary heating

If secondary heating, or provision for secondary heating (e.g. a fireplace), is specified it is assumed to be used and contribute a minimum 10 per cent to the overall space heating. It forms part of the DER calculation and the efficiency of the equipment to be installed is applied to the fuel used. The worst case is to not specify the equipment. So that if the drawings show a chimney and the specification states that there is a gas connection adjacent to the chimney but does not state which gas fire is to be installed, SAP calculation assumes that a gas fire will be fitted, that it will use the chimney and therefore have an efficiency of 20 per cent, with consequently devastating effect on the CO_2 emission rate.

Lighting

The regulation requires that a minimum of 25 per cent of all fixed light fittings are specifically for low energy lighting. That means that those fittings will not accept bayonet cap or Edison screw lamps. In all cases the DER is calculated using a fixed assumption of 30 per cent low energy lighting irrespective of the number of low energy light fittings actual specified. This is done so that lighting is not tradable, i.e. the builder cannot increase the proportion of low energy lamps and off-set this against poorer insulation.

Achieving the Target

By which they mean achieving a good DER and this section deals with the potential impact of installing renewable energy systems and how they can be a more cost-effective option than increasing insulation or improving air permeability. The way that U-values are used means that, however big the renewable energy system, it will not compensate for a poor building envelope.

Design Limits for envelope standards

The technical guidance to the Regulations state that 'to achieve the TER, the envelope standards for most of the elements will need to be significantly better than those set out in the following paragraphs'. In other words the U-value is no longer the standard of measurement. It is now the TER and ultimately the CO_2 emissions that count.

U-values

BR 443 sets out a convention for calculating U-values and sets limits for each element of :

	Area weighted	Limiting
Wall	0.3	0.70
Floor	0.22	0.70
Roof	0.16	0.35
Windows & doors	1.8	2.2

The area weighted figure is the one usually used and the one quoted on insulation and other products. In practice these figures have to be improved on to achieve a good DER (in the SAP example shown the figures are walls 0.20, floor 0.15, roof 0.16, windows & doors 2.20).

Air Permeability

'A reasonable limit for the design air permeability is 10m³/h/m² at 50Pa.' Which may or may not be a good thing (see Section 2 – Insulation). The major problem with this issue is that it is calculated at the design stage and the SAP rating (and Pass or Fail) is based on the design air permeability.

The actual permeability must be tested (by independent testers) and the design rate achieved. Testing is not, and cannot be, carried out until the building is virtually complete, for obvious reasons. The consequence is that failure to meet the designed air rating will result in expensive remedial work.

The Regulations do allow a get out clause. If the specification calls for a design air permeability of 15m³/h/m² then testing is not required. However, if this route is taken then good insulation and/or renewable energy will be essential to achieve an acceptable DER.

DESIGN LIMITS FOR FIXED BUILDING SERVICES

Heating and Hot Water Systems

In terms of traditional heating systems, nothing less than a condensing boiler with an efficiency rating of more than 86 per cent will produce figures to enable a good DER. Heat pumps and biomass boilers will both qualify but heat pumps are not so favoured in 2010 Building Regs. It has been recognised that they typically use electricity from the grid which has a significantly higher CO_2 emission rate than, say, natural gas in a condensing boiler. This higher emission rate is reflected in the SAP calculation fixed data meaning that a heat pump alone will not be enough to get a good DER.

Insulation of pipes, ducts and vessels

This relates to the primary heating pipes (flow & return), ducting to mechanical ventilation and hot water storage tanks. In effect all of these items have to be insulated to the manufacturers specification – which is usually 15mm of pipe lagging.

Mechanical Ventilation

This sets out minimum standards for the provision of mechanical ventilation. So far as extract fans are concerned it is largely complied with by the manufacturers. Similarly, manufacturers of heat recovery systems ensure their products comply. The real question is by how much they exceed the regulation.

The minimum requirements are :-
- Specific Fan Power (SPF) for continuous extract   0.8 litres/s.W
- SPF for balanced systems (mechanical ventilation)   2.0 litres/s.W
- Heat recovery efficiency   66%

Mechanical cooling

On the basis that no house in the UK with any pretensions to sustainability will have air conditioning, this section is omitted. If you need air conditioning you have got the design wrong and need to start again.

Fixed internal lighting

To provide compliance at least 25 per cent (but not more than 30 per cent are counted) of the light fittings in habitable spaces (not cupboards) must be dedicated low-energy fittings. That is fittings that will not accept bayonet cap or Edison screw lamps. Fluorescent, compact fluorescent and LED lamps qualify.

A slight anomaly in the regulations is that these dedicated fittings are generally B-rated in efficiency terms, having a luminosity of perhaps 40 lumens per circuit watt. It is easily possible to buy Edison screw and bayonet cap compact fluorescent lamps with luminosity of 52 to 60 lumens per circuit Watt and A-rated, but that do not comply. This anomaly is set to change under 2010 Building Regs, and in light of the legislation around the availability of tungsten filament lamps.

Fixed external lighting

This is defined as lighting that is fixed to the external surface of the dwelling and supplied from the occupier's electrical system. There are two options available:

■ Lamps that are not more than 150W and that have PIR movement and daylight controls.
■ Lamps that are more than 40 lumens per circuit Watt (the same as used internally).

Lighting not fixed to an external surface of the dwelling, e.g. lighting to the drive, garden lights, etc. are not covered by this regulation and there are plenty of solar powered options available.

Limiting the effects of solar gains in summer

The purpose of this regulation is to limit the use of air conditioning (See Mechanical Cooling above). Solar heat gains form part of the SAP calculation and are a factor of the size and orientation of windows and the amount of shading. The installation of high thermal mass in front of the windows will also be a factor by allowing heat to be absorbed.

The light-tight structures currently being advocated, together with low levels of air movement and high levels of insulation tend to use lots of glass to reduce the load on the heating system. It is very easy to go too far, or to plan poorly for summer conditions and find the house intolerably hot. The use of glass to encourage passive solar heat gains is a good idea but the design needs to incorporate shading in some form for the summer months.

The shading can be internal or external, curtains or blinds, fixed or moveable, or indeed natural (deciduous trees planted an appropriate distance from the house).

If reducing the amount of glass is taken as a measure to reduce the solar heat gain, the design may run foul of the requirements for minimum daylighting.

Quality of construction – Building fabric

The regulation concerns itself with only two issues:
- the insulation be reasonably continuous over the whole building envelope.
- the air permeability be within reasonable limits.

Continuity of insulation

This section refers to the avoidance of thermal bridges (see Chapter 4), and for the first time appears in the Regulations. It sets out that insulation must overlap at joints in building elements (e.g. floor and wall) and at the edges of elements such as around window and door openings.

In addition the builder has to demonstrate that there is an adequate inspection system in place to ensure that the insulation is installed as specified. This effectively removes the burden from the building control officer and places it on the builder.

Air permeability and pressure testing

(See Air Permeability above). This section goes to some length to determine what must be tested and how it is to be done.

What comes from this section is that failing the pressure test does not automatically mean failing Part L if the measured test result is better than 10m³ per hour and the TER is still met. In reality if the design calls for low permeability there is a reason for it and failing to meet the design requirement means that the design fails, even if it passes Part L. To put it another way, if the design is for a light-tight structure, the builder has to be sure to achieve it, and that means two things:
- Far more attention to construction detail than the average builder is used to, and
- a return to wet plastering (board and skim is not air-tight as skim cracks and cracks leak).

Alternative to pressure testing on small developments

A small development is defined as one with no more than two dwellings. In this case there are two options:

■ Demonstrate that a dwelling of the same design has been constructed by the same builder within the previous 12 months and that that dwelling passed the pressure test

■ Adopt an air permeability of 15m³ in the SAP calculation

This last is an interesting idea. If we are building, say, a green oak frame house, which will be inherently leaky in time, as the oak dries and shrink, we might naturally design in a biomass heating system to compensate for that long-term leakiness. In which case trying to achieve an air tightness of 10m³ or less is of no real benefit. If it is achieved today, it is unlikely to be the same in 10 years time. So adopting that higher air tightness figure of 15m³ / hr means that we can design in the higher heat load that is likely to be needed in 10 years time, avoid having the test and save the test fee.

Commissioning of heating and hot water systems

The regulation requires that heating and hot water systems are commissioned by a suitably qualified person to certify that the plant and system is working in accordance with the manufacturers specification.

Operating and maintenance instructions

This regulation is given the same weight as all those foregoing. The requirement is that the builder provides a manual setting out sufficient information about the building and its fixed services (heating, ventilation and lighting) and their maintenance so that the building can be operated in a way as to use no more fuel than is reasonable. The manual must give specific reference to the systems and equipment actually installed in the building, rather than generic equipment of a similar type. This information then forms part of the Home Information Pack and must also include the SAP rating.

Building Regulations Parts L and F – Proposed changes to be implemented October 2010

The changes being implemented are being lauded as the first substantive legislative step on the road to zero carbon homes. In the last week of August 2009 the Labour Government re-affirmed its commitment to the idea of all new homes being zero carbon from 2016 and that these changes were the route map to achieving that. The focus of the new regulations is entirely on reducing carbon emissions, but the method they are adopting to achieve it is not what we expected.

The anticipation was that insulation levels would be stepped up, U-values, air-leakage and construction detail would all be changed.

But in fact all those factors, with the exception of construction detail, remain just the same. The elemental U-values for floor, walls, roof, windows & doors and air-leakage are all exactly the same as they were in the 2006 Building Regs. But they are now termed 'backstop' figures. That is, figures below which you must not fall. The reality is that if you design to those backstop figures you will not pass the SAP calculation and without that you don't get Building Regs approval.

The changes that have been wrought are more subtle, more tricky than simple things like U-values. The whole document is now a lot more technical than it was. It has always been a difficult document but its removal from access by the common herd is now complete. Experts are now needed to interpret and implement.

More information is required at the design stage, principally this amounts to a SAP calculation that gives a PASS. To achieve a Pass the SAP must show a minimum 25% improvement of Target Emission Rate (TER) over a notional 2006 standard Dwelling Emission Rate (DER) – more of this later. Until now, submitting a SAP calculation anytime prior to completion of the building was acceptable. Now an acceptable SAP must be submitted prior to Building Regs approval being granted and work commencing. What this means is that rather than CO_2 emissions being a consequence of design, they now become a design criterion.

Building control officers have been given more powers to test and enforce in an attempt to ensure that buildings are built and perform as specified. Most usually they don't. Poor quality materials, poor attention to detail, poor craftsmanship are all too common and all lead to a house that fails to perform as specified. The difficulty is that we don't know how much they fail by because we don't test. The zero carbon target is universally accepted as a stiff challenge and it means, above all things, that the building must perform as specified.

Which is why the focus in the Building Regs has shifted to the TER. It relates directly to CO_2 emissions. The requirement is that the building achieves a 25 per cent reduction on CO_2 emissions compared to the 2006 Regulations. There will be a new set of Building Regs in 2013 and these will have a flat rate of emissions rather than a percentage reduction. Insulation, air leakage rates, installed appliances, heating fuel, these all influence the SAP calculation and are used to establish the TER but only so far as their CO_2 impact is concerned. And the designer can look outside Part L1A for help. Part F – dealing with ventilation – sets out that using Appendix Q approved heat recovery systems will achieve up to 8 per cent CO_2 saving. Part G – dealing with water use – sets out similar savings if maximum water use is restricted to 125 litres per person per day (less hot water, less energy used). The biggest saving comes from using Accredited Construction Details to deal with thermal bridging, but again you have to prove that the detail has actually been constructed.

Conversely heat pumps have fallen out of favour. As they use mains electricity, although they use less energy than, say, a gas boiler, they can emit more CO_2 as grid electricity is massively inefficient. This has now been recognised and heat pumps get no better treatment than conventional boilers, in terms of the SAP calculation.

What these proposed Building Regs do is force us to design a house that performs to a given level of energy efficiency and given rates of CO_2 emission, and then build the house as it is designed. It will mean designing the house, doing the SAP calculation (at a cost), changing the design in light of the result, doing the SAP calculation again (at another cost), maybe changing the design again... and so on until we get it right. Practice and familiarity will shorten the process but it is only four years until there will be a whole new set. Maybe when we get to 2016 and zero carbon homes they will leave the Building Regs alone as there is nowhere else to go.

APPENDIX 4:
A PRÉCIS OF THE ECOHOMES STANDARD

Acomplete version of the Ecohomes standard is downloadable from www.ecohomes.org . From April 2007 the Code for Sustainable Homes replaced Ecohomes for new housing in England. It is still relevant to some extent but Ecohomes will gradually fade away across the whole of the UK as CfSH becomes the de facto standard. A somewhat shorter précis is provided, just in case the reader might bump up against it.

The Ecohomes standard is a step beyond Part L and moves from simple energy efficiency to a level of sustainability, dealing with all the principal issues:

- ■ Energy
- ■ Transport
- ■ Pollution
- ■ Materials
- ■ Water
- ■ Land Use and Ecology
- ■ Health and Wellbeing
- ■ Management

The standard has been devised by Buildings Research Establishment to 'balance environmental performance with the need for a high quality of life and a safe and healthy internal environment'. Points are awarded for a level of attainment in each category so that the standard is not a simple pass or fail but properties are rated through a fairly complex assessment process from Pass to Good, Very Good and Excellent.

Points are awarded for each element of the standard with greater weighting being given to some areas than others. Equally some areas are easier to deal with than others. For instance 1.83 points are awarded for installing all A-rated white goods (fridge, freezer, washing machine etc.) and virtually the same, 1.82 points, for reducing surface water run off. The first will probably be done as a matter of course, with only a trivial cost implication and the second will require thought, planning and not inconsiderable cost.

The assessment is carried out at the design stage and the normal process is for the owner / builder to decide what rating they want to achieve (Pass to Excellent) and use the services of an Ecohomes assessor to scrutinise the drawings and specification and suggest how best to achieve the desired rating. The maximum number of points available for each element is shown to give an idea of the influence of each element.

The Ecohomes standard covers all the main points of a sustainable build. It can be argued, with some justification, that some of the standards need a bit of re-consideration; water use would be a case in point. But if nothing else, Ecohomes provides a yardstick that the sustainable self-builder can measure their design by. You also get a pretty certificate with sunflowers on it to hang in the hall.

APPENDIX 5:
A PRÉCIS OF THE CODE FOR SUSTAINABLE HOMES
A complete version of the Code is downloadable from www.breeam.org

From April 2007 the Code for Sustainable Homes replaced Ecohomes for new housing in England. Ecohomes continues to be used for refurbished housing in England and for all housing in Scotland and Wales, but is predicted to be replaced by the Code by 2012.

The Code goes a step further than Ecohomes in setting out minimum standards for six main aspects of the property and the construction process.

■ Energy efficiency /CO_2
■ Water efficiency
■ Surface water management

THE **SUSTAINABLE** BUILDING BIBLE

- Site Waste Management
- Household Waste Management
- Use of Materials

The Code steps-up on Ecohomes in a number of ways: it introduces minimum standards for energy and water efficiency at every level, it uses a simpler system of awarding points, the weighting system is removed, it introduces new areas of sustainability such as Lifetime Homes and composting facilities.

The Code currently sits alongside Ecohomes and the planning system and is set to become an intrinsic part of planning and building regulation compliance control.

The Code uses a sustainability rating system – indicated by 'stars', to rate the overall sustainability performance of a home. A rating of one star to six stars is available. One star is the entry level – around 10 per cent above the level of 2006 Building Regulations – and six stars is the highest level – reflecting excellent performance in sustainability terms and specifically zero carbon emissions.

The following is an extract from the Code technical guidance to give an idea as to what the standards are.

Minimum standards		
Code Level	**Category**	**Minimum Standard**
	Energy/CO$_2$	
1(★)	Percentage improvement over	10%
2(★★)	Target Emission Rate (TER)	18%
3(★★★)	as determined by the	25%
4(★★★★)	2006 Building Regulation	44%
5(★★★★★)	Standards	100%
6(★★★★★★)		A 'zero carbon home' (heating, lighting, hot water and **all** other energy uses in the home)
	Water	
1(★)	Internal potable water	120 l/p/d
2(★★)	consumption measured in	120 l/p/d
3(★★★)	litres per person per day (l/p/d)	105 l/p/d
4(★★★★)		105 l/p/d
5(★★★★★)		80 l/p/d
6(★★★★★★)		80 l/p/d
	Materials	
1(★)	Environmental impact of materials[†]	At least three of the following 5 key element of construction are specified to achieve a BRE Green Guide 2006 rating of at least D – Roof structure and finishes

		– External walls – Upper floor – Internal walls – Windows and doors
1(★)	**Surface Water Run-off** Surface water management	Ensure that peak run-off rates and annual volumes of run-off will be no greater than the previous conditions for the development site

† A probable future development regarding the environmental impact of materials is to reward resource efficiency, as well as the use of resources that are more sustainable, by developing 'Ecopoints per m²' as a measure for this item. However, it may be that the 'Green Guide' route will remain as a simple route for smaller developments.

It can be seen that the Code moves the game on from Ecohomes. As an example, a one star rating for water use requires a usage of not more than 120 litres per person per day (l/p/d), falling to 80 l/p/d at six stars. Ecohomes starts at 142 l/p/d and falls to 88 l/p/d. The minimum standard for surface water is '…no greater than the previous conditions for the development site'. This effectively means that rain water from the roof, driveways etc. have to be contained on site rather than discharged into main drains. The thinking is that these minimum levels will be moved up over time encouraging (or forcing) us to achieve higher levels of sustainability and making ever more use of renewable energy.

Clearly the legislation is a bit of a muddle at the moment with three different instruments to deal with, each vying for contention – Building Regs, Ecohomes and the Code. The Code (and to an extent Ecohomes) requires energy performance at least 10 per cent better than Part L. The Government has suggested that these will be ratcheted-up to 25 per cent in 2010, 44 per cent in 2013 and zero carbon in 2016. It can be argued that Parts C, F and L of the Building Regs, the instrument we have grown to know and love, is valueless if the Code for Sustainable Homes, or Ecohomes, is the standard we actually need to adopt. I guess they will sort it out one day.

INDEX

The Housebuilder's Bible is unique - the first book in its field to mix information and advice with detailed yardstick costings for residential building projects. This edition has been completely redesigned with new tables and improved illustrations - all in colour for the first time. Experienced construction professionals have expressed amazement at the amount of detailed information in the book. It works for newbuilds and extensions alike.

How to Find and Buy a Building Plot is the first and only comprehensive book specifically about buying land on which to build a house. It gives you all the essential information you need to locate, assess and purchase a plot. With more than 65 illustrations, tables and examples it is written in a clear and accessible style and is of as much benefit to professionals as it is to the thousands of families who begin land-searching each year. Written by Roy Speer & Mike Dade this is a fully revised third edition of the book.